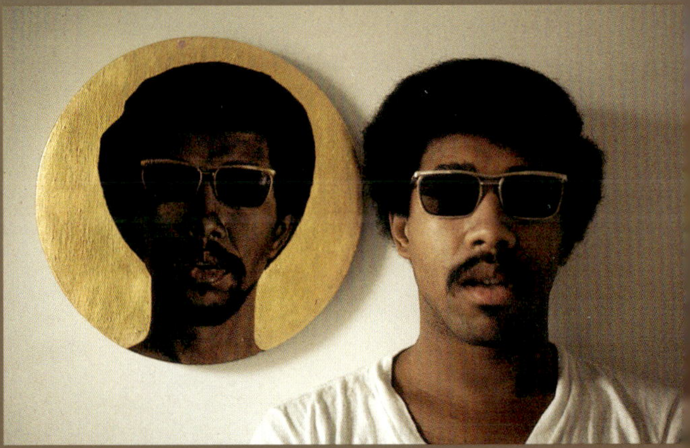

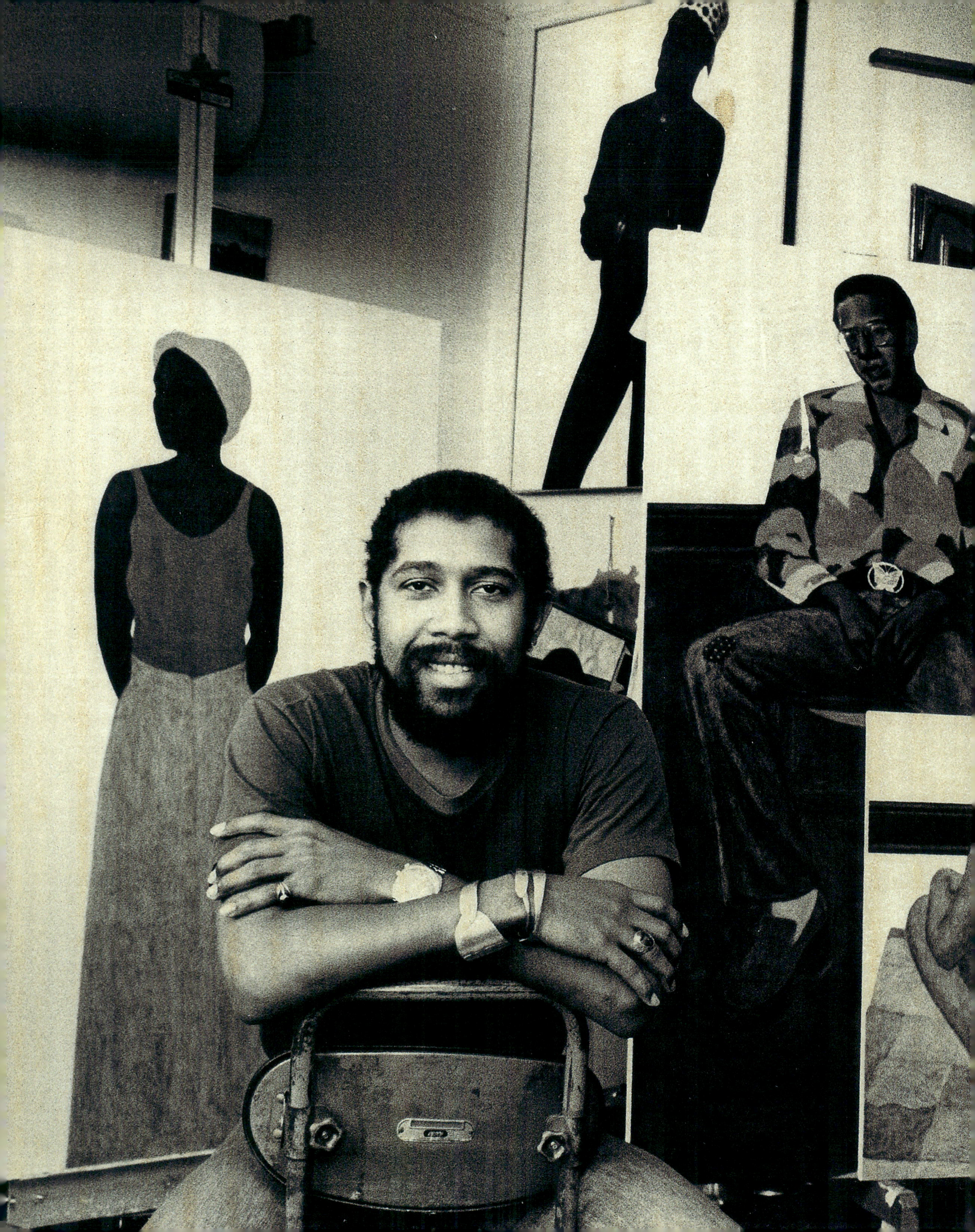

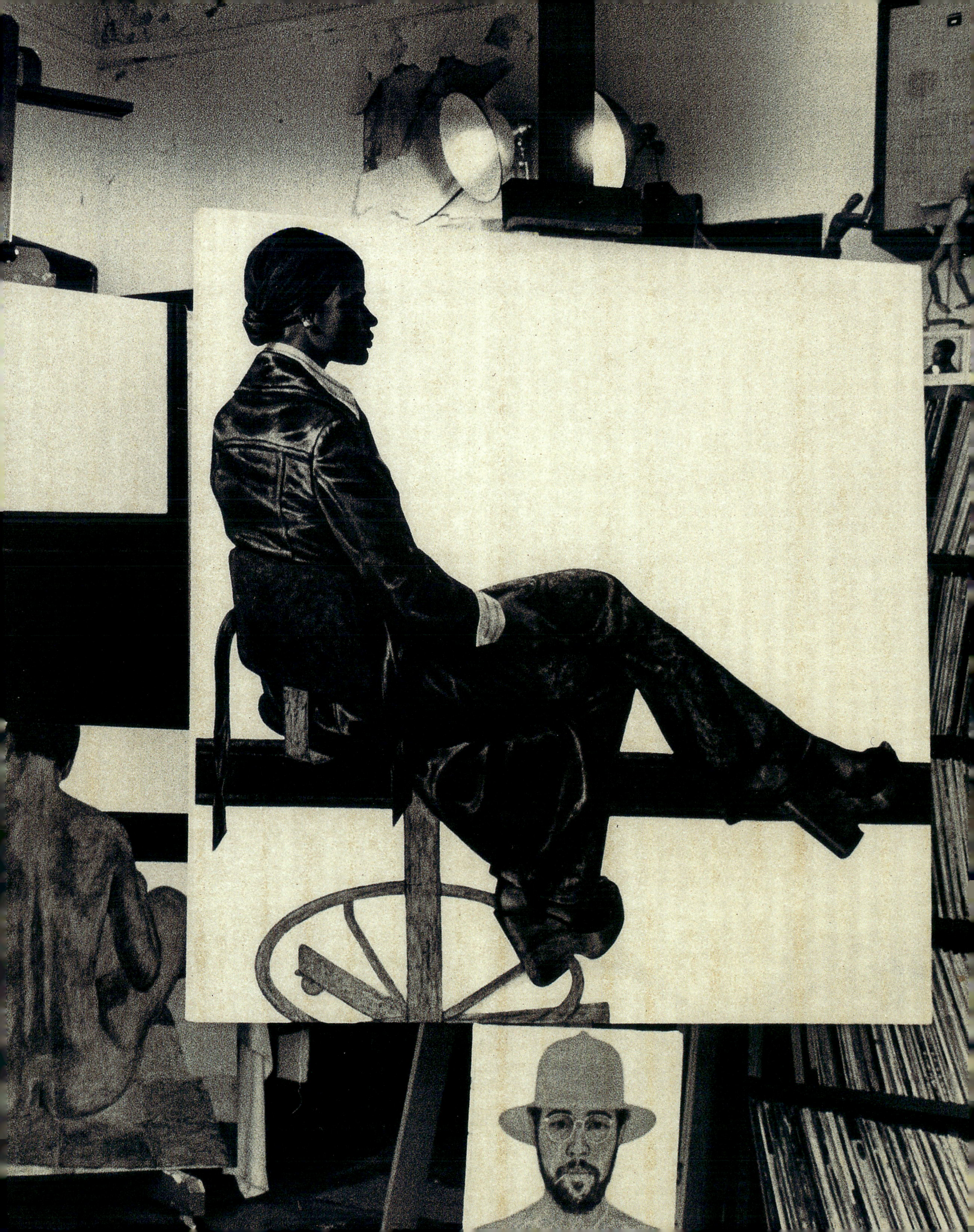

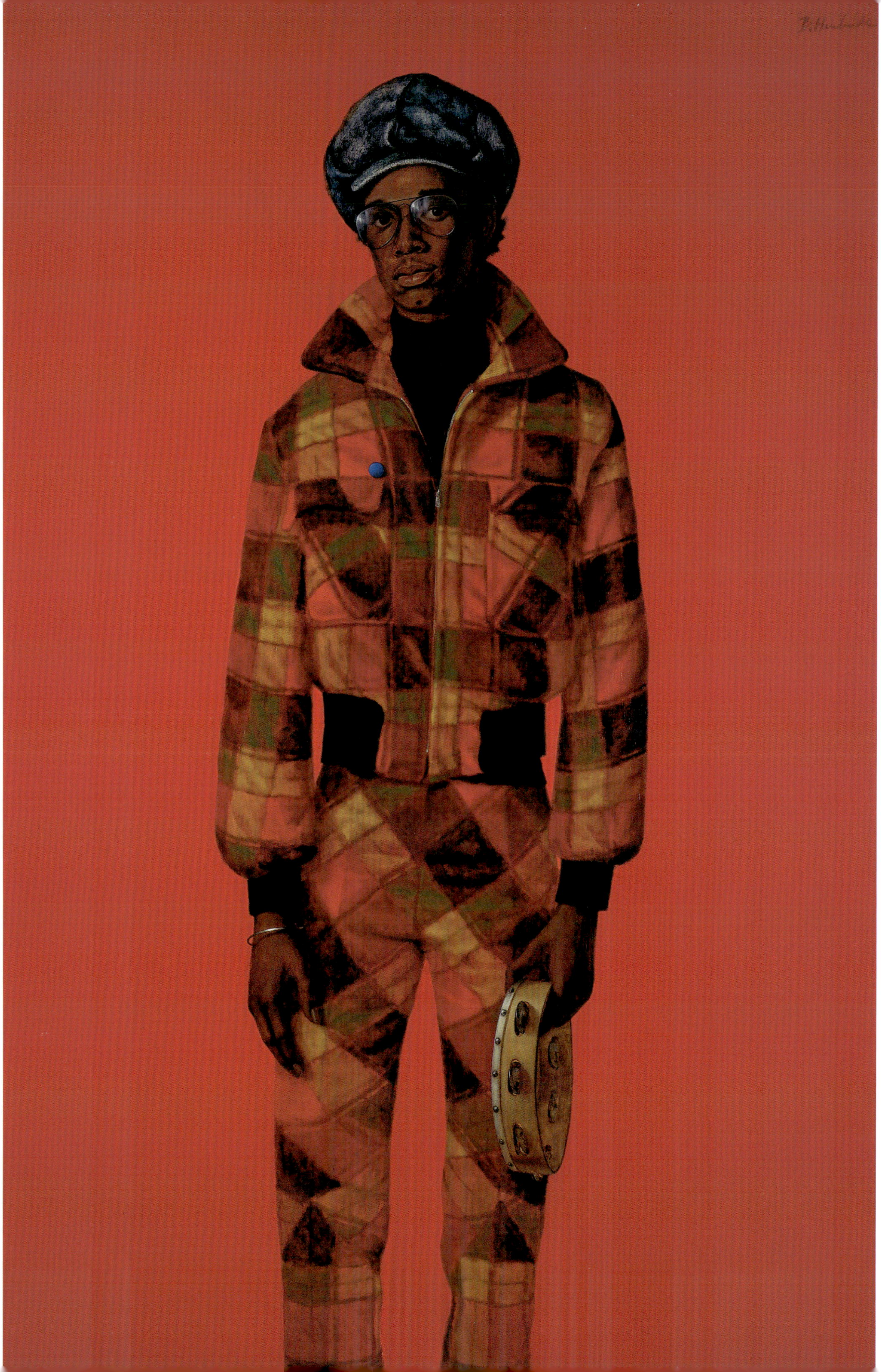

Birth of the Cool

Barkley L. Hendricks

Edited by Trevor Schoonmaker

Nasher Museum of Art
Duke University
2008 (reprinted 2023)

Published in conjunction with the exhibition, *Barkley L. Hendricks: Birth of the Cool.*

Nasher Museum of Art at Duke University, Durham, NC
February 7, 2008–July 13, 2008

Studio Museum in Harlem, New York, NY
November 12, 2008–March 15, 2009

Santa Monica Museum of Art, Santa Monica, CA
May 9, 2009–August 15, 2009

Pennsylvania Academy of the Fine Arts, Philadelphia, PA
September 18, 2009–December 20, 2009

Contemporary Arts Museum, Houston, TX
January 23, 2010–April 18, 2010

Nasher Museum of Art at Duke University
2001 Campus Drive, Durham, North Carolina 27705
(919) 684-5135
www.nasher.duke.edu

Third printing, 2023, in memory of Barkley L. Hendricks (1945–2017).

Cataloguing-in-publication data are available from the Library of Congress

Library of Congress Control Number: 2007941302

ISBN: 978-0-938989-44-8

Distributed by Duke University Press

We extend our tremendous gratitude to the Estate of Barkley L. Hendricks for making the third printing of this exhibition catalogue possible.

The exhibition, *Barkley L. Hendricks: Birth of the Cool,* and related programs were sponsored in part by the Andy Warhol Foundation for the Visual Arts, Inc., the National Endowment for the Arts, the Mary Duke Biddle Foundation, and the North Carolina Arts Council with funding from the State of North Carolina.

NATIONAL ENDOWMENT for the ARTS
arts.gov

North Carolina Arts Council

Edited by Trevor Schoonmaker

Project management (2023 reprint) by Melissa Gwynn

Copyediting by Laura Poole, Durham, NC

Color separations by Professional Graphics, Inc., Rockford, IL

Printing and binding by Friesens in Canada

Book design by Klugman Braude Design, Durham, NC

Typeset in Monotype Grotesque

Page 1:
Hendricks with *Butch*
Studio at 1605 Race Street, Philadelphia, 1968

Pages 2–3:
Hendricks with self-portrait in pith helmet, *Pretty Peggy's Black Box*, *Fast Eddie*, *Brenda's Sister Barbara Jean*, and unfinished *Greg* and *Adrienne*
Studio at 58 State Street, New London, CT, mid-1970s

Frontispiece:
cat. 25
Blood (Donald Formey), 1975
Oil and acrylic on cotton canvas
72 x 50 1/2 inches

Back cover:
Barkley L. Hendricks
Self-portrait with Red Sweater
Studio at 58 State Street, New London, CT, c. 1980

Page 8:
cat. 26
North Philly Niggah (William Corbett), 1975
Oil and acrylic on cotton canvas
72 1/2 x 48 1/2 inches

Contents

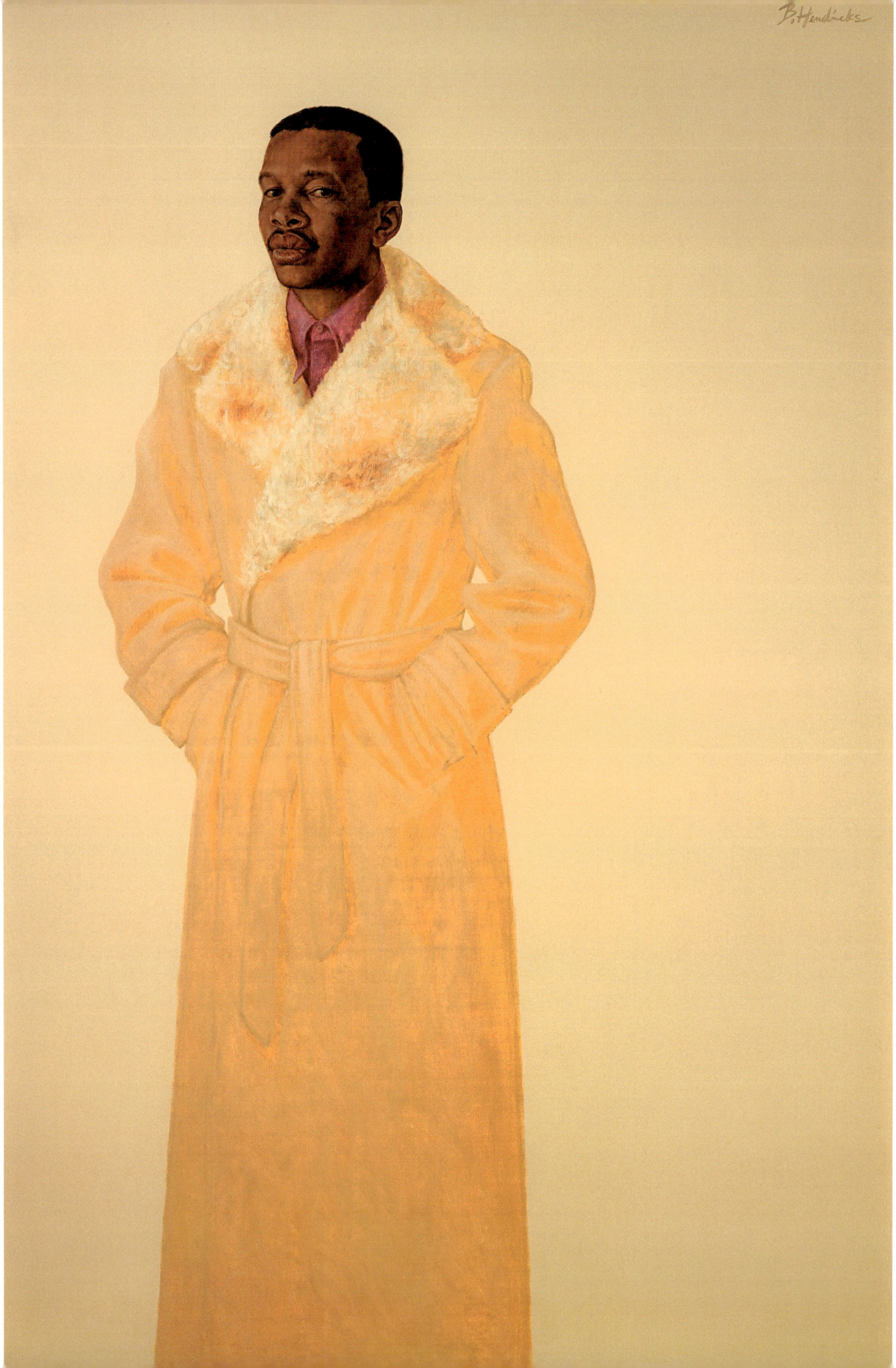
B Hendricks

Director's Foreword

We are extremely proud to present *Barkley L. Hendricks: Birth of the Cool*, the artist's first (and long overdue) retrospective exhibition. Barkley Hendricks is well known in the art world, but he is not as well known to the broader public as he deserves to be. Trained at the Pennsylvania Academy of the Fine Arts and Yale University, he is a tremendously accomplished painter, whose grand manner portraits of contemporaries from the 1960s and 1970s were revolutionary at the time they were created. These works retain their power today and, indeed, are even more relevant as a new generation of artists, many of whom have been influenced by Hendricks's achievements, continues to explore the issues of race, gender, and identity that he began to engage in such an exciting way over forty years ago.

A project of this magnitude could not have been realized without the support and contributions of many people. First of all, we are extremely grateful to Barkley L. Hendricks, whose long career and body of work made this exhibition possible. He and Trevor Schoonmaker, the Nasher Museum's Curator of Contemporary Art, have worked closely together over the past few years, and Barkley's openness and generosity have made this one of the most cordial and collaborative projects we have ever undertaken. We also thank Barkley's wife, Susan Hendricks, who worked tirelessly to make the exhibition and catalogue a reality.

We are also most grateful to Richard J. Powell, the John Spencer Bassett Professor of Art History at Duke University, for his generous and enthusiastic support and for his insightful essay on Hendricks, an artist he has followed for thirty years and about whom he has written extensively. We are also delighted that Thelma Golden, Director and Chief Curator of the Studio Museum in Harlem, and Franklin Sirmans, Curator of Modern and Contemporary Art at the Menil Collection, agreed to work with us on this project. Golden worked with Barkley Hendricks to produce a lively interview, and Sirmans's essay offers an understanding of Hendricks's influence on today's generation of figurative artists.

We thank the many lenders whose generosity helped us secure key works for the exhibition. Private lenders include Barkley and Susan Hendricks, Blake Byrne (with thanks to Barbara Schwann), Dr. Robert Clark and Mrs. Joan Clark, Mr. and Mrs. Alexander Miller (with thanks to Steve Miller), Dr. Kenneth Montague/The Wedge Collection, Charlotte and Gordon Moore, Monica and Rick Segal, Kathleen Spicer, and Dr. and Mrs. John T. Williams Sr. We also thank institutional and gallery lenders ACA Galleries (Jeffrey and Dorian Bergen), the Butler Institute of American Art (Rebecca Davis and Patrick McCormick), Chrysler Museum of Art (Catherine Jordan Wass), Columbus Museum of Art (Melissa Wolfe and Jennifer Wilkinson), Office of the Dean of Students at Cornell University (Liz Colucci), Forbes Collection (Andrianna Campbell and Gabrielle Schickler), Gibbes Museum of Art/Carolina Art Association (Todd D. Smith, Angela Mack, and Zinnia Willits), National Afro-American Museum and Cultural Center (Wendy Felder), National Gallery of Art (Alicia Thomas and Anne Halpern), North Carolina Central University Art Museum (Kenneth G. Rodgers and Patti Jones), Pennsylvania Academy of the Fine Arts (Lynn Marsden-Atlass, Alex Baker, and Robert Harman), Philadelphia Museum of Art (Shannon Schuller), Studio Museum in Harlem (Thelma Golden, Christine Y. Kim, and Susan Callanan), and Yale University Art Gallery (Jock Reynolds and L. Lynne Addison).

The Andy Warhol Foundation for the Visual Arts, the Mary Duke Biddle Foundation, the National Endowment for the Arts, and the North Carolina Arts Council provided essential financial support for the exhibition and related educational programs. We are most grateful for their assistance.

We are delighted that the exhibition will tour to several venues in major U.S. cities, so that a much broader audience will have the opportunity to see Barkley Hendricks's work and learn more about his contributions. We thank our colleagues at the Studio Museum in Harlem, the Pennsylvania Academy of the Fine Arts, the Santa Monica Museum of Art, and the Contemporary Arts Museum, Houston, for their enthusiasm and support.

As a teaching institution, the Nasher Museum of Art at Duke University provides opportunities for graduate students to work with our curators and staff on major exhibition projects. We are grateful to Samantha Noel, our Mary Duke Biddle Foundation graduate intern, who assisted with many aspects of the catalogue and the exhibition's organization, and to graduate students Rebecca Keegan, who organized research materials for the exhibition, and Anne-Marie Angelo, who helped create the artist's bibliography, for their contributions to the project.

At the Nasher Museum of Art at Duke University, we thank chief preparator Brad Johnson, registrar Myra Scott and assistant registrar Shelby Spaulding, manager of marketing and communications Wendy Hower Livingston, director of development and external affairs Rebecca Swartz, curatorial assistants Carolina Sánchez Cordova and Enid Maxfield, curator of education Juline Chevalier and associate curator of education Julie Thomson, and the installation and preparation team of Harvey Craig, Allan Dippy, and Patrick Krivacka.

Finally, special thanks are due to Trevor Schoonmaker, the Nasher Museum's Curator of Contemporary Art, who proposed this exhibition and worked to realize it in the most exciting and ambitious fashion. He has known the artist for many years and believes deeply in the work. We are enormously proud to present the fruits of his thinking and research on Barkley Hendricks and delighted to have been able to support such a productive collaboration between artist and curator.

Kimerly Rorschach
Mary D.B.T. and James H. Semans Director
Nasher Museum of Art at Duke University
2008

Curator's Acknowledgments

I express my infinite gratitude to Barkley Hendricks, who throughout the challenging process of producing this exhibition and catalogue has been a generous, thoughtful, enthusiastic, and humorous collaborative partner. My introduction to his work was in graduate school in 1994, and we first met in 2000. Since then my curatorial work has been inspired by his art, and he has enriched my life with his friendship. It has been an honor to work with Barkley on several projects over the past eight years, but to organize with him the first historical survey of his portraits and landscapes from 1964 to 2007 has truly been an incredible experience. The openness, trust, and respect that he has shown over the years are what made a project of this scope and scale possible. For that I am sincerely grateful.

To know and work with Barkley Hendricks is to also know and work with his wife, Susan. It would be an understatement to say that her contributions to this project were both monumental and essential. Her boundless energy and enthusiasm made it a joy to work with her while handling the necessary tedious tasks and pressing deadlines. On a daily basis she juggled emails and phone calls, investigative research, digging through archives, and endless fact checking to help create this catalogue. I am very grateful for her friendship, generosity with her time, and indefatigable spirit. Without her commitment, this project would have never been possible.

I thank my wife, Teka Selman, whose feedback and support throughout the development of this project were instrumental in shaping the exhibition and catalogue. As always, she is both my greatest critic and supporter, and I am forever thankful for that. She makes everything I do both better and more worthwhile.

Special thanks to my colleagues Thelma Golden, Rick Powell, and Franklin Sirmans for their exceptional texts in this catalogue, which will surely contribute to a greater understanding, appreciation, and investigation of Hendricks's work. I further thank Rick Powell for leading the way with his scholarship on Barkley Hendricks. His enthusiastic support of this exhibition and his thoughtful advice during its development were invaluable. Julie Klugman Braude worked with grace under pressure to design a terrific catalogue for which we are very thankful. Laura Poole, Kim Rorschach, and Teka Selman all provided insightful editorial suggestions for this text.

I join our director, Kim Rorschach, in thanking the generous lenders to the exhibition. Their commitment to this project has been vital. I additionally thank the following individuals for their assistance in obtaining images and information for the catalogue and making the tour possible: Valerie Cassel Oliver and Toby Kamps at the Contemporary Arts Museum, Houston; Lynn Marsden-Atlass, Alex Baker, Robert Cozzolino, and Brian Duffy at the Pennsylvania Academy of the Fine Arts; Amey Hutchins at the University of Pennsylvania (Philadelphia Art Alliance); Christian Haye and Lizzy Cross at The Project; Elsa Longhauser at the Santa Monica Museum of Art; Jack Shainman, Judy Sagal, and Brooke Mellen at Jack Shainman Gallery; and Thelma Golden, Christine Y. Kim, Naomi Beckwith, Liz Gwinn, Renee E. Turner, and Thomas J. Lax at the Studio Museum in Harlem.

Finally, I am grateful to the entire staff of the Nasher Museum of Art for having such genuine enthusiasm for this exhibition. To curate a retrospective survey of Barkley's paintings has been a dream of mine for many years, and I am grateful to our director, Kim Rorschach, and Senior Curator Sarah Schroth for immediately and wholeheartedly believing in this exhibition from the moment it was presented. The entire Nasher staff has frequently gone above and beyond the call of duty to help realize this exhibition to the fullest, and without their concerted efforts this project could not have become a reality. For that I am exceptionally grateful.

Getting to know the man behind the work continues to be rewarding, and I hope that this exhibition and catalogue will inspire a wider audience to experience, discuss, and appreciate the work of Barkley L. Hendricks.

Trevor Schoonmaker
Curator of Contemporary Art
Nasher Museum of Art at Duke University
2008

Artist's Acknowledgments

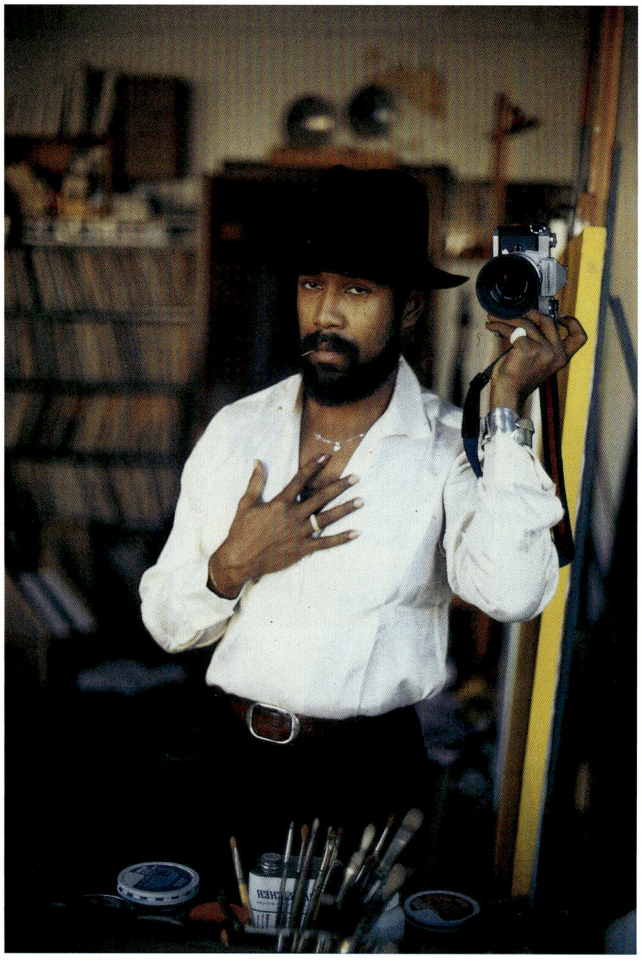

fig. 1
Barkley L. Hendricks
Self-Portrait with Black Hat
Studio at 58 State Street,
New London, CT, c. 1980

There is a significant and important list of acknowledgments inspired by this presentation.

Doc and Ruby Hendricks, my parents, are first to get their props.

Mere thank-yous do not come close to recognizing the contributions given to this exhibition by Trevor Schoonmaker and Susan Hendricks. So knowing where to start is certainly beyond words.

Susan, my wife, has been a total wonder woman. There was an almost daily dialogue with her about every aspect of this exhibition. From her sharp eyes and sparkling mind, to her constant stream of questions and inquiries, to the literally hundreds of emails she was responsible for, this truly would not have been possible without her contribution. Will a million thank-yous cover her contribution? I doubt it. Perhaps fifty-'leven trillion will approach a reasonable number. She is indeed my own "Susan Mingus." Just like one of my favorite musicians, Charles Mingus, I, too, have a wonder woman and wonderful woman named Susan.

In that same numeric thank-you category would reside my indebtedness to Trevor Schoonmaker. Now there's a name that will be a part of art history for many moons to come. Stay tuned to his channel of visions and insight. The word *hip* evolved from an African expression "hep," to be in the know. Trevor's hipness puts him very much in the know about many relevant and poignant pedagogical perspectives. Julian "Cannonball" Adderley, while introducing one of his tunes, stated, "Hipness is not a state of mind, it's a fact of life." You don't decide to be hip, it just happens that way. Trevor does his homework, which fortifies his being in the know, thus making him genuinely and spiritually hip. It has been my honor and pleasure to be a part of his visions for several exhibitions and a number of years. I look forward to many future collaborations that will bear the Schoonmaker seal of insight, hip, and cool.

Duke University has hit the double jackpot with Schoonmaker and Professor Rick Powell. Powell was first on my art radar screen. There is, I thought, an art historian for the here and now. A scholar necessary for the times with visions crafted and honed from having an ear to the cultural shouts and raps as well as the moans and sighs. He was early on the case to see and understand, as they say, where I was coming from. The scale and direction of this show allows Powell to expand his probe and prose to fit the occasion. Again I thank him for his insight and comprehension of the human and the artist in me that seeks to live with and cultivate the energy, the mystery, and the muses.

I learned this proverb from the works of Langston Hughes: "Blessed is he who expects nothing, for he shall not be disappointed." My only expectation for much of what I have created has been the personal joy and enlightenment it has given me. On many occasions, I have been surprised and gratified to know that what I produced was also enjoyed and appreciated by many, probably too many to name here. For all those who have shared their admiration and appreciation, mere thanks seem inadequate. Although I feel it is almost beyond words, words are all I have to convey how deeply I feel about those who have supported and encouraged me over the years to follow my various muses in whatever form they have emerged.

I am deeply humbled and gratified by the amazing commitment and passion that have been invested in and for *Barkley L. Hendricks: Birth of the Cool* by the Nasher Museum administration and staff. Starting with Kim Rorschach, who has been enthusiastically hands-on at every level, to Wendy Livingston who is working her creative magic in the public relations and marketing realm, to Brad Johnson who brings his genius to the design and layout of the exhibition, to Myra Scott and Shelby Spaulding who have calmly gathered information and artworks from lenders all over the country, to Trevor and the entire curatorial team, as well as the many others I have yet to meet, I say thank you, thank you! *Thank You!* I so appreciate this opportunity to share my work at the Nasher Museum and for the effort that has been made to organize and secure what are now four traveling venues for the exhibition, including my alma mater, The Pennsylvania Academy of the Fine Arts.

My most sincere gratitude to the lenders, public and private, and to friends near and far, all of whom have been so wonderfully willing to allow my works to be a part of *Barkley L. Hendricks: Birth of the Cool*, making it possible to take it on the road for the next two years.

Special mention goes out to the members of the band I play in. We call ourselves Other Issues. After one of our musical communions, we were trying to find time in our schedules for the next practice get-together. After we came to the conclusion that the various situations in our respective lives were conspiring against us, I quipped, "It seems we've all got other issues." And we did; something about those words described our lives to a T. So thanks, guys. At this time in my life, you have joined a special group of folks who have my utmost respect, love, and praise.

To all those who have inspired me in this search for the proper words, many thanks going out to you "from this ol' heart of mine."

Barkley Hendricks
2008

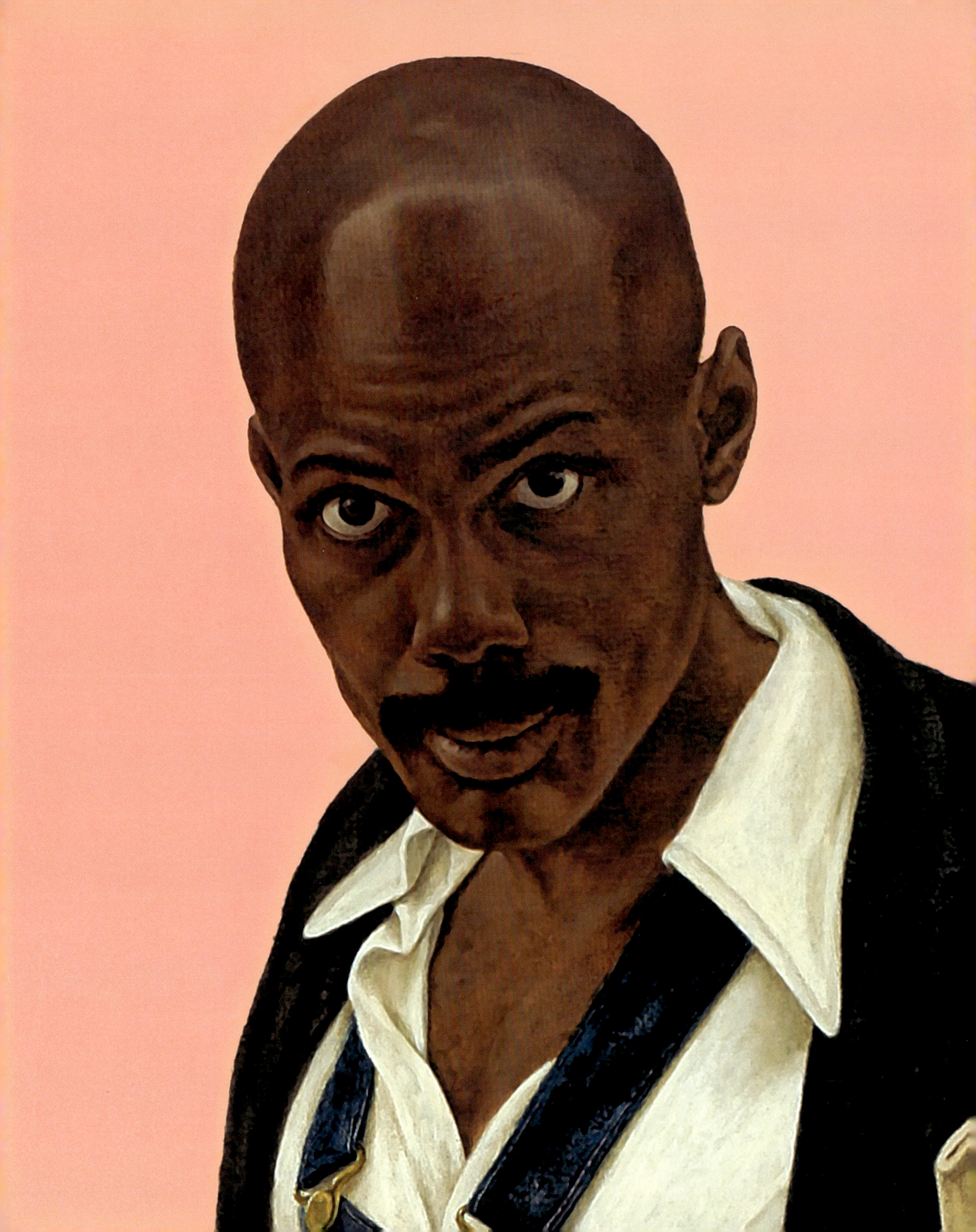

Birth of the Cool Trevor Schoonmaker

Entering the home of Barkley L. Hendricks is a transporting, kaleidoscopic visual experience. Floor to ceiling, wall to wall, the house is covered with a barely imaginable assortment of objects. Hendricks's own oil paintings, portraits, landscapes, still lifes, watercolors, photographs, assemblage sculptures, and pencil and black-light drawings live, in true democratic fashion, side by side with mass-produced odds and ends that overlap, touch, balance, and teeter. There are women's heels (lots of them), wigs, fake fur, feathered carnival masks, religious icons, magazine covers, exhibition posters, musical instruments, stacks of vinyl records and CDs, books, post-cards, sculptures, and generally anything that has caught Hendricks's eye over the years. An unfinished self-portrait head with a gold-leaf background sits by a blue Smurf and a high-heeled shoe with a string of beads dangling from it. A Xena the Warrior Princess action figure is pinned to the wall next to taped-up black and white images of Miles Davis, Billie Holiday, and the famous 1969 Marsha Hunt *Vogue* cover photo.[1] By the front door are rows of shiny gold, silver, or beaded hats (ranging from ball caps to pith helmets), piles of sunglasses, wind chimes, license plates, a green and white 1970s environmental American flag, JFK memorabilia, Virginia Slims life-sized cardboard cutouts of women selling the sexiness of smoking, Courvoisier liquor store pinups, and an old Frankenstein movie poster.

You get the idea. No surface is left uncovered. The entire house is Hendricks's sprawling studio, a living installation, with objects of inspiration piled high at every turn. These items serve multiple functions. They are fashion accessories for portraits, ready-made still lifes for paintings, materials for assemblage works, visceral stimulation, and material reminders of our cultural history. It is sensory overload, a visual feast, and a passageway into the mind of the artist.

This is what I encountered when I first met Hendricks at his home in early spring of 2000. It was one of those moments that is immeasurably memorable in the way that one is instantly transported and completely immersed in another environment, much like my experience of stepping off a plane into the swirling energy of Lagos, Nigeria, while in college. Having never met or spoken to Hendricks, I had called him to see if he might be interested in being part of an exhibition I was organizing that summer at a Chelsea gallery where I worked. At the time he was as surprised that I knew something about his work as I was that he invited me out to visit him in Connecticut. In our initial phone conversation, we made a connection over our mutual admiration for the late Nigerian Afrobeat musician and political activist Fela Kuti.[2]

It occurred to me then that Hendricks and Fela have some strong commonalities. They were both incredible talents who, since their prime in the 1970s, had been grossly overlooked by the mainstream in the United States. They were staunchly independent, rugged individualists who followed their respective visions to create innovative new artistic expressions, despite a lack of commercial success. They both called attention to and even championed people in society who had been underserved and otherwise rendered invisible. Most important, looking back, their bodies of work from more than thirty years ago stand out as unique among their contemporaries and are as fresh today as when produced. Like Fela's Afrobeat, Hendricks's portraits are of their time, yet still timeless. The inevitable consequence is that over the past several years both have been rediscovered by and are having a profound impact on a younger generation of creative minds. If a relative contemporary realist painter like Chuck Close (born in 1940) can be likened to a best seller, Hendricks would be the cult classic. Best-known for his bold life-sized portraits, Hendricks is also an accomplished photographer, landscape painter, watercolorist, draftsman, assemblage artist, carpenter, and jazz musician. The breadth of these varied media demonstrates a desire to continually learn, experiment, and take risks. That Hendricks adheres to his desire to pursue such varied interests also speaks to his faith in artistic intention and integrity, whether or not the art world has been willing to follow along.

Barkley L. Hendricks was born in Philadelphia in 1945 to parents who had moved north from rural Halifax County, Virginia, for the promise of better employment opportunities and to escape the Jim Crow laws of the South. As the child of two hard-working parents who had no choice but to leave school early to help their families earn a living, Hendricks had his own set of challenges to face in the city. Growing up in a tough African American neighborhood, he learned to navigate the streets of North Philadelphia at a young age, but his interests in art, basketball, and music (most specifically jazz) helped keep him out of trouble. Hendricks's parents were enthusiasts of blues and jazz vocals, and Philadelphia in the 1960s was a hotbed of modern music with sophisticated jazz and soul radio stations, well-stocked discount record stores, and a variety of first-class nightclubs that Hendricks began frequenting as a teenager.[3] Consequently, it is not surprising that he took up music himself, and many of his painting titles contain musical references.[4]

Though Hendricks was deeply engaged with music at a young age, it was his talent in the visual arts that gave him his first significant opportunity to move beyond the world of urban Philadelphia. He admittedly was not the most dedicated student; even so, with the encouragement of his high school art teachers to pursue his ability to draw, he produced an art portfolio strong enough to gain him admittance into the prestigious Pennsylvania Academy of the Fine Arts (PAFA), where he was a student from 1963 to 1967. Those were important developmental years for Hendricks, and he credits his teachers with inspiring him to maximize his potential as an artist.

My Black Nun, painted in 1964, was Hendricks's first portrait, albeit a fanciful one. At first glance it might seem small, dark, and unremarkable, far removed from the performative, eye-catching portraiture he arrived at a few years later. But as a statement, it was both audacious and alluring when it was painted. Having noted the dearth of black nuns in Philadelphia, Hendricks took corrective action and, from his imagination, created his own. With a confident gaze and arms defiantly crossed, she is a self-possessed figure with attitude. Perhaps taking his cues from soul musicians like Ray Charles and Al Green, Hendricks mixed the sacred with the profane, giving his nun modest sex appeal by drawing our eye to the curve of her waist and hips with a glimmering golden rope from which a pendulum-like cross dangles.[5] With this early work, Hendricks was beginning to set the stage for the development of his portrait painting. At the age of

cat. 29 (page 14)
Misc. Tyrone (Tyrone Smith), (detail) 1976
Oil and magna on linen canvas
72 x 50 1/4 inches

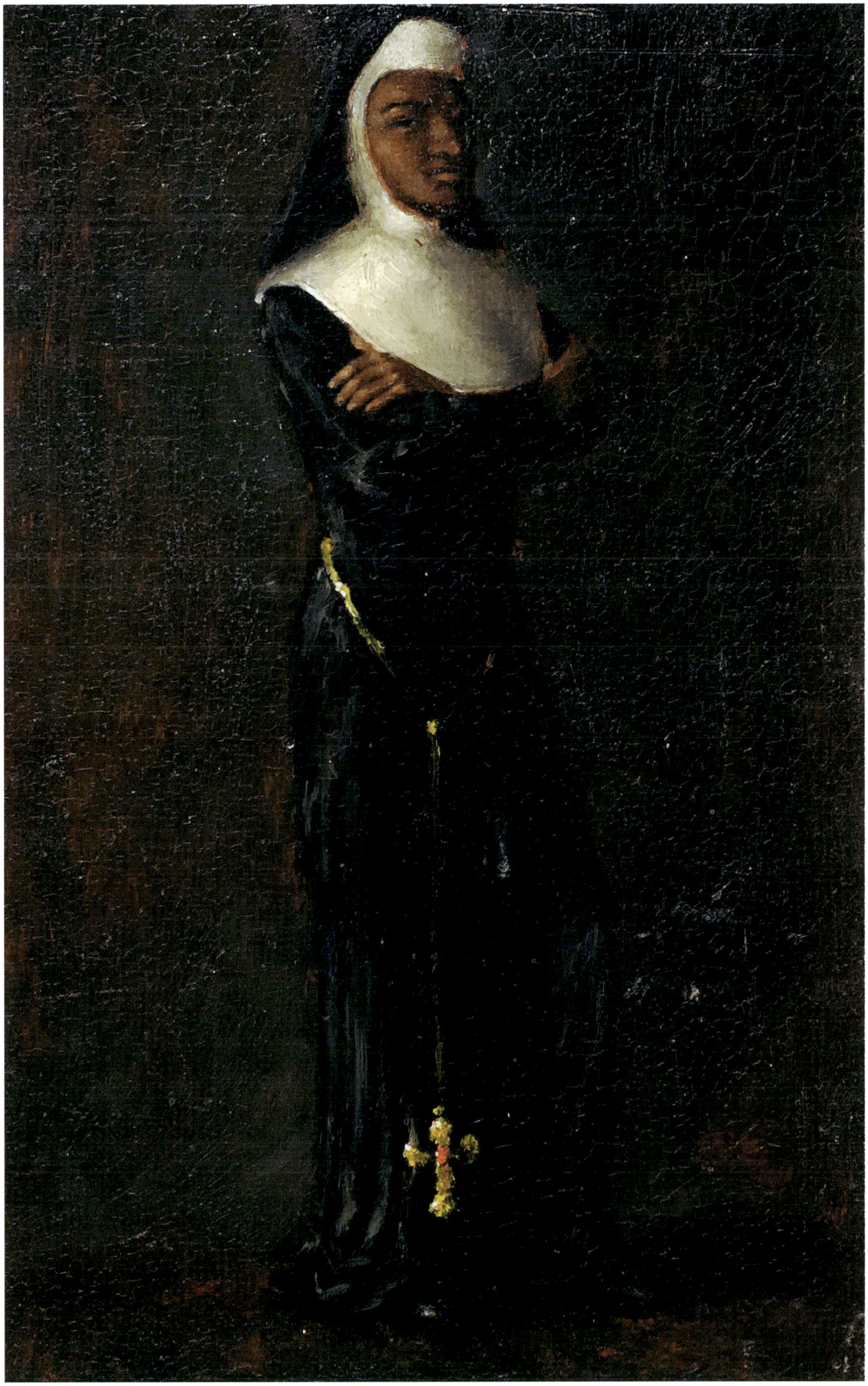

cat. 1
My Black Nun, 1964
Oil on masonite board
11 3/4 x 7 1/4 inches

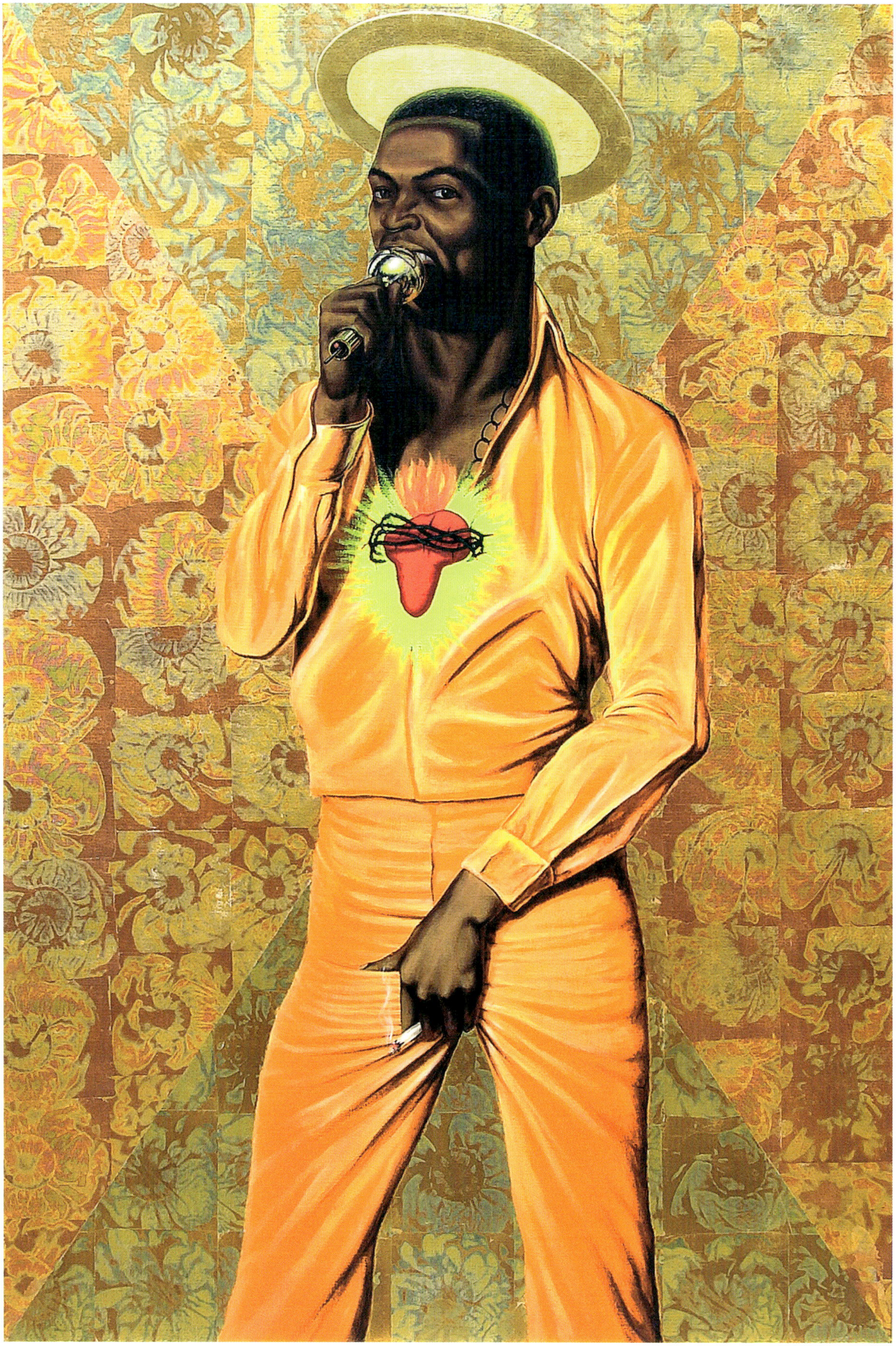

nineteen, he revealed his interest in creating new representations of black individuals. *My Black Nun* also demonstrated both the limited color palette and attention to light and reflection that have been ongoing investigations throughout his career. His melding of religious iconography with irreverent secular playfulness is a recurring theme, perhaps most clearly exemplified in his 2002 work *Fela: Amen, Amen, Amen, Amen*.[6] With one hand grabbing his crotch and a joint between his fingers, a crown of thorns around a flaming heart in the shape of the reversed African continent, gilded background, and halo over his head, Fela in Hendricks's portrait is a potent concoction of bad-boy rock star, man of the people, and religious icon.

While in school at PAFA, Hendricks worked as an arts instructor at the Philadelphia Department of Recreation and quickly became a visible figure in the local art community when some of his students won art awards in city-wide competitions. His own artwork earned him many honors at PAFA; he was the first African American student to be awarded two consecutive travel scholarships, which brought him to Europe in 1966 and then North Africa in 1968. Already familiar with the impressive art collections at the PAFA and the Philadelphia Museum of Art, his first trip to Europe and first airplane ride in 1966 extended his knowledge to those of the National Portrait Gallery and Tate Gallery in London, the Rijksmuseum in Amsterdam, the Uffizi in Florence, the Prado in Madrid, and the Louvre in Paris. There he encountered works by the old masters of European painting, as well as complex tile and textile patterns in Morocco, the pyramids in Egypt, and Moorish architecture in southern Spain. As Hendricks visited the major art museums across Europe, he noticed just how limited the representation of black figures has been in Western art history, and how few of those depicted have been truly humanizing or personalized portraits. At the same time, he was fascinated by the elaborate portraiture of wealthy individuals that was so often present in museums—the work of such artists as Rembrandt, van Dyck, Caravaggio, and van Eyck.[7] Shortly after his return home, Hendricks began painting life-sized representations of

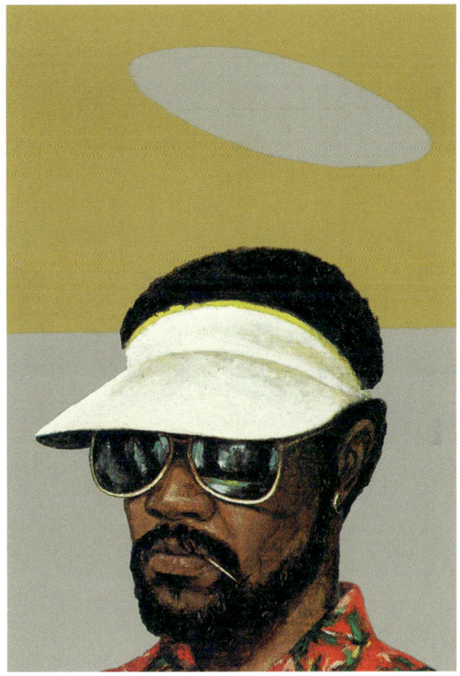

people of color, blending his interest in the history of portraiture with the growing consciousness of black self-representation, in the process creating some of the most remarkable portraits of people of color of the time.

At Hendricks's first PAFA exhibition for travel award winners in 1966, Philadelphia art dealer Harry Kulkowitz saw his work and offered him the opportunity to exhibit at his space, Kenmore Gallery. Kulkowitz was a great promoter of Hendricks, representing the young artist and introducing his work for the first time to collectors and curators until he closed the gallery and retired in 1975. In 1970 Hendricks enrolled at Yale University in a program that accepted his four years of credits at PAFA and offered him the opportunity to earn both a BFA and MFA in two years. Shortly before, on returning home from his travels in Europe, Hendricks had joined the New Jersey National Guard for the beginning of a six-year stint from 1968 to 1974. Consequently, while at Yale, Hendricks spent a lot of his time taking the train back and forth to and from New Jersey to fulfill his duties in the National Guard, the unfortunate result of which was his inevitable separation from conventional student life. He was enrolled in the art program at Yale at the same time as acclaimed postminimalist sculptor Martin Puryear, but his obligations to the

cat. 45 (opposite page)
Fela: Amen, Amen, Amen, Amen..., (detail) 2002
Oil and variegated leaf on linen canvas, wooden frame, altarpiece armature
66 3/4 x 46 3/4 inches
(60 x 40 inches unframed), with 60 inch altarpiece

fig. 1
Me (Self-Portrait), 1978
Oil, gold, and aluminum leaf on canvas
5 x 3 inches

National Guard and ties to his family and gallery in Philadelphia divorced him from any real sense of an artistic community in New Haven. Perhaps more significant, Hendricks was one of only two figurative painters enrolled at Yale at a time when most artists were working with abstraction and minimalism. As a result, he spent more time with Yale's photography students and professors than those in the painting department. With the camera that he bought in 1966 for his first trip to Europe, he put together a portfolio of photographs that allowed him to enter Walker Evans's advanced photography course.[8] Hendricks quickly became an accomplished photographer in a love affair that has continued to follow him throughout his life, winning his first award in the medium in 1971 and more recently exhibiting his photographs in the cutting-edge Wrong Gallery's contribution to the 2006 Whitney Biennial. Photography became such a passion that to this day, Hendricks rarely leaves home without his camera.

Before enrolling at Yale, Hendricks had produced a series of basketball paintings as an early investigation of color and geometry through the lens of abstraction and minimalism, artistic movements that were ubiquitous in the art world at the time. Because of his examination of basic forms like the square and circle, when he arrived at Yale it was assumed that he knew the work of abstract painter and former Yale professor Joseph Albers.[9] Hendricks's practice, however, actually came from both his love of the game that he grew up playing and the simplicity of the theme of basketball. Looking to one of his favorite pastimes was the most logical place to find the inspiration he needed for his work, and the ball, backboard, rim, and lane provided basic geometric forms that he could easily utilize in this exploratory series. The painting *Granada* (1970) is a linear depiction of two basketball lanes painted in black oil on a black acrylic background, with one lane inverted for symmetrical balance. The title of the work comes from a town in southern Spain that Hendricks visited in 1966, where he first saw the Islamic palace known as the Alhambra, built by Moorish monarchs. Impressed by the classical Islamic architecture, Hendricks mirrored and abstracted its lunette archways in the jump ball circles at the top of the lane in his painting. Though *Granada* is primarily a formal work, Hendricks's choice of black on black paint suggests a conceptual and cultural connection both to the Moors of North Africa and the urban sport of basketball.

In 1971, while a student at Yale, Hendricks participated in his first major museum exhibition, *Contemporary Black Artists in America*, at the Whitney Museum of American Art in New York. There he exhibited his painting *Brown Sugar Vine* (1970), a life-sized nude self-portrait humorously detailed with sunglasses and stocking cap. Ironically, Hendricks did not attend the opening of the exhibition, not because he was one of the many artists boycotting the controversial exhibition of black artists but because he was an outsider to the New York art world. His location and military obligations did not afford him the opportunity to know many of his colleagues in New York or become part of a peer group that worked, talked, and exhibited together. Then again, Hendricks was accustomed to going against the grain; it was much more his style to do his own thing, independent of any group or movement. Upon graduation from Yale in 1972, Hendricks was offered a teaching position in the art department at Connecticut College in New London. There, with the convenience of his relative proximity to New York and affordable studio space, he pursued his rapidly developing art career while handling his teaching responsibilities.

By the mid-1970s Hendricks began to garner serious attention for his work. He had been in significant exhibitions at the Museum of Fine Arts in Boston and the Philadelphia Museum of Art and had solo shows at the Gibbes Museum of Art in Charleston, SC, and ACA Galleries in New York. His work was beginning to be acquired into important collections, and he even had a Dewar's scotch magazine profile that was printed in *Playboy*, *Essence*, and other magazines. But as was the case for most African American artists of his generation, large-scale mainstream commercial success was harder to come by.

In the volatile social climate of the time, Hendricks's hard-hitting and true-to-life portrayals of African American and Latino culture were challenging to the status quo of the art world.

cat. 11 (opposite page)
Granada, 1970
Oil and acrylic on cotton canvas
48 x 46 inches

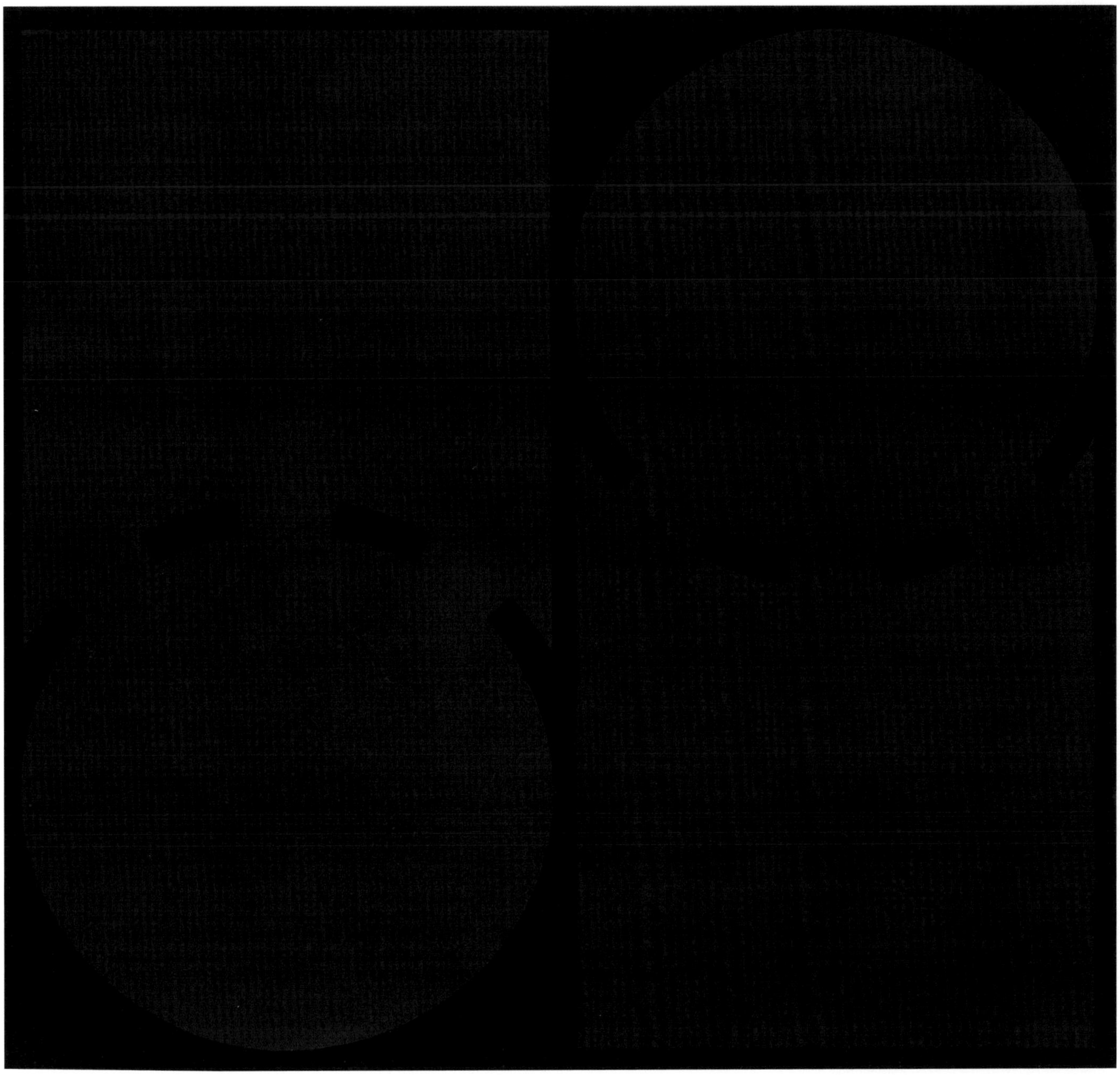

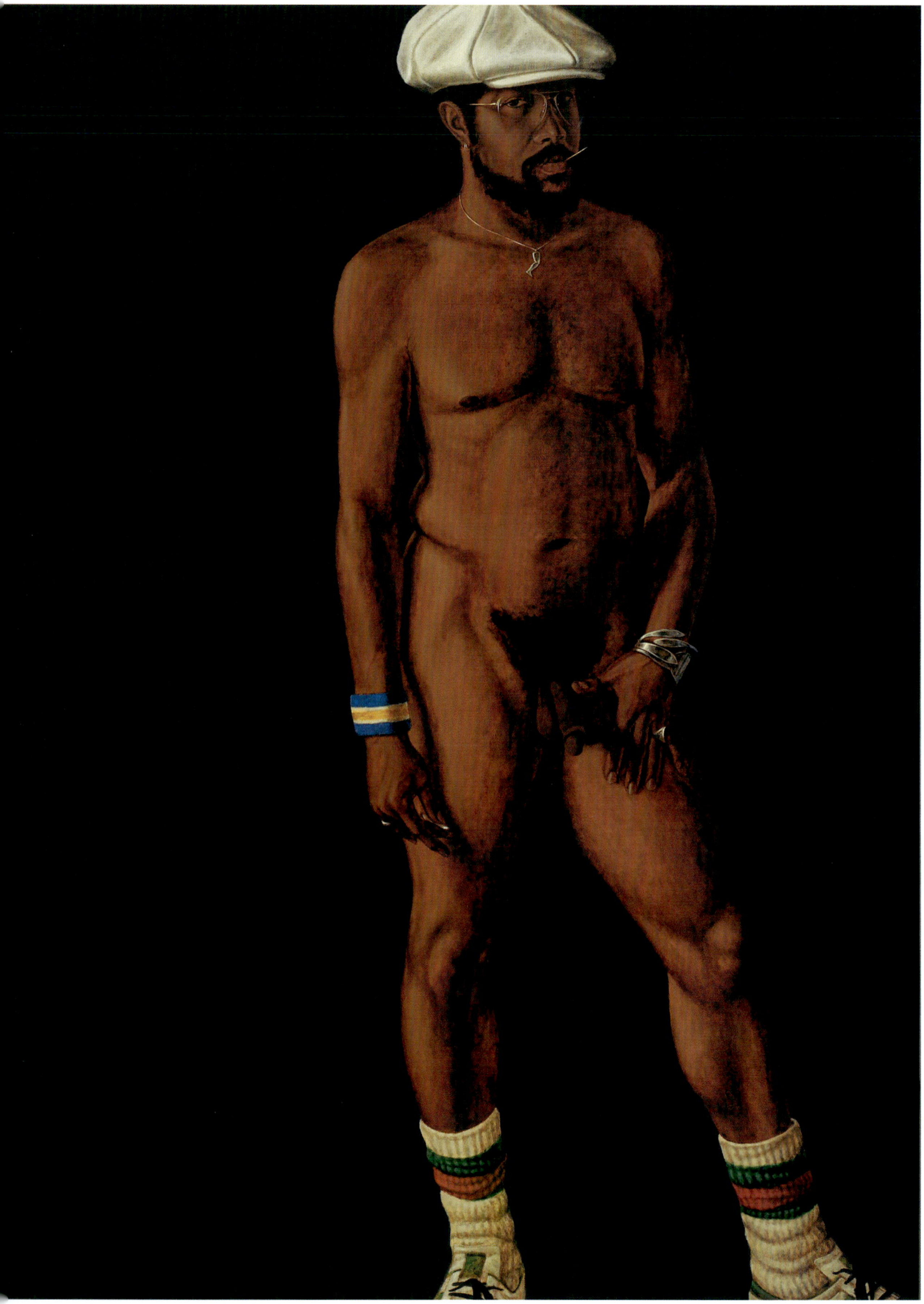

cat. 31
Brilliantly Endowed (Self-Portrait), 1977
Oil and acrylic on linen canvas
66 x 48 1/4 inches

cat. 37 (opposite page)
Tequila, 1978
Oil and acrylic on linen canvas
60 3/4 x 50 1/4 inches

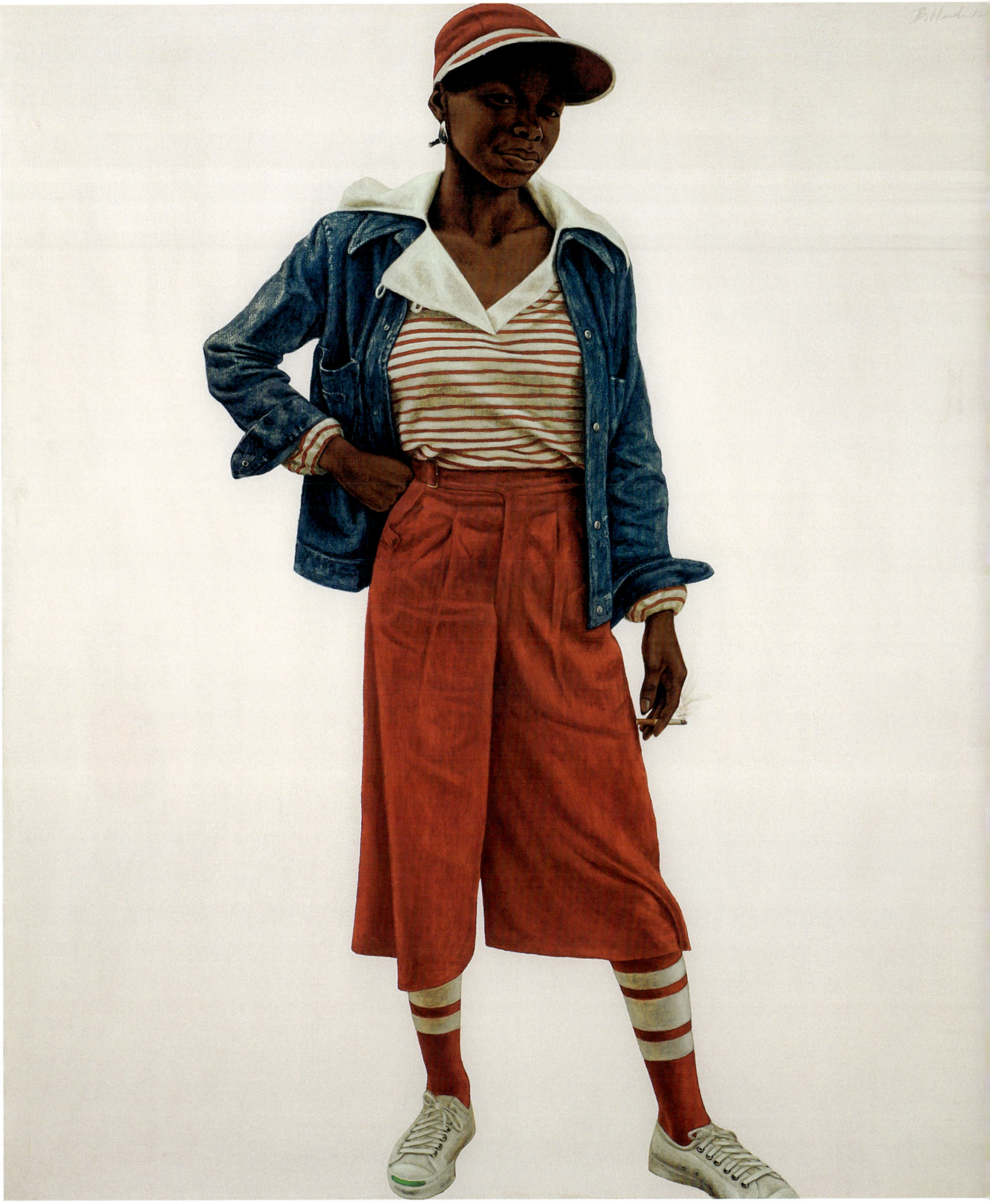

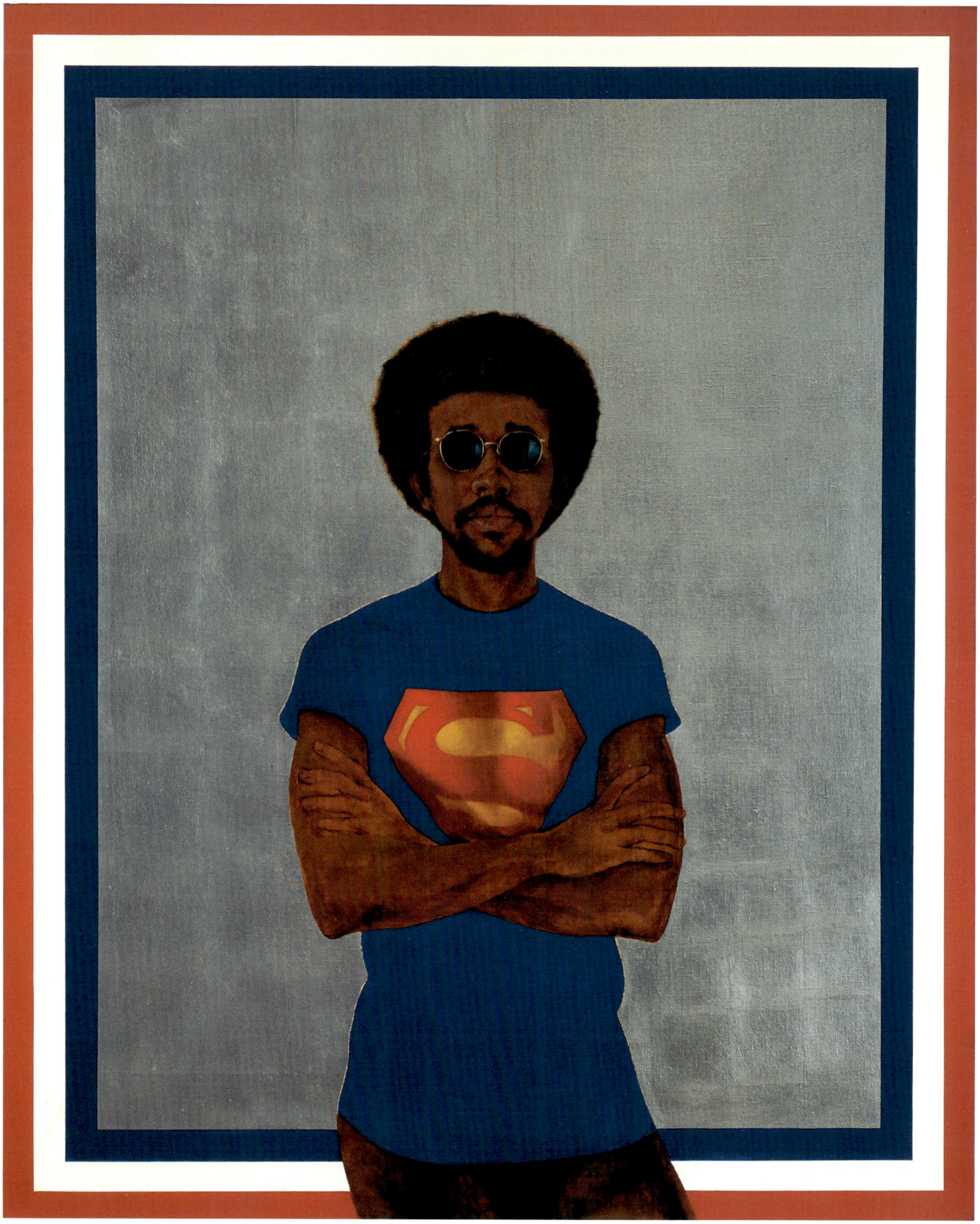

His portraits are unique in that they are neither clinically rendered photorealist representations nor culturally idealized or romantic images. Rather, they are tightly rendered and emotionally stirring, honest portraits of everyday people—his family, friends, associates, students, and local characters from the neighborhood. They are people with distinctive style, personality, and attitude that caught his attention and inspired a creative response. But to mainstream society of the 1970s, these images were both visually and conceptually loaded and thus potentially dangerous. To recognize the validity of many of Hendricks's portraits, one would have to also acknowledge the racial, cultural, and economic divides between the upper- and underclass of the time. To further complicate matters, Hendricks depicted the human nude not as the passive white female most commonly portrayed and sanctioned by art history but as a self-aware and self-assured black male. In his 1974 painting *Family Jules: NNN (No Naked Niggahs)*, the subject sits languidly in the nude, stretched across a pristine white couch, with his head relaxed against Moroccan tile and hash pipe in hand. Hendricks makes it known through his title how representations of African American nudes have been received, feared, and censored; in doing so, he directly tackles the widely accepted notion of the hypersexualized black body that continues to be codified and consumed around the globe. His response seems to say, "If this is what you expect, then this is what I am going to give you."

As much as Hendricks has exhibited a defiant and provocative streak through the years, he has equally shown a playful sense of humor. In the case of *Brilliantly Endowed (Self-Portrait)* from 1977, he displays a little of both. He depicts himself in the nude with a stern, self-assured gaze that looks the viewer in the eye and a strong, idealized physique that plays to stereotypical public perceptions of the hypermasculine black male. But within the apparent machismo is a healthy dose of sarcastic self-parody. The title of the painting is taken from a review earlier that year by New York art critic Hilton Kramer, who described Hendricks as a "brilliantly endowed" painter.[10] Hendricks plays up the tongue-in-cheek title by resting his hand on his upper thigh to draw the viewer's attention to the title's double entendre. The inherent sarcasm in his nakedness is emphasized by carefully detailing the many accessories that the artist wears, even though he is nude—a white applejack cap, earring, glasses, the ever-present toothpick in his mouth, a necklace with a shiny leg-shaped amulet, a blue and yellow wrist band, a joint between the fingers of his right hand, a silver cuff bracelet and rings, white low-top athletic shoes, and green and red striped tube socks. The red and green of his socks set against the solid black background create the colors of the Black Liberation flag in what is perhaps the artist's subtle and joking way of engaging the "black power" and "black is beautiful" ideology of the era. Despite the pervasive humor in *Brilliantly Endowed*, neither the general public nor the mainstream art world was ready for such a bold, sarcastic, and in-your-face portrayal of the black male.

Hendricks painted two other self-portraits that year that are each so different from *Brilliantly Endowed* in style and attitude that they almost function as alter egos, suggesting that the complex personality of the artist cannot be depicted in a single portrait. In *Slick (Self-Portrait)*, Hendricks paints himself in an

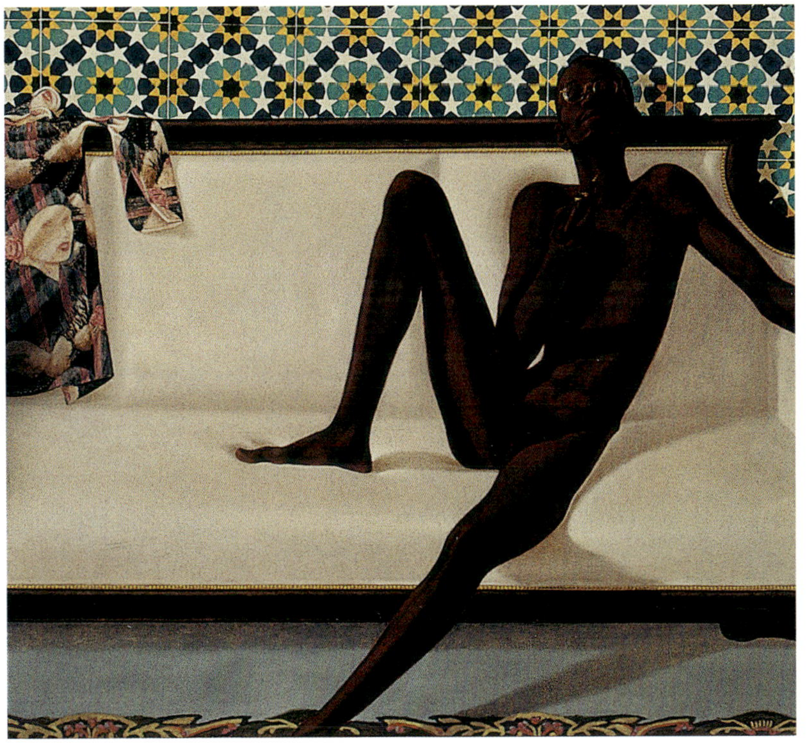

cat. 7 (opposite page)
Icon for My Man Superman (Superman never saved any black people–Bobby Seale), 1969
Oil, acrylic, and aluminum leaf on linen canvas
59 1/2 x 48 inches

fig. 2
Family Jules: NNN (No Naked Niggahs), 1974
Oil on linen canvas
66 x 72 inches

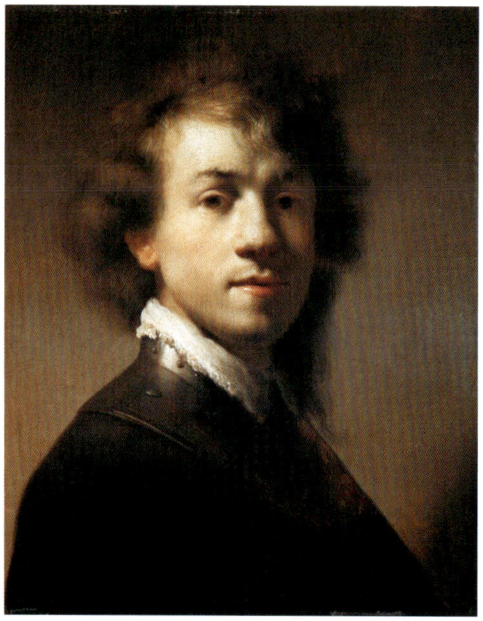

all-white suit and multicolored knit cap against a white background that enhances the contrast with his brown skin. He comes across as cool, cosmopolitan, and stylish, in a look that is reminiscent of late soul singer Marvin Gaye. *Doc and Ruby's Oldest Boy (Self-Portrait)*, on the other hand, is a seemingly earnest portrayal of himself as country artist, with toothpick-clinched smile, paintbrush in hand, and a wide-brimmed straw hat that he picked up while visiting family in rural Virginia.[11] Instead of white on white, here Hendricks painted black clothes against a black background. These works are part of what Hendricks describes as his "limited palette" series, in which he paints the clothes of the subject on top of a solid, flat background within the same color field. The series builds on his earlier basketball work, using the abstract, reductive quality to isolate the figure and heighten its immediacy. Most prominent in this oeuvre are the white-on-white works, such as *Dr. Kool* (1973), *Steve* (1976), and *Lagos Ladies (Gbemi, Bisi, Niki, Christy)* (1978), but he also produced limited palette paintings in a variety of other colors such as red, black, and green. Through their monochromatic backgrounds, flattened space, and simplified palette, this series demonstrates Hendricks's limited but willful engagement with minimalism through the unlikely genre of figurative representation.

Hendricks's stylized portraits also reveal the artist's rare talent for capturing and expressing the personality of his sitters through their unique gestures and expressions. Through an insightful eye and formal devices that enhance his subject's individuality and style, Hendricks can simultaneously convey the depth of one's psychology and elevate the common person to iconic status. His portrait *Tequila* (1978) captures the street smarts of a stylish young woman who seems to be a self-conscious, collaborative partner who is as much in control of her depiction as the artist is. Posed with one hand confidently resting on her hip and the other coolly holding a burning cigarette, her eyes look squarely at us with a soft but inquisitive gaze. Hendricks paints her at life-size scale, crops the tip of her hat and left sneaker, and sets her against a monochromatic pink background that enhances the blues and reds of her outfit, while pushing her off the canvas and out toward the viewer. Her denim jacket and canvas and rubber-toed sneakers look so real that they invite the viewer to touch them and feel their texture. The folds and drape of her clothing are as convincingly defined as the subtle shadowing around her collar bone, the drifting smoke from her cigarette, and the reflection in her earring. With the knowledge that the ability to convincingly portray different types of fabric was once a sign of a great painter, Hendricks makes evident his own mastery of simulating different textiles through color and shading.

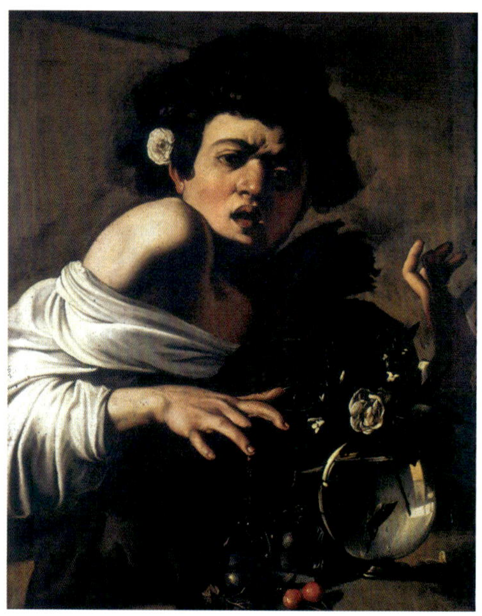

fig. 3
Rembrandt Harmensz van Rijn
Self-portrait as a Young Man, 1629
Mauritshuis, The Hague, The Netherlands

fig. 4
Caravaggio (Michelangelo Merisi da)
Youth Bitten by a Lizard, c. 1594
Longhi Collection, Florence, Italy

In developing his artistic voice, Hendricks has continually taken technical and stylistic cues from art history, refashioning elements of historic illusionism to reflect the here and now of his contemporary reality. Hendricks himself has noted many examples that help highlight his various influences. For example, drawn to the shine and luster of Greek and Russian icons, Hendricks began experimenting with metallic leaf in his paintings, producing the small self-portrait *Butch* in 1968 as his first test using gold leaf as a background. This successful effort led to more ambitious leaf works, including *Icon for My Man Superman (Superman never saved any black people—Bobby Seale)* (1969), *Lawdy Mama* (1969), *Icon for Fifi* (1982), and *Fela: Amen, Amen, Amen, Amen* (2002). Likewise, Hendricks's appreciation of Rembrandt's longtime engagement with self-portraiture and attention to the smallest detail can be seen in *Butch* and *BLH* (1968), both of which bring to mind Rembrandt's early work *Self-Portrait as a Young Man* (1629). Also a great admirer of Caravaggio, Hendricks observed the manner in which his theatrical use of light, shadow, and reflection bring an emotional quality to the work. The dynamic pose and intense look on the face of *Misc. Tyrone (Tyrone Smith)* (1976), for example,

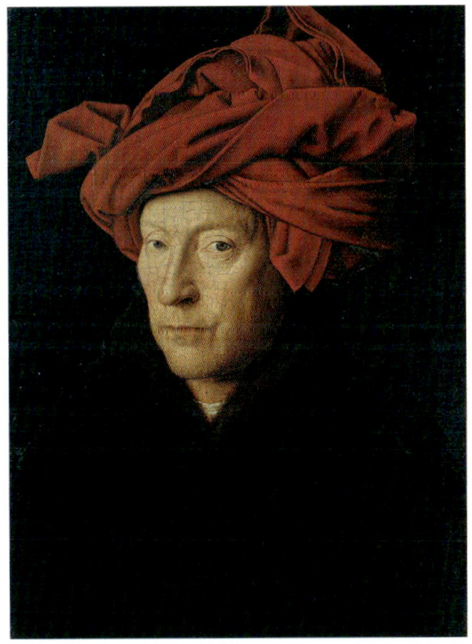

fig. 5
Jan van Eyck
A Man in a Red Turban (Self-portrait of Jan van Eyck), 1433
National Gallery, London

embody some of the theatricality that Hendricks gleaned from Caravaggio. In portraits like *Bedroom Eyes* (1975) and *Steve* (1976), Hendricks's depiction of the reflection of the windows of his studio in his subject's glasses is reminiscent of the reflection of a window in the vase in Caravaggio's *Boy Bitten by a Lizard* (c. 1594). Hendricks also noted that Jan van Eyck's *Portrait of a Man in a Red Turban* (1433) impressed him with its handling of the richly folded red fabric of the turban and the unique formal relationship created

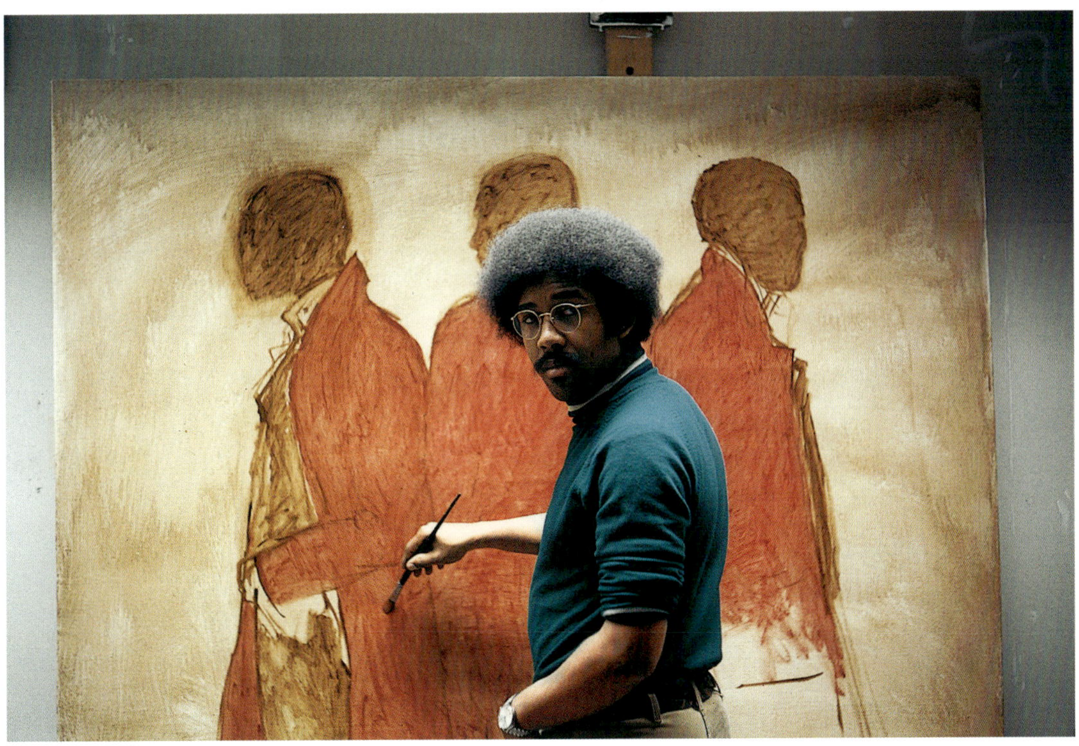

fig. 6
Hendricks painting *Sir Charles, Alias Willie Harris*
Studio at Yale University, New Haven, CT, 1972

cat. 24
Bedroom Eyes (Self-Portrait), 1975
Oil and acrylic (iridescent) on cotton canvas
10 x 10 inches

cat. 29 (opposite page)
Misc. Tyrone (Tyrone Smith), 1976
Oil and magna on linen canvas
72 x 50 1/4 inches

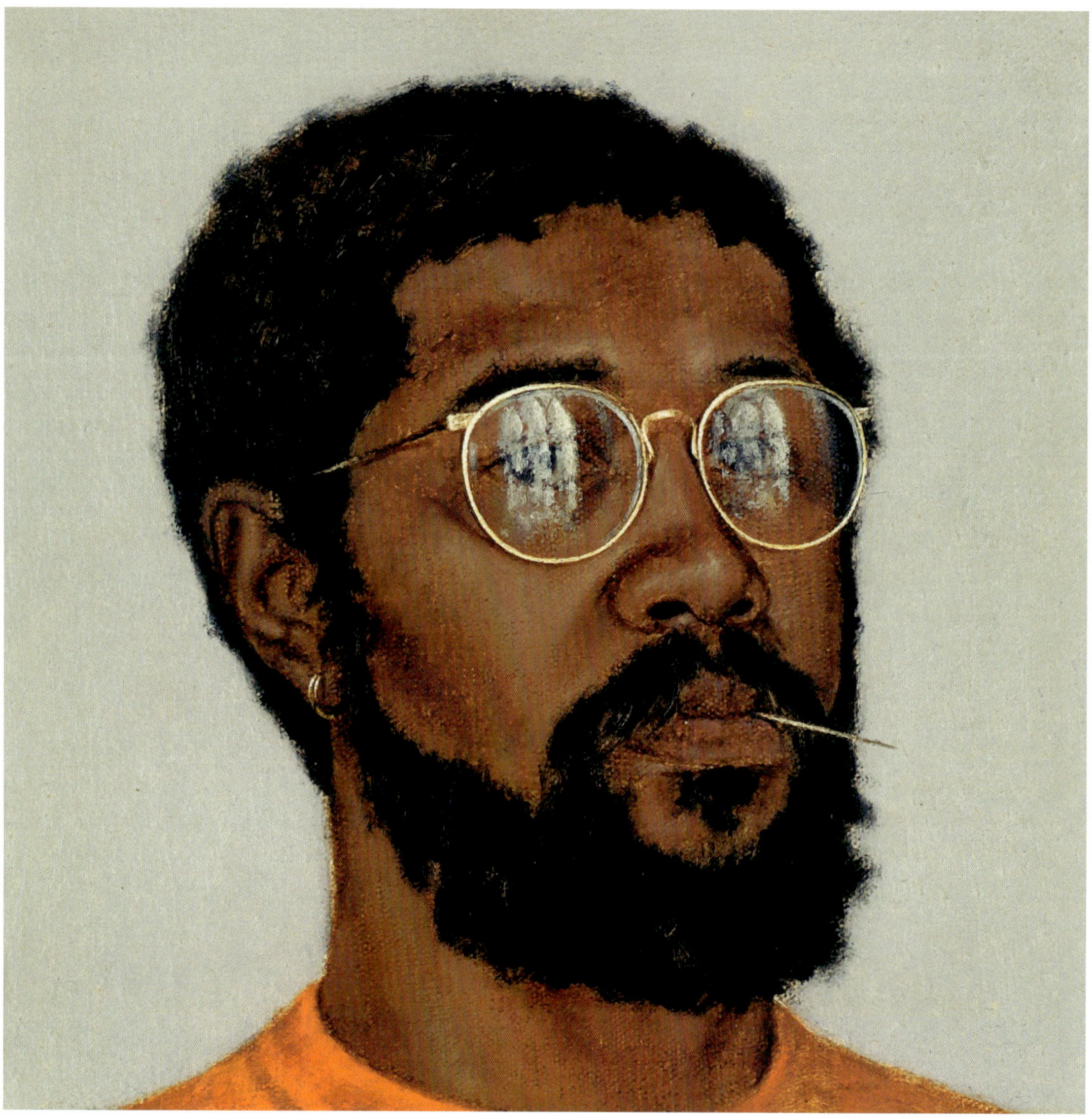

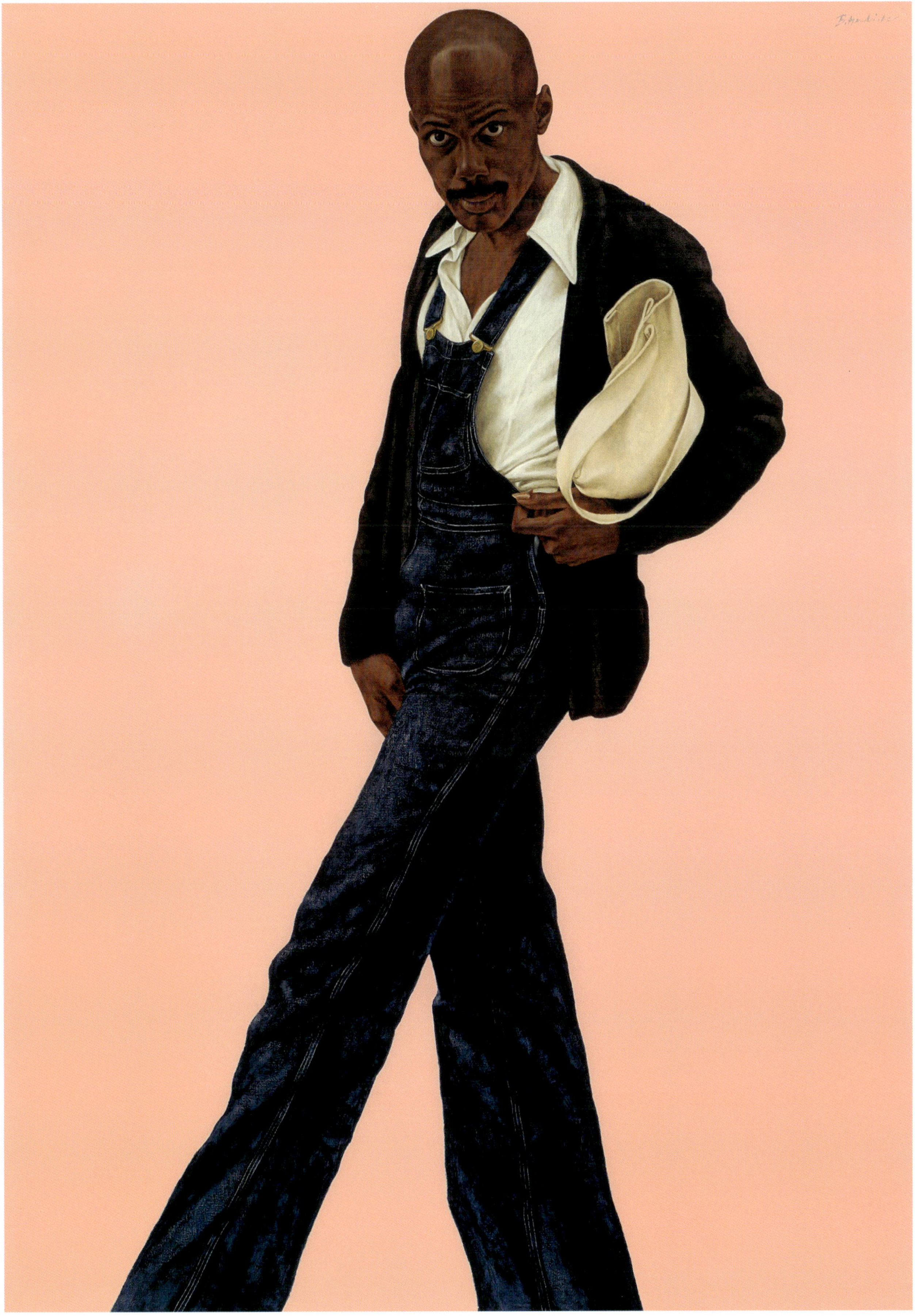

cat. 46
Lunch with Picasso: Curry Goat for Two, 2003
Oil, acrylic, and gold variegated leaf on cotton canvas
15 3/4 x 19 3/4 inches

cat. 41 (opposite page)
Ma Petite Kumquat, 1983
Oil, acrylic, white gold, and silver leaf on linen canvas
72 1/4 x 40 1/8 inches

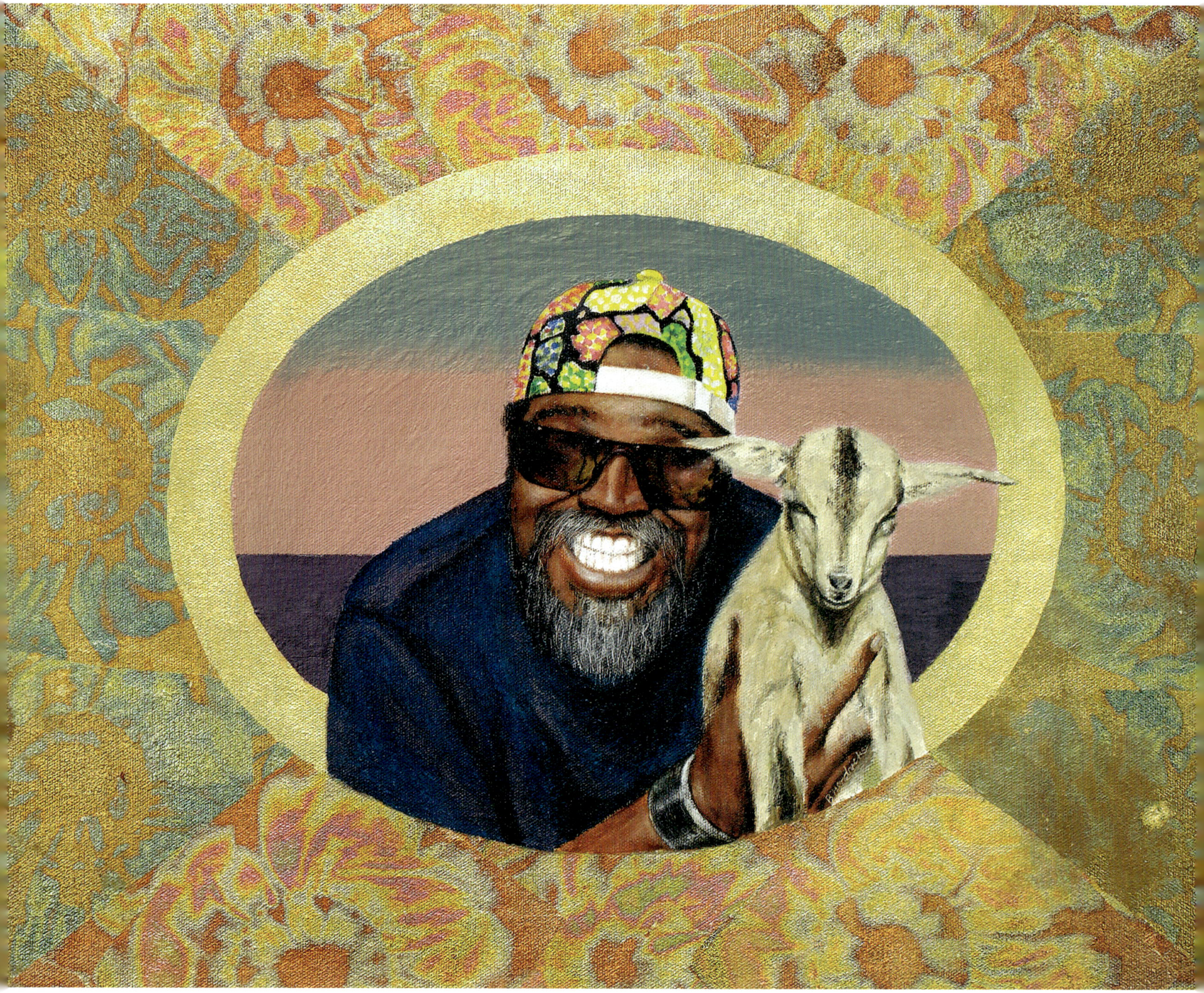

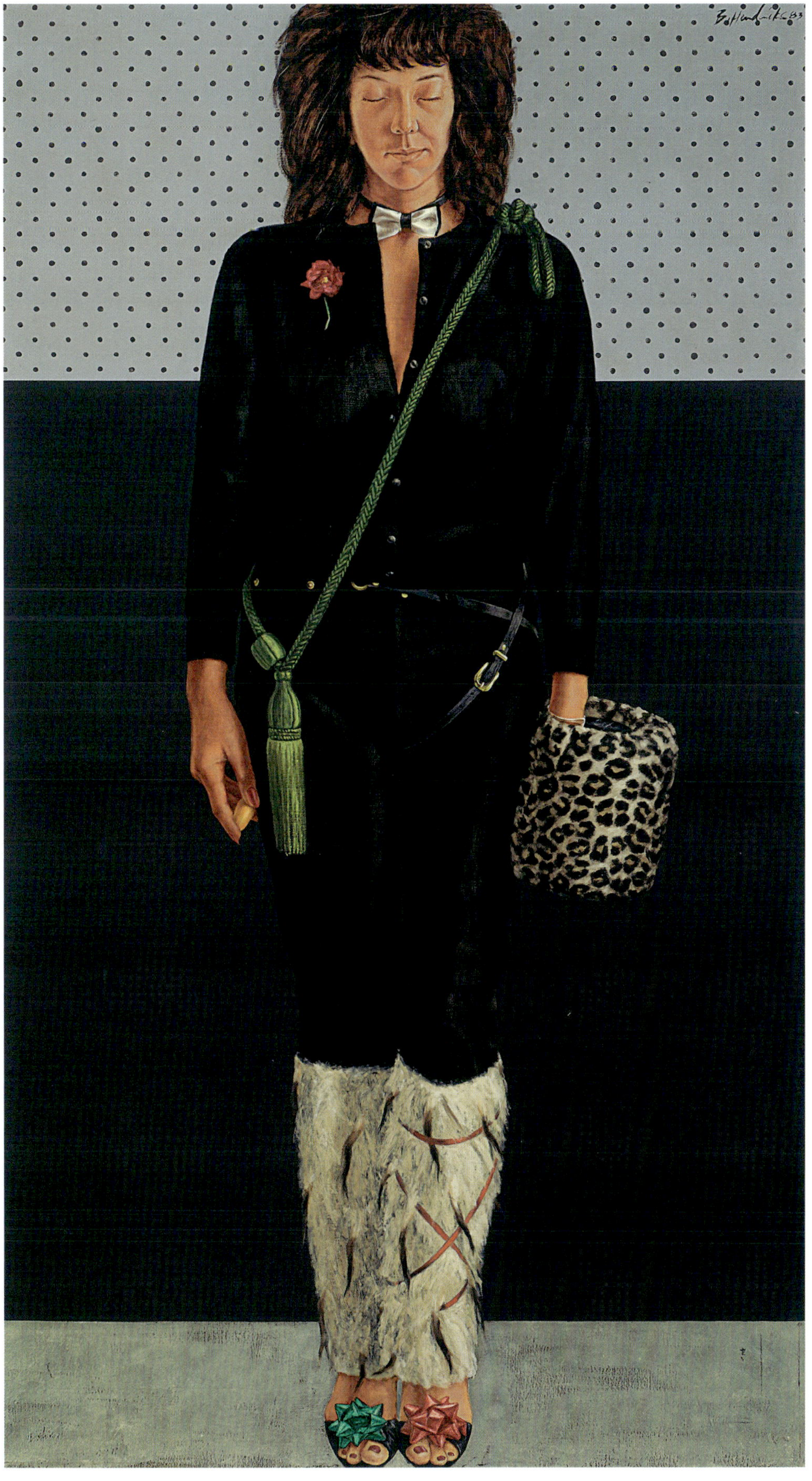

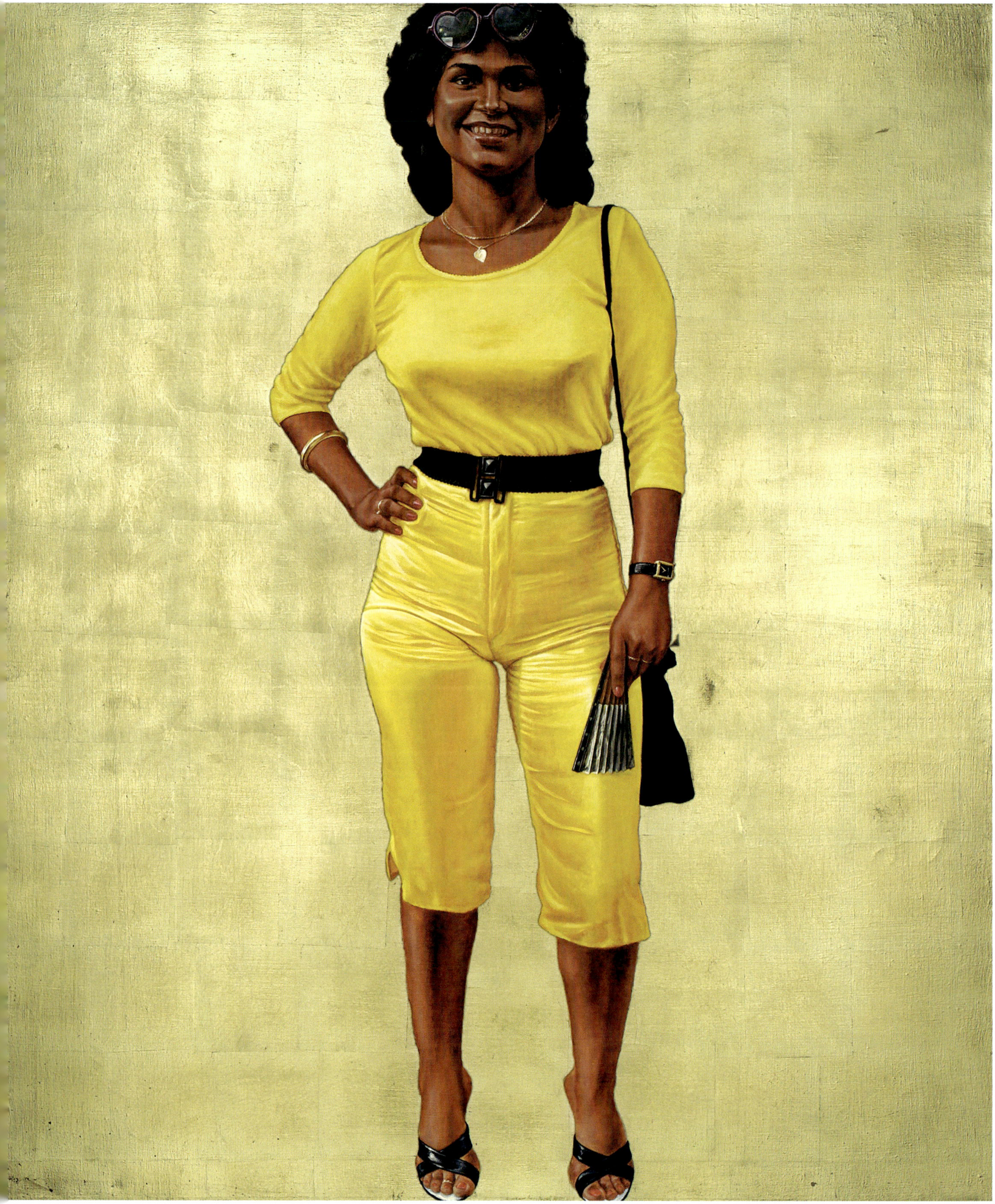

cat. 40 (opposite page)
Icon for Fifi, 1982
Oil and combination leaf
on linen canvas
60 1/4 x 50 1/4 inches

cat. 12
Dixwell, 1971
Oil and acrylic on
linen canvas
38 1/4 inches diameter

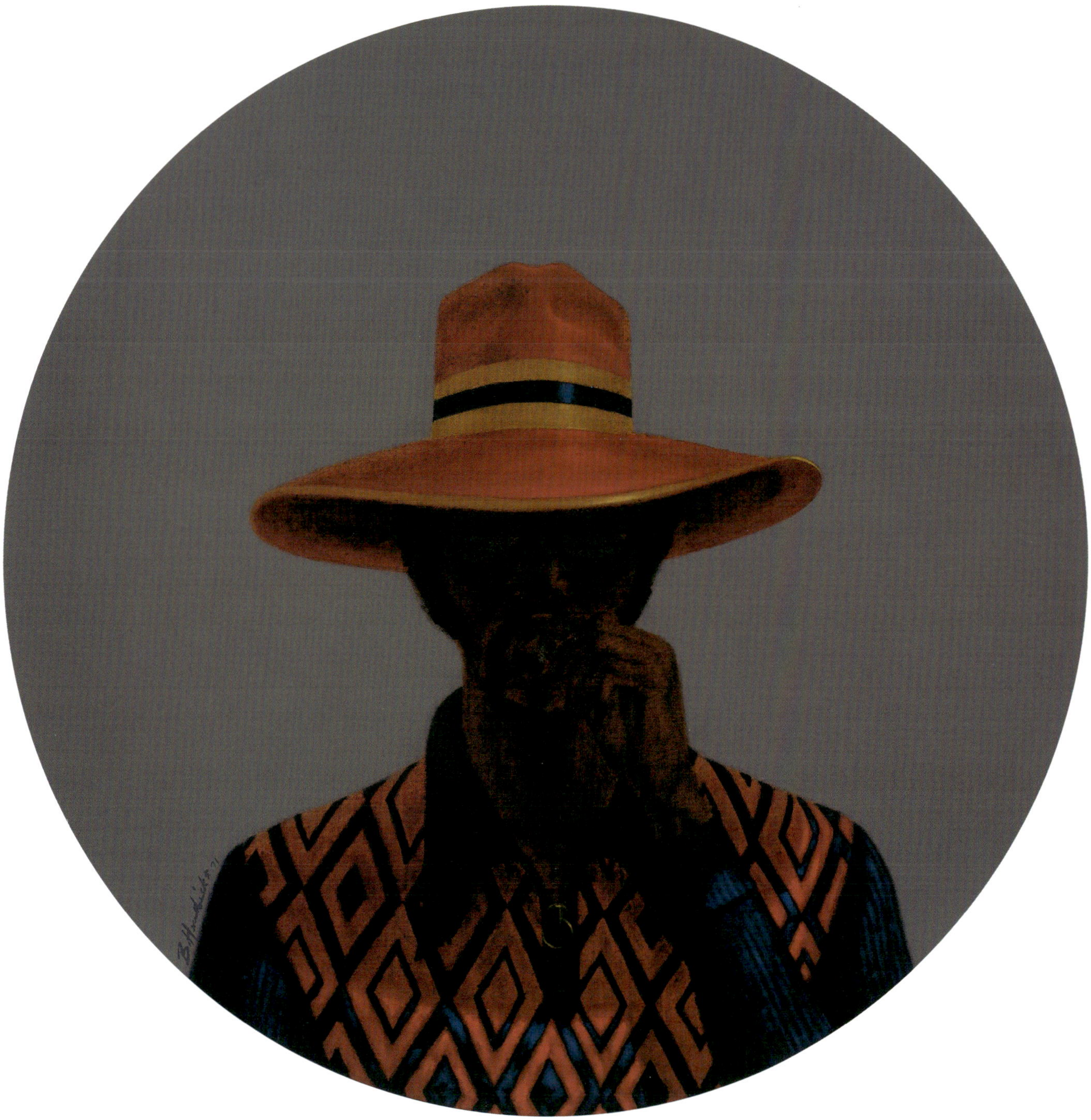

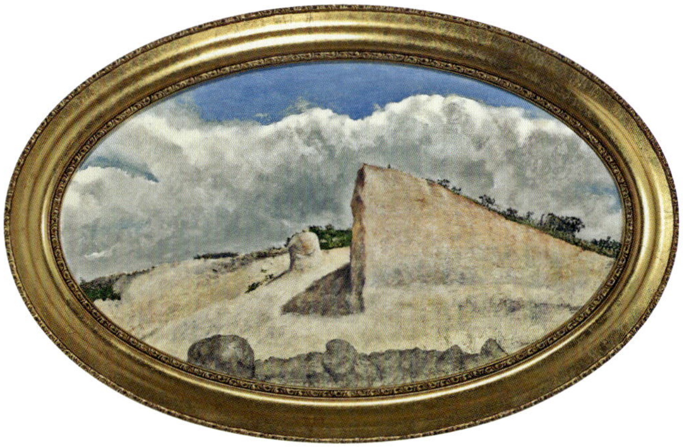

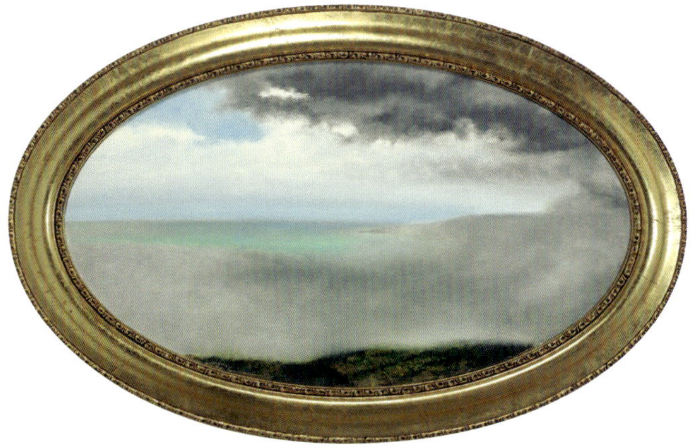

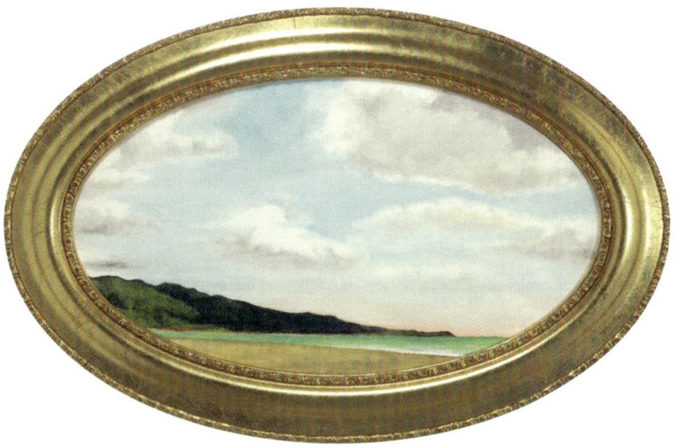

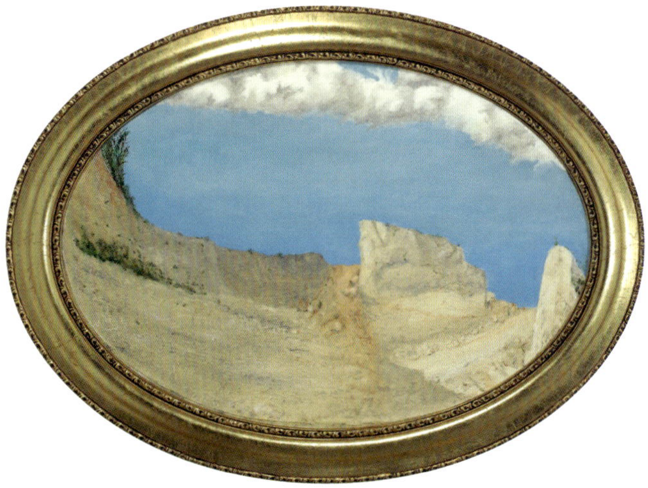

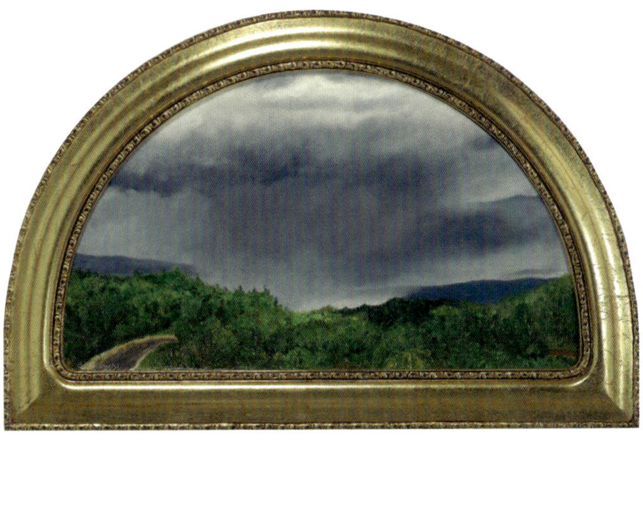

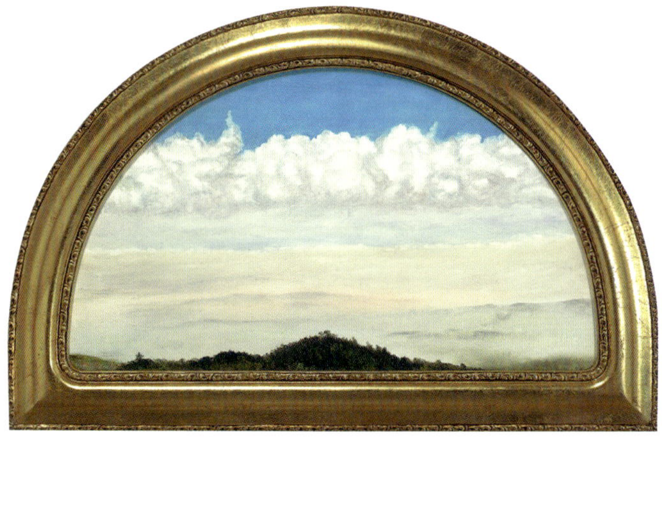

by positioning dark clothes on a dark background. Hendricks had already produced a black-on-black work in *My Black Nun* prior to seeing van Eyck's portrait, but works such as this reinforced and pushed forward his formal practice. The luscious red silk clothing simulated in van Dyck's *Portrait of Cardinal Guido Bentivoglio* (1621–1623) became direct inspiration for Hendricks's treatment of the long red overcoat in the 1972 painting *Sir Charles, Alias Willie Harris*.[12] In Hendricks's painting, the cardinal is replaced by a small-time New Haven drug dealer, but the sense of style, fashion, and splendor that van Dyck portrayed in his subjects is captured even centuries later.

Sweet Thang (Lynn Jenkins) (1975–1976) is one of the clearest examples of Hendricks's embracing of the Netherlandish tradition of embellishing the image for our visual consumption. From the woven carpet and Moroccan-tiled wall, to the subject's shimmering skirt, striped head wrap, and sparkling jewelry, a rich array of complex patterns and luxurious surfaces abounds. Such abundance is there not only to catch our eye but to convince us of the ability of the artist to represent materials, fabrics, and light. Hendricks's 1983 portrait of his wife, Susan, *Ma Petite Kumquat*, goes a step further to create a sumptuous still life within a portrait. Susan wears tight black corduroys, a vintage sweater, a leather bow tie, a red flower, a double wrap-around disco-era belt, fuzzy leg warmers, Christmas bows on the toes of her shoes, a leopard print muff in her left hand, a bright green window curtain tie-back worn as a sash, and to top it off she holds a kumquat in her right hand. Even the background is broken into different patterns, colors, and materials. By representing such an excess of objects that do not naturally go together, Hendricks appears to be showing us what he is capable of creating as a painter and inviting us to appreciate each individual element of the portrait as pure visual pleasure.

Similar to the way that Hendricks's figurative paintings demonstrate an engagement with the techniques of the old masters of European portraiture, his intimate Jamaican landscapes of the past twenty-five years share a dialogue with the centuries-old tradition of painting en plein air. His treatment of sea and sky invites particular comparisons to seventeenth-century Dutch landscape painter Jacob van Ruisdael, who was known for his many coastal scenes and the way his well-defined clouds often dominated the space and lighting of a composition. Hendricks shares similar interests in composition, but his pursuit is one of immediacy in the landscape. He paints on site, challenging himself as a painter to produce work out in the elements as natural light changes color and tone from moment to moment and wind and rain test one's ability and mettle. As much as his portraits, Hendricks's landscapes are about the act of painting. If being outdoors in the beauty of nature gives him the inspiration to paint landscapes, Jamaica provides a historic location that adds cultural significance to the formal exercise. As a geographically small island, it has played a major role in the development and dissemination of black ideology and culture, from Marcus Garvey to Bob Marley. The very fact of being set in Jamaica connects his landscape paintings to his long-standing practice of painting the black body. Just as Hendricks's portraits isolate the figure and rarely include a setting to contextualize his subject, his landscapes are devoid of the people who live there. Isolating the landscape and framing it within a porthole-like frame invites reflection and escapism, despite the specificity in depicting the location. The round and oval canvases that Hendricks uses give the paintings a portal-like feeling that magically transport the viewer to another time and place.[13]

Even with their transforming quality, Hendricks's landscape paintings are more connected in form and practice to his other paintings than one might initially realize. The oval and round formats build on some of Hendricks's earliest work, such as *Serpent's Tooth* (1968–1969), *Vertical Hold* (1967), *Butch* (1968), *Dippy's Delight* (1969), and *Dixwell* (1971). Their ornate, gilded frames draw parallels to those of Italian Renaissance and Byzantine art and reinforce the artist's interest in adornment, light, and reflection. Like his portraits of people, Hendricks's landscapes are not based on imaginary places or generalized types but reflect specific locations that he

Opposite page:

cat. 48 (top left)
Boxing Day in the Quarry #3, 2004
Oil on linen canvas
16 1/2 x 28 inches

cat. 49 (center left)
Alligator's Head, 2005
Oil on linen canvas
12 x 21 inches

cat. 53 (bottom left)
The Anglican Perspective on January 3rd, 2006
Oil on linen canvas
14 x 24 inches

cat. 50 (top right)
Black River from the Elgin Road View, 2005
Oil on linen canvas
16 1/2 x 28 inches

cat. 57 (center right)
New Year's Marl Hole, 2007
Oil on linen canvas
18 3/4 x 26 1/2 inches

cat. 56 (bottom right)
St. Mary's Blues (Sky), 2006
Oil on linen canvas
14 x 24 inches

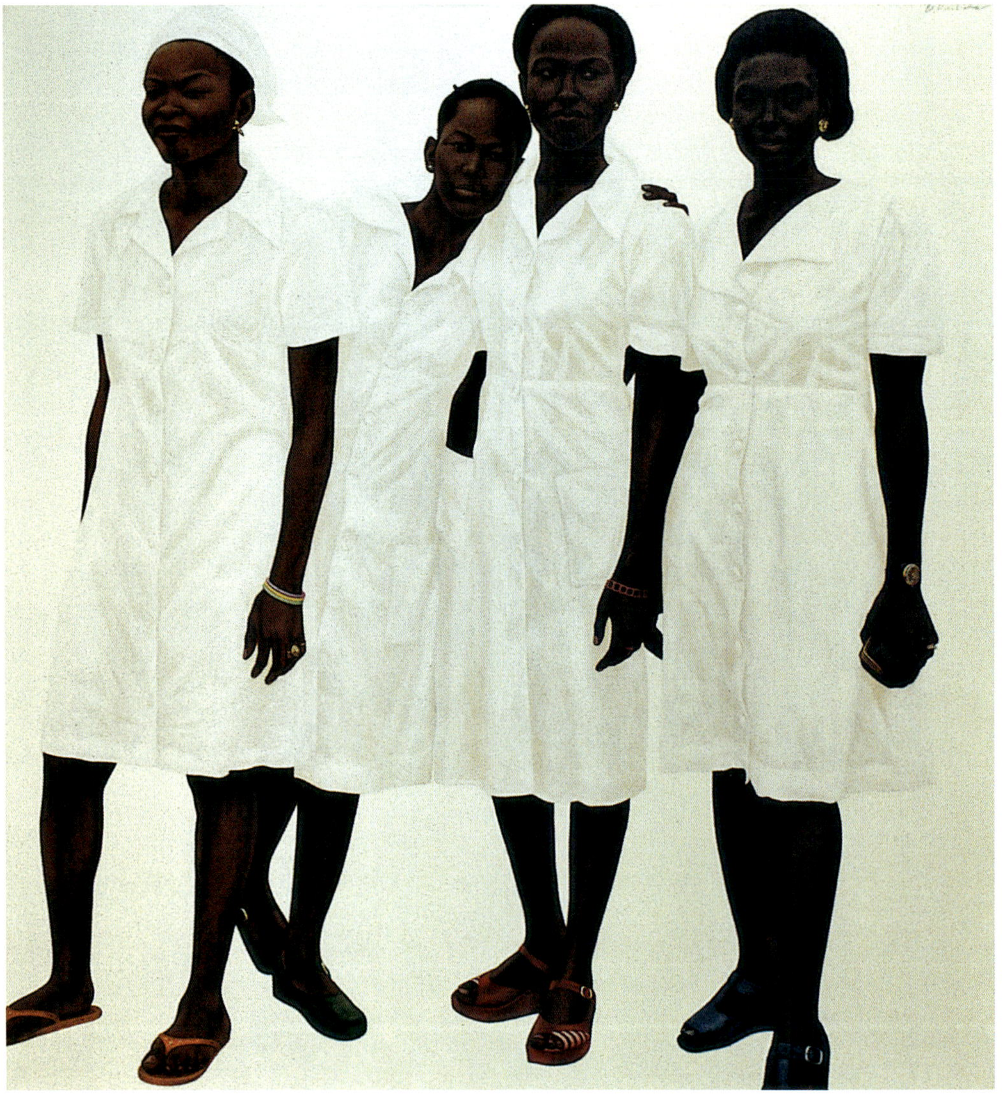

fig. 7
Lagos Ladies (Gbemi, Bisi, Niki, Christy), 1978
Oil, acrylic, and magna on cotton canvas
72 x 66 inches

fig. 8 (opposite page)
Fela: Amen, Amen, Amen, Amen..., (installation view) 2002
Oil and variegated leaf on linen canvas, wooden frame, altarpiece armature, 27 pairs of high heels
66 3/4 x 46 3/4 inches (60 x 40 inches unframed), with 60 inch altarpiece

strives to depict with great accuracy. Perhaps most significant, even in his pursuit of a very traditional art form, he continues go against the grain to follow his own interests. With little concern for what is popular or accepted, he has revived a realist landscape tradition that has been dismissed by many as an outdated practice. Some might call it romantic; others might call it dedicated, or even brave. But whatever the case, Hendricks has demonstrated over and over again integrity in his vision that is independent of popular movements and styles in the contemporary art world.

With a career spanning more than forty years, Hendricks stands out as an artist ahead of his time. His work has defied easy categorization, and his unique individualism has landed him outside of the mainstream, but his bold and empowering portrayal of those who have been overlooked and underappreciated has positioned him squarely in the hearts of many. His personalized realism has a timeless appeal; speaking with today's younger generation of artists gives one a sense for just how respected he is. By representing the black body in new and challenging ways, Hendricks's pioneering work has unwittingly helped pave the way for future generations of artists of color to work with issues of identity through representation of the black figure. Today his body of work is as vital and vibrant as ever, and it should prove him to be a lasting figure in the history of American art.

Notes

The title of this catalogue and essay, *Birth of the Cool*, is borrowed from the seminal 1949 Miles Davis album of the same title. Hendricks plays the trumpet himself and is a devoted Miles Davis enthusiast who has met and photographed Miles in concert.

1. Marsha Hunt is an African American singer, model, and actress from Philadelphia. She was the star of the London production of the 1968 rock musical *Hair*, and was Mick Jagger's girlfriend who inspired the Rolling Stones' 1971 song "Brown Sugar."

2. At the time I was also organizing an exhibition about the influence of Fela Kuti, which was realized in 2003 at the New Museum of Contemporary Art. Hendricks was introduced to Fela's music at a friend's studio in Brooklyn around 1974/1975 and traveled to Lagos, Nigeria, in 1977 for FESTAC '77 (the Second World Black and African Festival of Arts and Culture). In the early 1990s he met Fela and photographed him during various performances in Connecticut.

3. Barkley L. Hendricks in conversation with Trevor Schoonmaker, May 13, 2007.

4. Some examples of Hendricks's painting titles that contain musical references are *Arriving Soon*, borrowed from Eddie "Cleanhead" Vinson and Cannonball Adderley; *What's Going On* from Marvin Gaye; *Lawdy Mama* from Nina Simone; *Miss Brown to You* from Billie Holiday; *Down Home Taste* from Jimmy Smith; *Bid 'Em In* from Oscar Brown Junior; *Sophisticated Lady* from Duke Ellington; *Take All the Time You Need* from Ashford and Simpson. *Fela: Amen, Amen, Amen, Amen* is taken from Fela's composition "Coffin for Head of State."

5. Mixing of the secular and sacred has been a long-standing tradition in soul music that is rooted in gospel. It continues today with artists ranging from Prince to Cee-Lo Green.

6. Hendricks's portrait of Fela was produced for the 2003 New Museum exhibition *Black President: The Art and Legacy of Fela Anikulapo-Kuti*, and was his first completed portrait since *Ma Petite Kumquat* in 1983.

7. Hendricks in conversation with Trevor Schoonmaker, May 13, 2007.

8. Hendricks in conversation with Trevor Schoonmaker, May 13, 2007.

9. Hendricks in conversation with Trevor Schoonmaker, May 13, 2007.

10. Hilton Kramer, "Art: To the Last Detail," *New York Times* (June 17, 1977).

11. Hendricks in conversation with Trevor Schoonmaker, May 13, 2007.

12. Hendricks in conversation with Trevor Schoonmaker, May 13, 2007.

13. Floyd R. Thomas Jr., "A Personal Reflection on the Barkley L. Hendricks Experience— As I See It," in *The Barkley L. Hendricks Experience* (New London: Lyman Allyn Museum of Art, Connecticut College, 2001), p. 8.

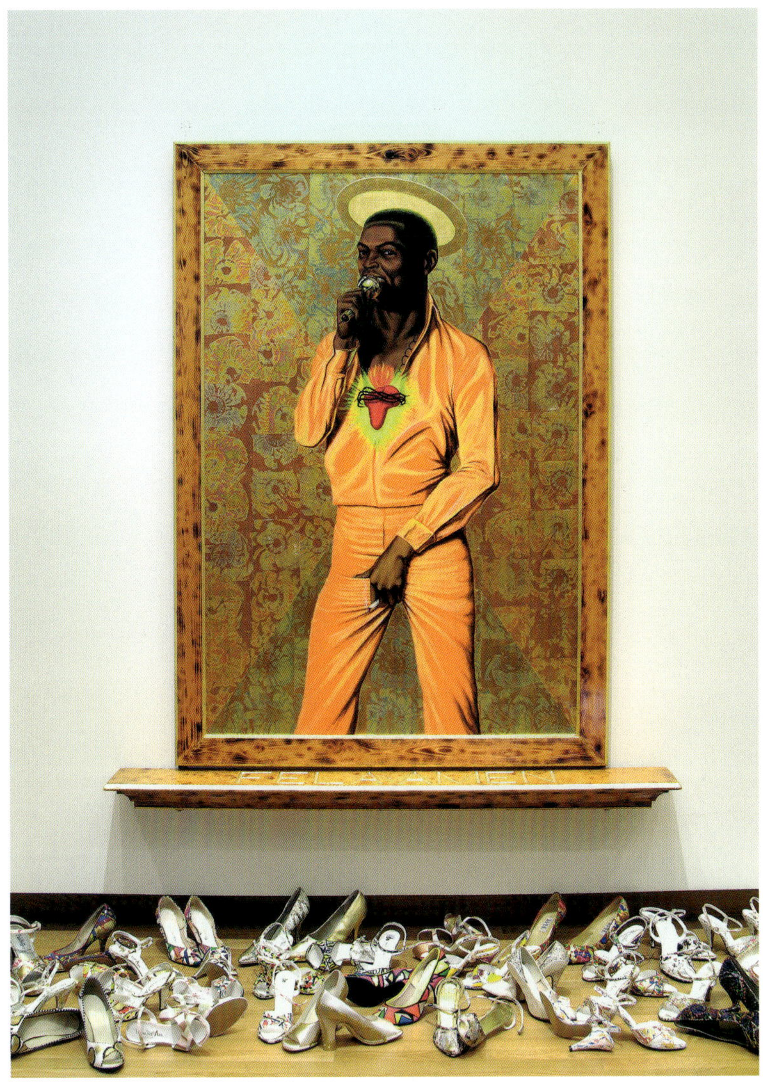

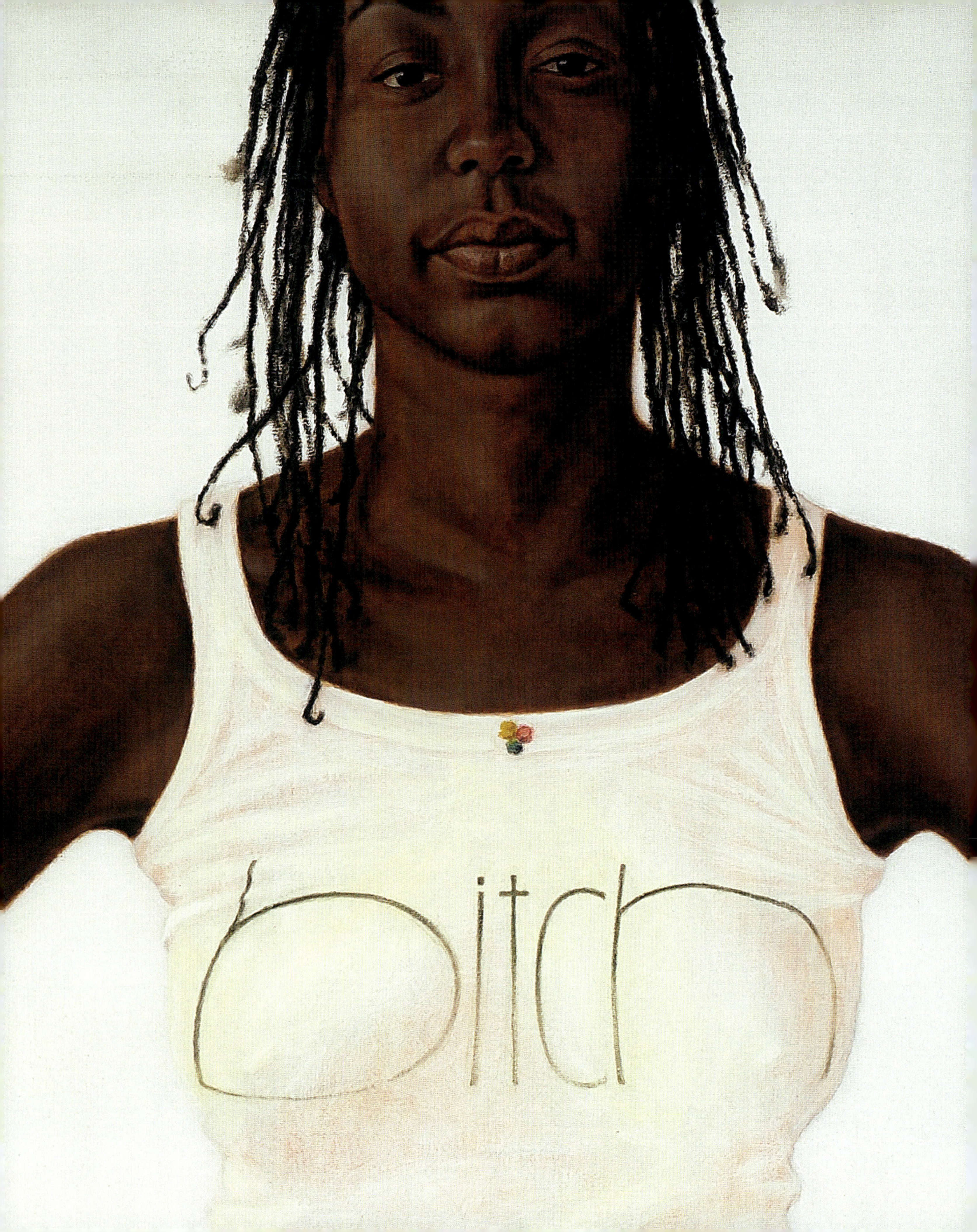
bitch

Barkley L. Hendricks, Anew Richard J. Powell

On May 20, 1978, I attended the ACA Galleries' opening reception for Barkley L. Hendricks. I remember taking lots of photographs that afternoon of Barkley, his paintings, and the invited guests (with the prescient sense that I would refer to these pictures someday). I was especially fascinated by those in attendance whose portraits were on view. Shifting my focus between the real-life subjects Vendetta, Barkley, and others, and then turning to the portrayals of these same people in oils and acrylics, I recall being intrigued not only with the virtuoso technique and verisimilitude on display but with the uncanny transference onto canvas of personality and character. It was as if Hendricks had captured something integral and constitutive about his subjects: individual essences that physical and sartorial aspects, while remarkable in their own right, only hinted at.

I remember the same feelings when, some sixteen years later, I was again in New York, viewing the Whitney Museum of American Art exhibition *Black Male: Representations of Masculinity in Contemporary American Art*. At first taken aback by unexpectedly encountering former associates there (like filmmaker Isaac Julien and poet/performance artist Essex Hemphill), I was then astounded and deeply moved to see one of Hendricks's paintings of an old acquaintance, Jules Taylor, on exhibition. Shoeless and sockless, but wearing a flamboyant cape and poker-faced expression, Jules—who had passed away almost a decade earlier during the AIDS epidemic—was his outrageous, funny self once more, and through Hendricks's visual magic attracting his own audience among the throngs gaping at Lyle Ashton Harris in crinoline and Fred Wilson's row of headless museum guards.[1]

Every intermittent sighting of Barkley L. Hendricks's work over the past few decades has been a revelation. Paintings previously seen (and about which I claimed some critical expertise) were invariably a surprise and an

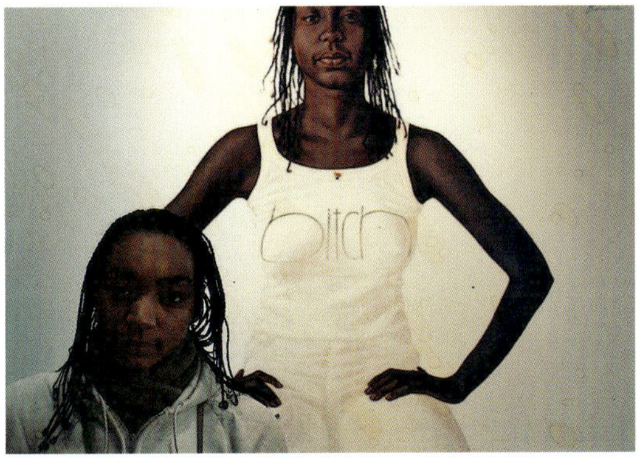

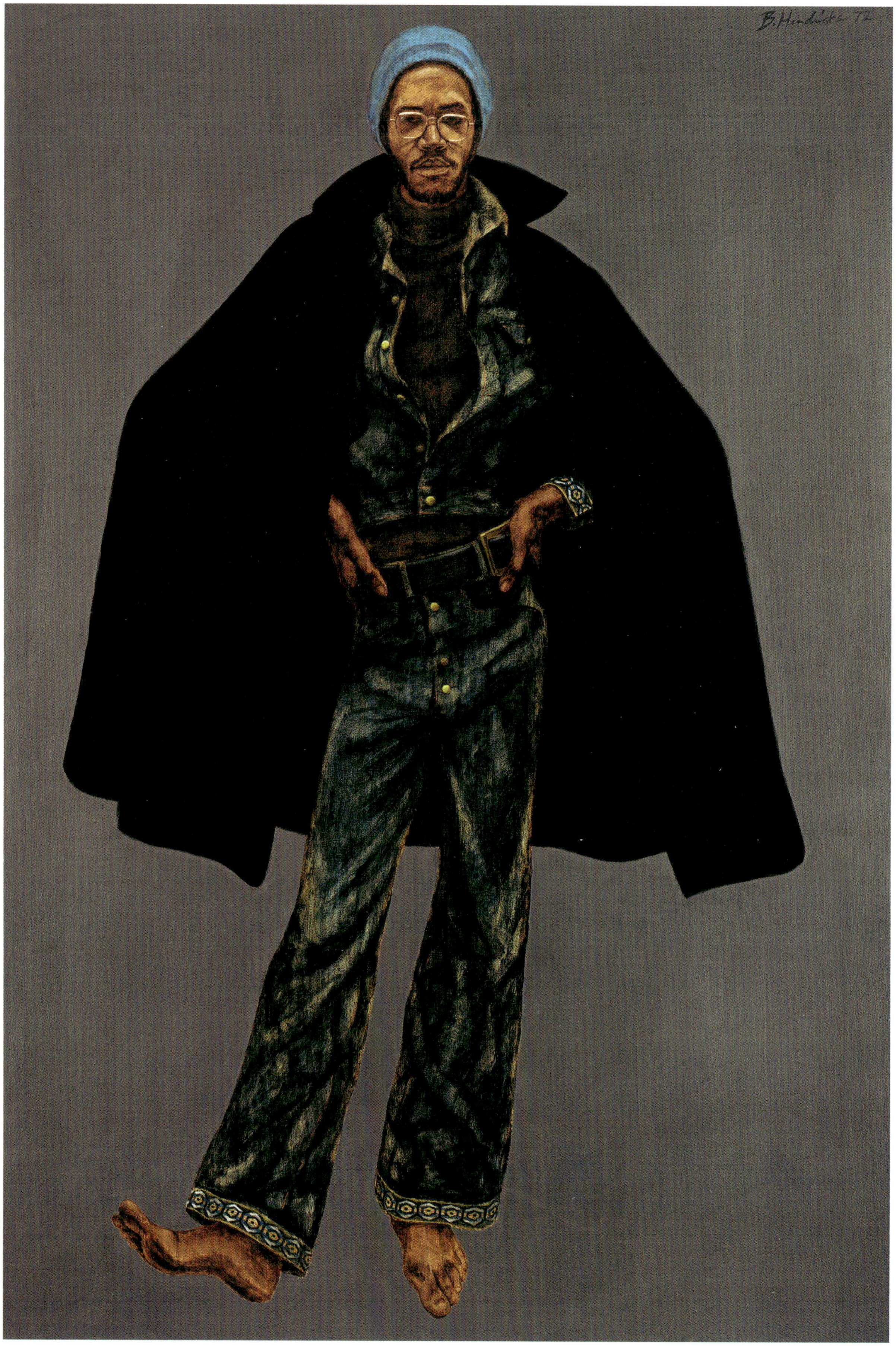
B. Hendricks 72

art historical conundrum to behold again and again. The particular modes of dress to which Hendricks's subjects subscribed were not only a lens onto a prior history of fashion and style but a close-up view of the multiplicity of personas that Hendricks and his subjects adopted, outwardly crying out it seemed for postportrait examinations. The few recognizable subjects in paintings whom I later met and had a chance to compare to their artistic portrayals always elicited a barrage of questions in my mind (What were the circumstances of the picture? How does the subject feel about his/her portrayal? Who is *really* calling the shots here?). Much of this work has been in existence since the 1960s, and yet its pictorial weight and eternal allure is a mystery in today's guileless world of visual excess and hypervisibility.

To account for these omnipresent yet surprised and applauded sightings, the knowing apperceptions and critical engagements with the renderings of these remarkable subjects, and the fundamental drawing power of Hendricks's paintings, I want to discuss this work in three art historical settings. The first frame of reference is the art world of the late 1960s and early 1970s when, largely in opposition to visual abstraction, minimalism, and the universal charisma of pop art, figurative painters readjusted their channels of artistic expression through various conceptual stratagems, mostly in reaction to photography. The second context for a reappraisal of Hendricks's work is this same chronological period, but in sharp contrast to the aforementioned scenario, a world where many African American artists, under the banner of the black arts movement, realigned their aesthetic barometers to racial and cultural determinants. The third historical framework is today's art scene, where painters, photographers, and others two-dimensional artists employ figural realism in a critical, ironic, and often highly referential manner.

What each of these comparative models yields is the sense that for all of Hendricks's connections to a particular moment in art history, his art transcends the times in which it was produced. He has created paintings of people, places, and things that, amazingly, extend themselves across the boundaries of

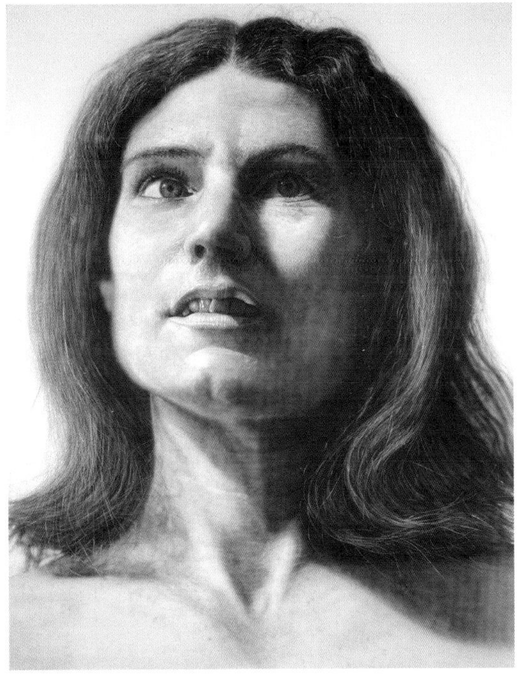

subjectivity and conventional representation, and into an at times indescribable world of information age spectatorship. "If three different people were asked how they responded to the portraits of Barkley Hendricks," wrote museum curator David Katzive, "it would be entirely possible to have one person reply that they were overpowering, sensual, and physically exciting; for another person to reply that they were cool, remote, and photographic; and for a third person to reply that they exemplify Black dignity, pride and self-affirmation."[2] As suggested in Katzive's curatorial observations, Hendricks's work has long transcended simple categorizations and elicits an array of critical responses to its seemingly straightforward but profoundly nuanced depictions of the figure.[3]

With a curious mixture of cool objectification, brash exhibitionism, and, paradoxically, a heartfelt empathy, the art of Barkley L. Hendricks vaults the temporal limitations of, say, late pop or postmodern art and becomes a testimony to the artistic challenges and infinite possibilities within an art tradition *proper*. As we ponders these canvases of "everyday people," we unconsciously bear witness to the magnetism and visual power of a retrofitted academism, dressed in polyester and extreme attitude, and, with a touch of the subversive, deconstructing before our very eyes against a

cat. 35 (page 38)
Vendetta, (detail) 1977
Oil, acrylic, and magna on linen canvas
36 x 48 1/8 inches

fig. 1 (page 39)
Vendetta (subject) with painting *Vendetta* in studio at 58 State Street New London, CT 1977

cat. 14 (opposite page)
George Jules Taylor, 1972
Oil and acrylic on cotton canvas
91 1/2 x 60 1/4 inches

fig. 2
Chuck Close
Nancy, 1968
Acrylic on canvas
108 3/8 x 82 1/2 inches

blank, white expanse. An assessment as to how Hendricks has "worked" this conceptual sleight of hand is at the root of this inquiry and, in a related vein, informs the bigger picture of modern portraiture, its destabilization of identity, and its assumed propensities for revealing an inner, unvarnished truth.

One of the challenges in discussing Barkley L. Hendricks's materialization in the late 1960s is the heterogeneous nature of the art scene at that time. The competing aesthetics of late 1960s pop art, minimalism, conceptualism, and earthworks, among other artistic directions, make it very difficult to identify any single philosophical development or cultural context for these works. The same could be said of the considerably smaller sphere in which just American painters operated. Notwithstanding the range of perspectives as well as the gamut of painting techniques by artists as diverse as John Baldessari, Romare Bearden, Judy Chicago, Sam Gilliam, Philip Guston, Sol Lewitt, Alex Katz, Ellsworth Kelly, Brice Marden, Alice Neel, Kenneth Noland, Robert Rauschenberg, Frank Stella, and Nancy Spero, among others, it could be said that American painting circa 1969 was undergoing an identity crisis of sorts. Even within the subset of "figurative realists" with whom Hendricks would have been categorized, the reconceptualization of reality, artistic representations, and modern painting itself called into question the cultural relevance of such a category.

These misgivings about figuration and painterly realism circa 1969 appeared in journals like *Artforum International*, which published several articles that grappled with these and other ostensibly conservative approaches to art-making.[4] The most notable of these published critiques were comments made by artist Chuck Close, whose massive paintings of people's heads (dispassionately transferred onto canvas from scaled photographs) were just then making their New York debut. When asked by *Artforum* interviewer Cindy Nemser if he felt any kinship with other figurative artists, Close replied, "I have very little sympathy or interest in the figurative art being shown today, and I object to the lumping together of everybody who works from life or from photographs under the title of realism or superrealism." Works by Close such as *Nancy* aesthetically challenged both the traditional painters and the more innovative minimalists, with its grid-informed deployment of a photographic realism, but monumentally conceived and unfettered by "outworn humanist notions."[5]

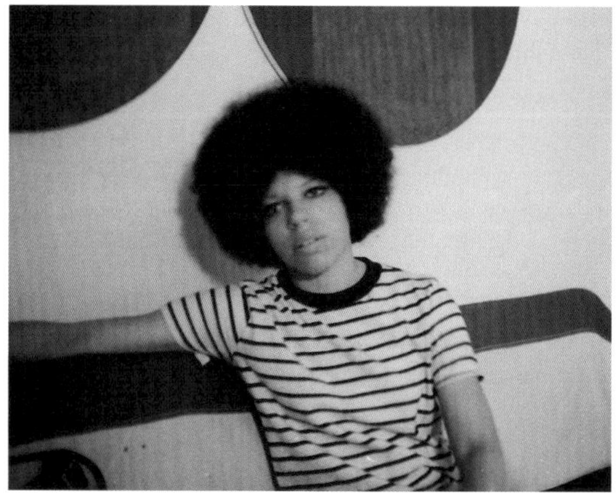

fig. 3
Photograph of Kathy Williams (subject of *Lawdy Mama*) in studio at 1605 Race Street, Philadelphia, 1970

cat. 8 (opposite page)
Lawdy Mama, 1969
Oil and gold leaf on linen canvas
53 3/4 x 36 1/4 inches

If Close and the other critics of figural realism had encountered Hendricks's *Lawdy Mama*, they probably would have struggled to make artistic sense of it. Unapologetically giving his cousin Kathy Williams an iconic, Byzantine-like context, Hendricks nonetheless put equal weight on corporeal veracity, as well as abetting the painting's inferred "authenticity" with its vernacular, "down-home" title (taken from a verbal aside in a recording by Nina Simone).[6] Whereas *Lawdy Mama* would have immediately launched viewers into the political symbolism of an *au-courant*, physically confrontational racial blackness (described by one art reviewer as portraying a "Negro girl with a big Afro hairdo"), her silhouetted form and its emphatic two-dimensionality—against a nonillusionistic, gold-leaf ground—short-circuited any straightforward cultural readings and interjected an unexpected but welcomed formalism.[7]

Commenting on Alfred Leslie and Philip Pearlstein (two 1960s luminaries of figural realism in painting), art critic Sidney Tillim wrote, "Theirs is a kind of Minimalism in figurative terms." "Some ineluctable modality," Tillim continued, "seems to conspire to keep [Leslie's and Pearlstein's] figures from being much more than presences." Paintings such as Pearlstein's *Model with Legs Up*,

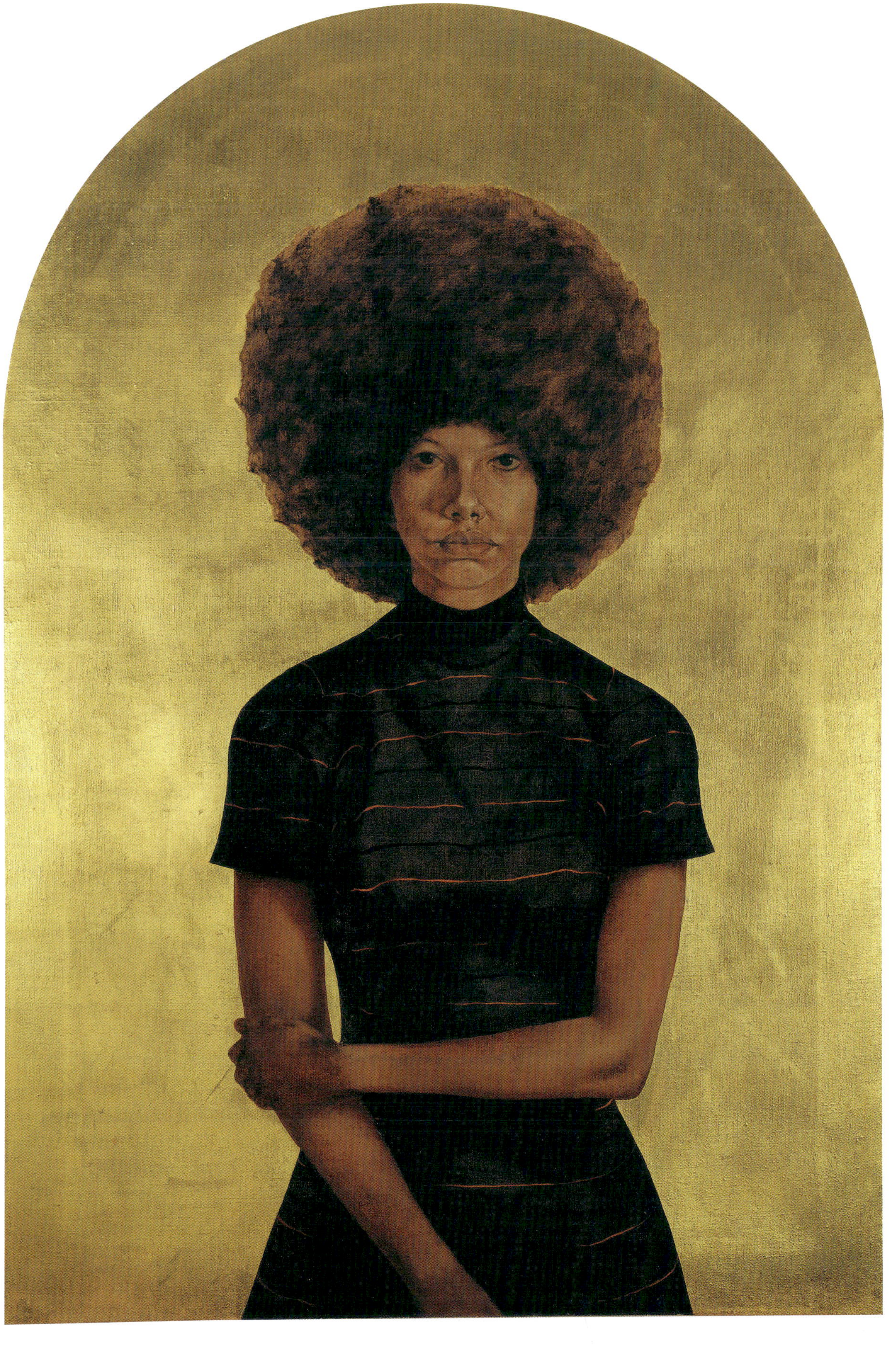

while conceptually as far removed from Chuck Close's *Nancy* as one could possibly imagine, nonetheless conveyed a similar emotional detachment and spiritual economy that critics of the "new realism" either championed or disparaged. It was especially in Pearlstein's reformulations of the academic renderings of nudes that even skeptics like Tillim found a small measure of hope: a humanity-centered realism that like "the essential idealism at stake in [the] civil rights [movement]" "executed the deeper social and psychological function of form, as opposed to a particular aspect of vanity called taste."[8]

Again, Hendricks's paintings—with their masterful yet uneasy "mingling [of] art and life"—resist easy categorization within the figurative realist vein.[9] These works are neither in alliance with Alfred Leslie's confrontational figures, nor with Pearlstein's neo-academic tributes to the live model. Hendricks's *Fast Eddie—JN*, while sharing the superficial trappings of Leslie's torsos and Pearlstein's nudes, revels in a restless mixture of idiosyncrasy and self-exhibitionism. Reverberating with an unbridled physicality that by comparison turned the pop eroticism of contemporaries Tom Wesselmann and Allen Jones into glib vulgarities, *Fast Eddie—JN* broached the underside of the "swinging '70s": a crisp depiction of a model/hustler that in sharp contrast to Tillim's civil rights "idealism" introduced a problematic and unsettling realism into the art world.

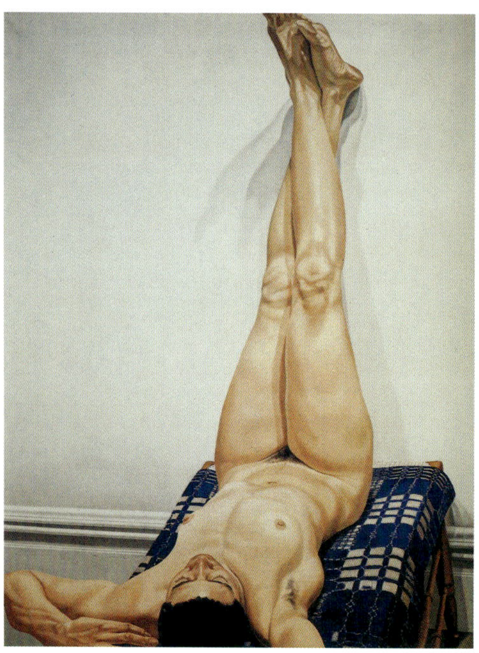

fig. 4
Philip Pearlstein
Model with Legs Up, 1975
Oil on linen canvas
72 x 54 inches

Both *Lawdy Mama* and *Fast Eddie—JN* negotiated their realism through the *idea*—if not the mechanics—of photography. In spite of having studied at Yale University with legendary photographer Walker Evans, Hendricks moderated the camera's representational intransigence with painting's inherent variability and potential for mythologizing (skills he obtained and perfected years before while studying at the Pennsylvania Academy of the Fine Arts, PAFA). Using both photography and painting as conceptual templates, Hendricks fashioned subjects whose physical characteristics, in addition to being faithfully rendered with camera-like specificity, were enhanced and emotionally charged vis-à-vis the art of painting. In addition, Hendricks employed a collage sensibility in these works, and because of his placement of people against stark, monochromatic areas, a sense of montage and materiality was achieved. Figure/ground distinctions—created by painting figures with oils and glazes and, in contrast, painting backgrounds with matte acrylics—underscored the formalist thinking behind these depictions, and Hendricks's adherence in painted portraiture to a sequestered yet sympathetic presentation.

Although Hendricks was trained at two prestigious art schools and consequently was an active participant in the mainstream art world, circa 1969, the social and artistic spheres in which he largely operated *outside* of the PAFA and Yale were of an entirely different cultural constitution. Hendricks's "other" context—as a rising star in the burgeoning black arts movement—took place along with his overtures to a deeply divided, realist painting scene, and introduces yet another intriguing frame through which one can consider his work.

As a young man in the late 1960s Hendricks was attuned to the widespread changes taking place within post–civil rights-era African American communities, as expressed in an updated, culturally enlightened nomenclature; in ethnic apparel and customs of self-fashioning; and generally in racially informed concerns and policies within the society at large.[10] He was aware of the ever-increasing numbers of new black artists' organizations, recently opened museums and galleries that prominently featured works by black artists, and the rise in racially themed exhibitions, both in the Northeastern United States and nationwide.[11] The Boston-to-D.C. black artists network (of which Hendricks was an active component) kept him apprised, for example, of the 1968 founding of the Studio Museum in Harlem, the protests in 1969 against the Metropolitan Museum of Art's controversial *Harlem on My Mind* show, and the heated debates swirling around the equally contentious 1970 exhibition *Afro-American Artists, New York and Boston*.[12]

Based in Philadelphia at the time of the *Harlem on My Mind* show (and the ensuing protests), Hendricks participated that year in his first major African American art exhibition. *Afro-American Artists, 1800–1969* at the Philadelphia Civic Center featured an impressive collection of paintings and sculptures by historic and contemporary artists. Many in the contemporary category (like Paul Keene, Faith Ringgold, Charles Searles, and others) were proponents of a widely embraced aesthetic among black artists, celebrating African sensibilities in designs and colors and depicting African American subject matter with an explicit social and political perspective.[13] Although not included in *Afro-American Artists, 1800–1969*, Chicago-based painter Jeff Donaldson was nationally recognized during this period for works of art and organizational activities that epitomized this racial reprioritizing in the visual arts. As one of the founding members of the black artists group AfriCOBRA (the African Commune of Bad Relevant Artists), Donaldson penned their broadly declaimed manifesto "10 in Search of a Nation"; brought his cultural nationalist philosophy of art to Howard University's College of Fine Arts; and painted exemplary, Afro-centric compositions like *Ala Sango*, with its idealized figures and visual passages of rhythmic, abstract patterning.[14]

Lawdy Mama, by sheer virtue of Kathy Williams's high-flying Afro, would have been viewed by many at this time as representative of the black arts movement. But in other works Hendricks clearly raised the ante on what "black art" could be or should look like. A few years prior to *Lawdy Mama*, Hendricks created a series of circular and square paintings depicting basketballs, illusorily fixed at various stages of proximity to the hoop and/or the backboard.[15] Formally reminiscent of the geometric abstractions of Ellsworth Kelly, works like *Black on Black in Black* were wry commentaries on both minimalism in painting and the black arts movement, utilizing the visual and titular trappings of both, yet maintaining an allegiance to realism and, perhaps more significant, to a form of cultural portraiture.[16] In Donaldson's published manifesto for AfriCOBRA, the idea of a black cultural portrait was articulated and advanced (in the section

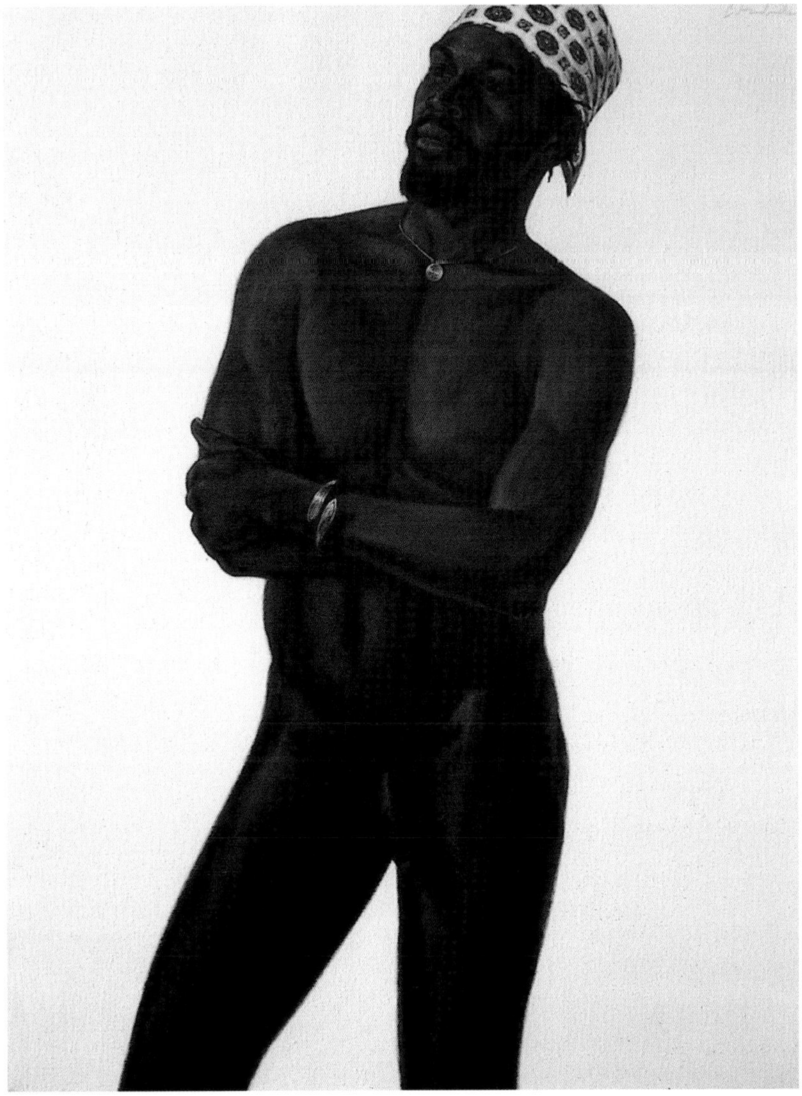

fig. 5
Fast Eddie–JN (Jive Niggah/ Eddie Clanton), 1975
Oil and acrylic on linen canvas
48 1/2 x 36 1/2 inches

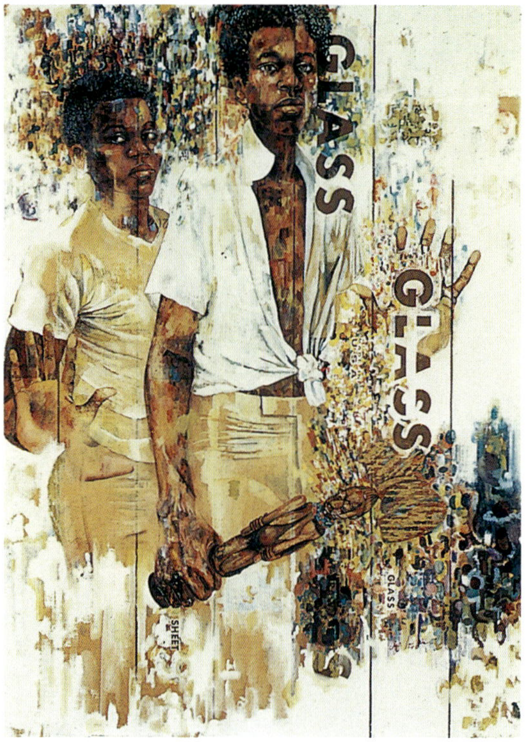

fig. 6
Jeff Donaldson
Ala Sango, 1968
Mixed media on canvas
28 x 23 inches

describing the "expressive awesomeness" of the quotidian African American experience) but subsumed, arguably, by other visual and political prescriptions (such as the call for incorporating contrastive color schemes, projecting onto one's art patterns reminiscent of African textiles, and the utilization of sociopolitical allegory and agitprop).[17] Unlike the overt references to Africa, or to the "black power" and "black is beautiful" attributes found in much of the work made by that era's loosely affiliated consortium of black painters and sculptors, Hendricks, through his basketball still lifes and realist portraits, was in quest of a *fundamental* blackness. What Hendricks aspired toward in *Black on Black in Black* was a racial and cultural quintessence that rather than functioning as something symbolic or being superficially retrieved through a discursive rhetoric or mere phenotype, operated conceptually and metonymically and could be intuited through informed representations, a canvassing of cultural predilections and mores, and an exact understanding of what might be described as a "black reality."[18]

Having already veered away from the new black corporeal stereotypes in several early portraits (including *Lawdy Mama*'s somewhat vague, racial indeterminacy, sans the Afro), Hendricks painted scores of men and women in the 1970s whose inferable eccentricities and imaginative dress (or, in the case of *Fast Eddie—JN*, the lack thereof) expanded the popular perceptions of African Americans. If any bias can be ascertained from Hendricks's black scopic regime during this period, it overwhelmingly converges on young, urbane adults, whose characteristic joie de vivre and *in-process* identity formation—emblematized in revelatory fashion statements and expressive poses and body language—ably manifested themselves through his painterly devices.

Neither content with an *Ebony* magazine–styled black man and woman whose dress-for-success look approximated the corporate mainstream, nor completely at ease with the Afro-centric vogue of black cultural nationalists, Hendricks painted the spectrum of young, contemporary African Americans circa 1970s whose perceived aesthetic difference, coupled with a core universality, individuated his portrayals. "The subjects of Hendricks's portraits are generally people from the community who

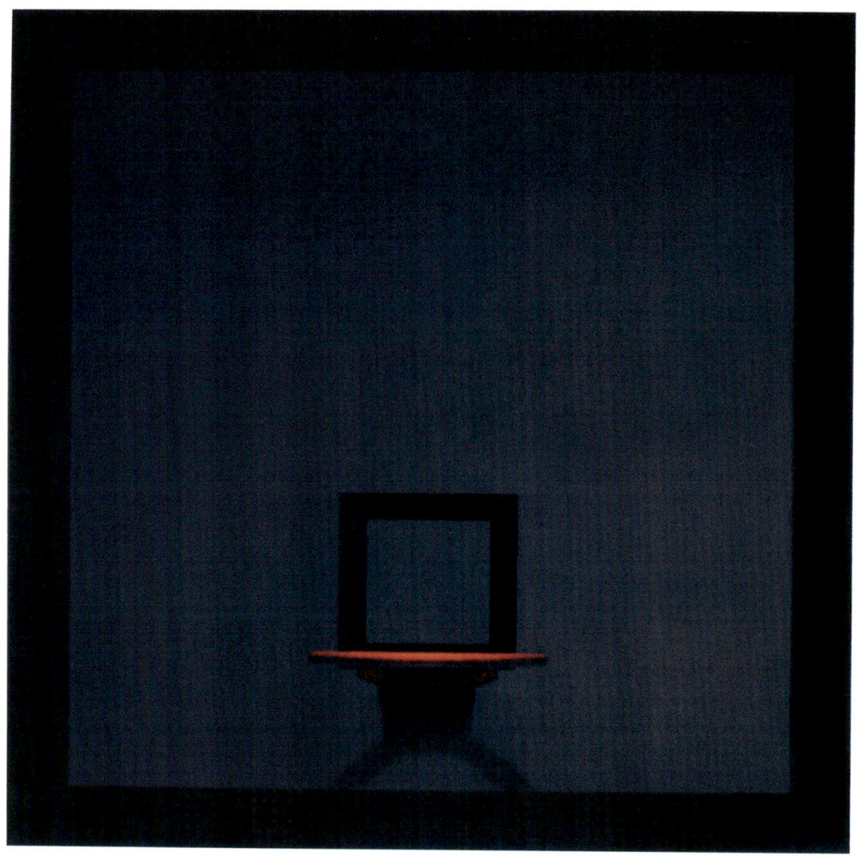

fig. 7
Black on Black in Black, 1967
Oil and acrylic on canvas
50 x 50 inches

one might see on the street but not *really* see," perceptively wrote museum curator Floyd R. Thomas Jr. about this subtle imponderability in Hendricks's figures.[19] Rather than painting his black subjects with that era's prevailing mood of racial idealism, Hendricks frequently interjected an element of irony into common notions of blackness, as in *Blood (Donald Fomey)*. Inducing viewers to choose from several possible meanings for this portrait's title (i.e., the vascular fluid, the racial colloquialism, a color allusion, a metaphor for life itself, etc.), Hendricks complicates the notion of blood (and by extension, blackness), but does so through a relatively straightforward representation of a typical African American. As seen in his former student Donald Fomey's plaid jumpsuit–clad figure (strategically placed against a solid red rectangle), Hendricks's *typikós* is often cloaked in the trappings of the *phainómenos*.[20]

In a painting of another former student, titled *Sweet Thang (Lynn Jenkins)*, Hendricks again troubled conventional portraiture, in that his young, attractive, and flippant sitter presented a stark, physical alternative to the standard (re: conservative) African American image, circa 1975. Lynn's languorous, cavalier posture and her partial disappearance behind a bubble gum buffer conveyed a subtle irony and irreverence rarely depicted in figurative paintings of African Americans (or for that matter, in figurative and realist painting in general).[21] More likely to appear in the photographs of a disaffected, post-Vietnam and post–civil rights generation (as seen in camera portraits by Larry Clark, Roland L. Freeman, and Nan Goldin), these disaffected subjects, along with their artistic consecration by Hendricks, pioneered a figural prototype in late twentieth-century painting that with the advent of artistic dissidents like John Currin, Lisa Yuskavage, and Kerry James Marshall, has finally achieved a significant degree of art world currency. Postmodern critiques of black romanticism and identity politics sui generis, as evidenced in Kerry James Marshall's tongue-in-cheek *SOB, SOB*, owe at the very least a small debt to Hendricks's women and men and their visceral ambivalence to portrait protocols and more idealized states of a bodily existence.[22]

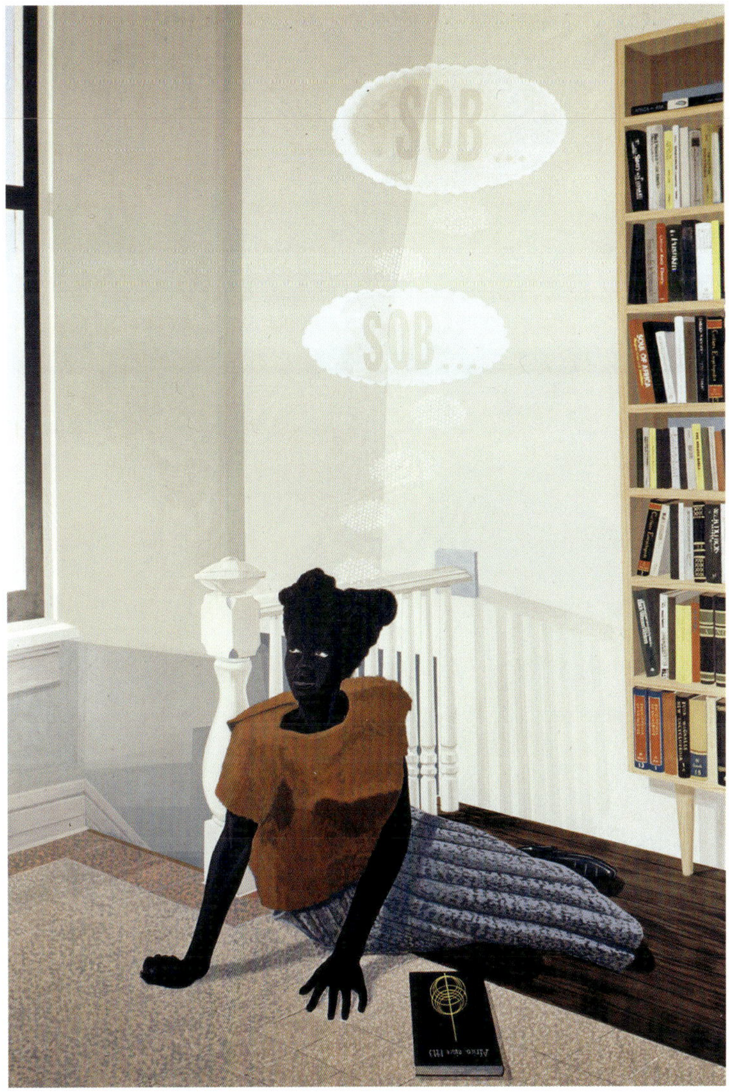

fig. 8
Kerry James Marshall
SOB, SOB, 2003
Acrylic on fiberglass
108 x 72 inches

The visual gulf that audiences might initially assume is present between Hendricks's work and the postmodern attitudes of a contemporary portraitist like Belgian painter Till Freiwald dwindles (or at least becomes more clearly mapped) with close, critical examinations of works by both artists. Freiwald's *Untitled* watercolor of the head of a black man—painted from memory and diffused with an ocular and classificatory disinterest—has some of the same qualities that an earlier generation of minimalists like Chuck Close fostered in their work. This tendency to make a real-life subject generic, along with monumentalizing the portrait and then disallowing it of an identifying title, reflects the latest fin-de-siècle fatigue with evidentiary excesses and a sense of indiscernibility in contemporary life.[23]

cat. 18
Bid 'Em In/Slave (Angie), 1973
Oil and acrylic on linen canvas
72 x 50 inches

cat. 28 (opposite page)
Sweet Thang (Lynn Jenkins), 1975–1976
Oil on linen canvas
52 1/8 x 52 3/4 inches

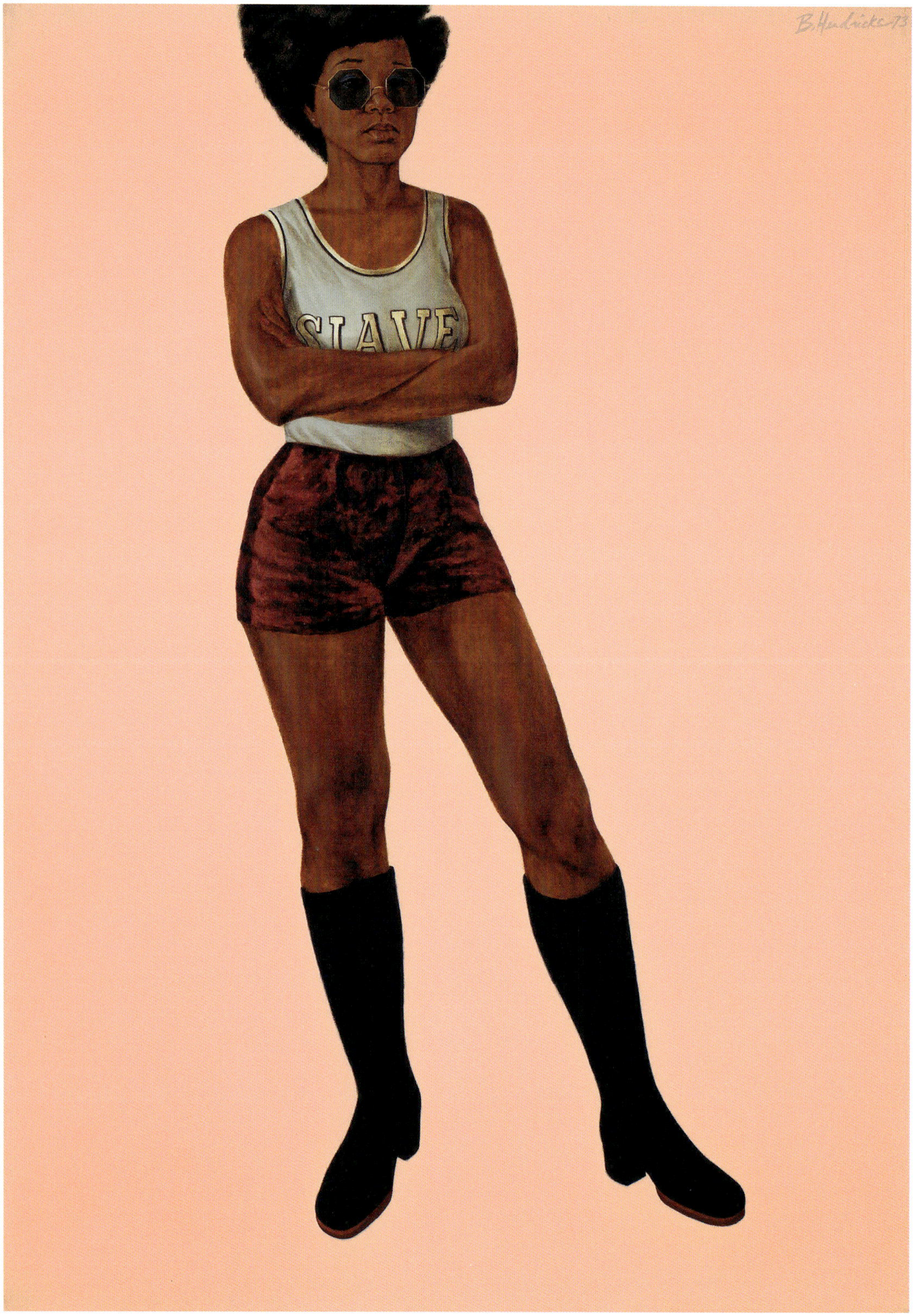

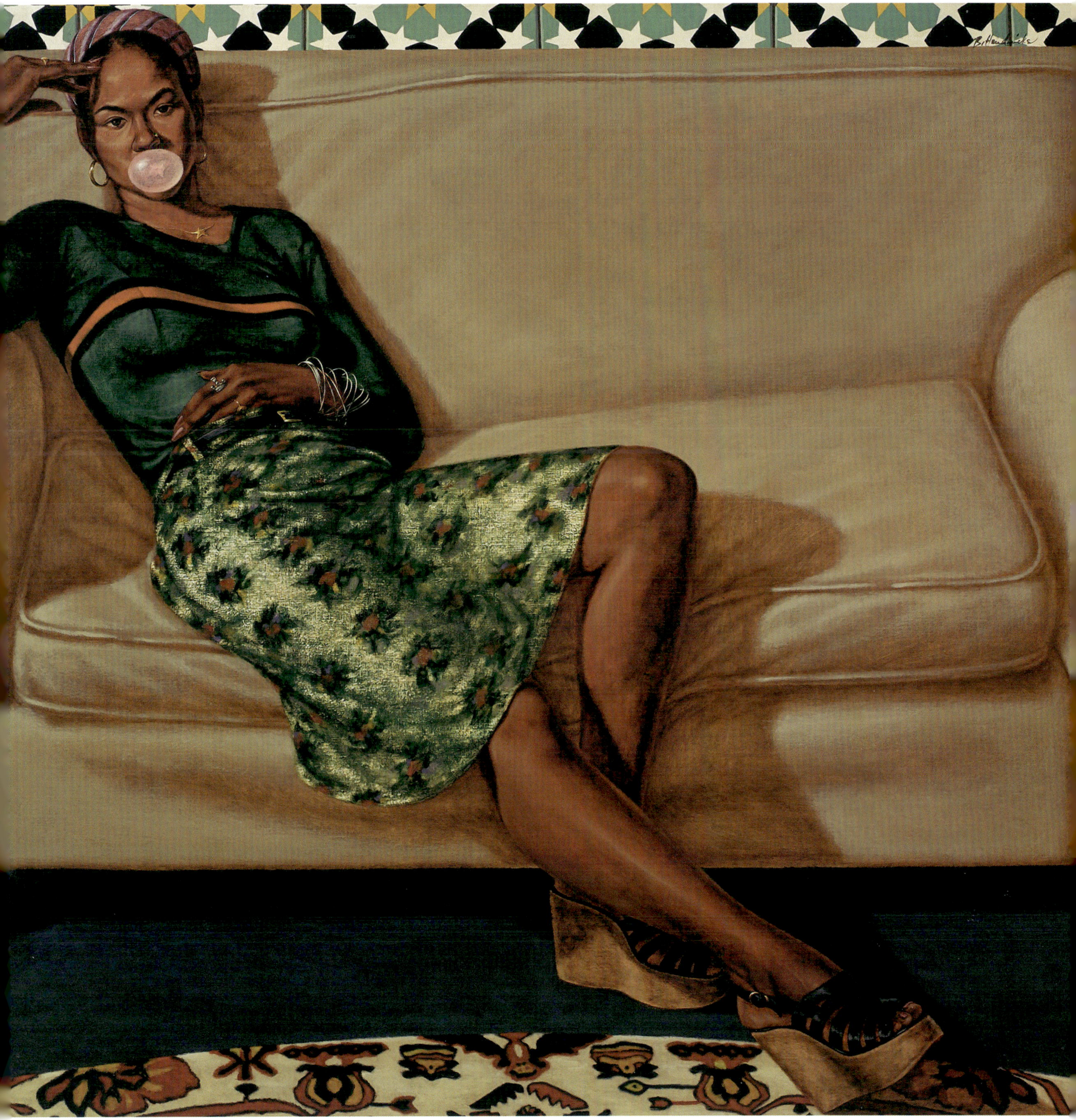

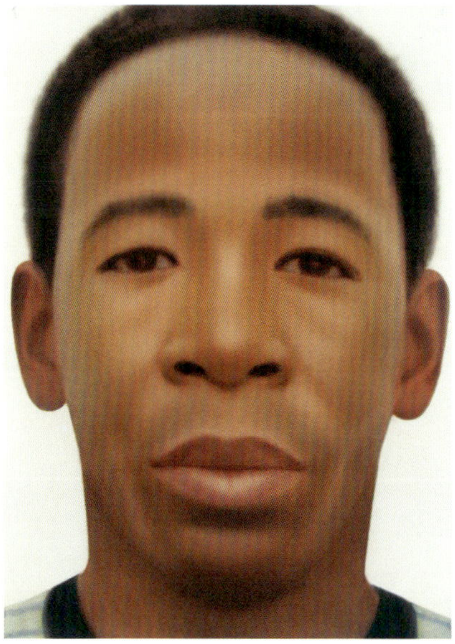

Almost thirty years before Freiwald's *Untitled*, Hendricks had entered a similar but different theoretical terrain with his populist portraiture. For example, in his cryptically titled *New Michael* he flirts with an obscure and generalized figure saved from complete anonymity by sartorial distinctiveness and a modicum of barely visible facial characteristics. Shifting his conscious disengagement with time-worn, identifying physical features to a shadowy, half-lit silhouette, Hendricks nevertheless gives himself over in *New Michael* to the pictorial aggrandizements of the circular canvas (re: *tondo*), which, through its Renaissance-rooted, window-like form, subliminally invites spectators into its inveigling, oil-on-canvas world by way of an imaginary portal.[24]

Whereas Freiwald's paintings invoke the current anxieties concerning unwarranted surveillance and today's global portrait gallery of often unreliable, mistaken identities, Hendricks's paintings, while similarly preoccupied with notions of spectatorship, bring to the fore issues of exhibitionism, voyeurism, and self-invention in a mass media-influenced society. For all of the cultural differences between art and life in the 1970s and art and life during the first few years of the twenty-first century, what Hendricks's and Freiwald's paintings have in common is a preoccupation with the unlikely subjects and processes of portraiture, in all of that genre's recuperative and reconstructive glory in art history.[25]

Hendricks's reconceptualization of portraiture is what he is best known for, but beginning in the 1980s, he turned to still lifes and landscapes for fresh subject matter, as well as a new perspective on the revitalization of easel painting. Working for extended periods on the Caribbean island of Jamaica during his winter breaks from teaching, Hendricks created dozens of watercolors and oil paintings of farmlands, mountain vistas, and distant village scenes, suggestive of John Constable, Jean-Baptiste Camille Corot, and other nineteenth-century European painters. In "Lover's Leap in Southfield, Jamaica" Hendricks begins an account about his favorite *plein air* site on the island that "has inspired my many paintings and watercolors, all of which, like words, only minimally describe the indescribable."[26] Although individual works like *Rooftop View* betray Hendricks's academy ideals and respect for traditional landscape painting, when collectively exhibited by the artist in amassed, parlor-oriented displays reminiscent of the multicomponent 1990s wall installations by Allan McCollum, Raymond Pettibon, and others, these paintings transmitted something

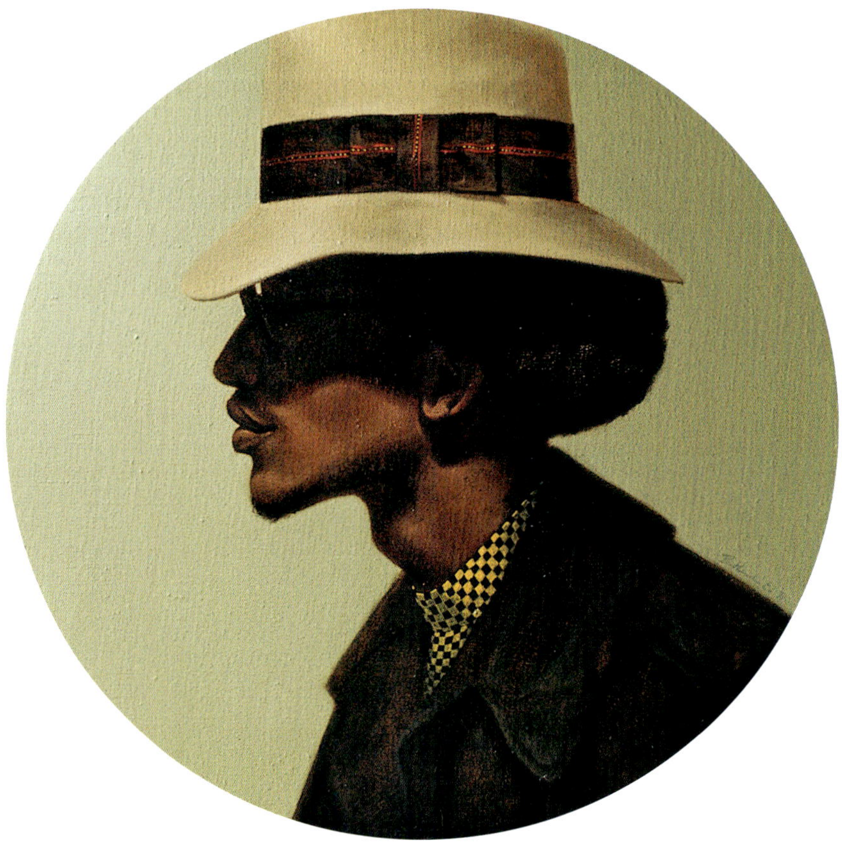

fig. 9
Till Freiwald
Untitled, 2003
Watercolor on paper
59 x 39 inches

fig. 10
New Michael, 1971
Oil and acrylic on canvas
22 inch diameter

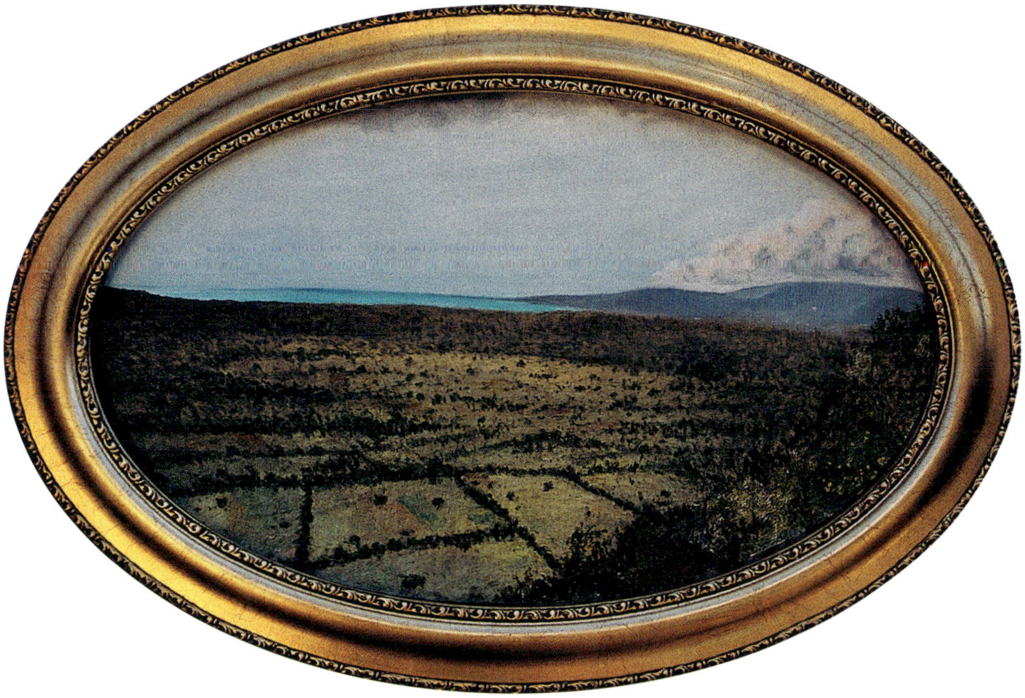

fig. 11
Rooftop View, 1999
Oil on linen canvas
17 x 27 inches

else: an aesthetic experience more about the mise-en-scène of a contemporary, archive-driven pictorialism than simply a sublime and majestic landscape. Deploying circular and oval formats and ornate, gold-leaf frames, these landscapes oddly yet aptly complemented Hendricks's portraiture, with their shared preoccupations with an ancillary, glimmering splendor.

Indeed, the glint and glare in Hendricks's paintings are just as important as the subject's themselves, in that these optical effects refer to the auras and energies that humans exude in their day-to-day interactions with one another.[27] For example in the painting *Roaring River Apostle*, a succession of rainbow-colored horizons (appearing behind the figure of a Jamaican Rastafarian) resituates Hendricks's friend to a part illusionistic, part abstract world of the artist's own making. Similar to Hendricks's earlier figure-on-flat-ground paintings, *Roaring River Apostle* shifts the Renaissance perspective in conventional portraiture from an implied, studio/interior spatiality to a two-dimensional and centrifugal insistence on the figure. Hendricks's coincidental updating of Russian theologian Pavel Florensky's icon theory—here transposed to a secular, historically self-conscious, and early twenty-first-century context—puts these paintings in telling comparisons with works by contemporary iconographers like Chris Ofili, Kehinde Wiley, and Jeff Sonhouse.[28] That black people and especially African American men are the principal objects of each of these artists' works is the art historical link they have to Hendricks, whose visual forays into questions of race, gender, and self-invention are pivotal (if not canonical) to figurative realism in modern painting.

In 2001 I traveled to New London, Connecticut, to see, again, another Hendricks exhibition.[29] After taking in the breadth of his forty-odd-year career with this show, I interviewed Barkley at his home the next day. As I entered his house that morning and proceeded to the kitchen where I would conduct my interview, my eyes caught sight of *Bahsir*: a painting I was familiar with from reproductions but hadn't before seen in person.[30] Viewing *Bahsir* at that moment—in an informal setting, and the way an unexpected person happens upon you from around a corner while you're completely preoccupied with other thoughts and agendas—reminded me of why Hendricks's portraits have a sweeping, timeless fascination.

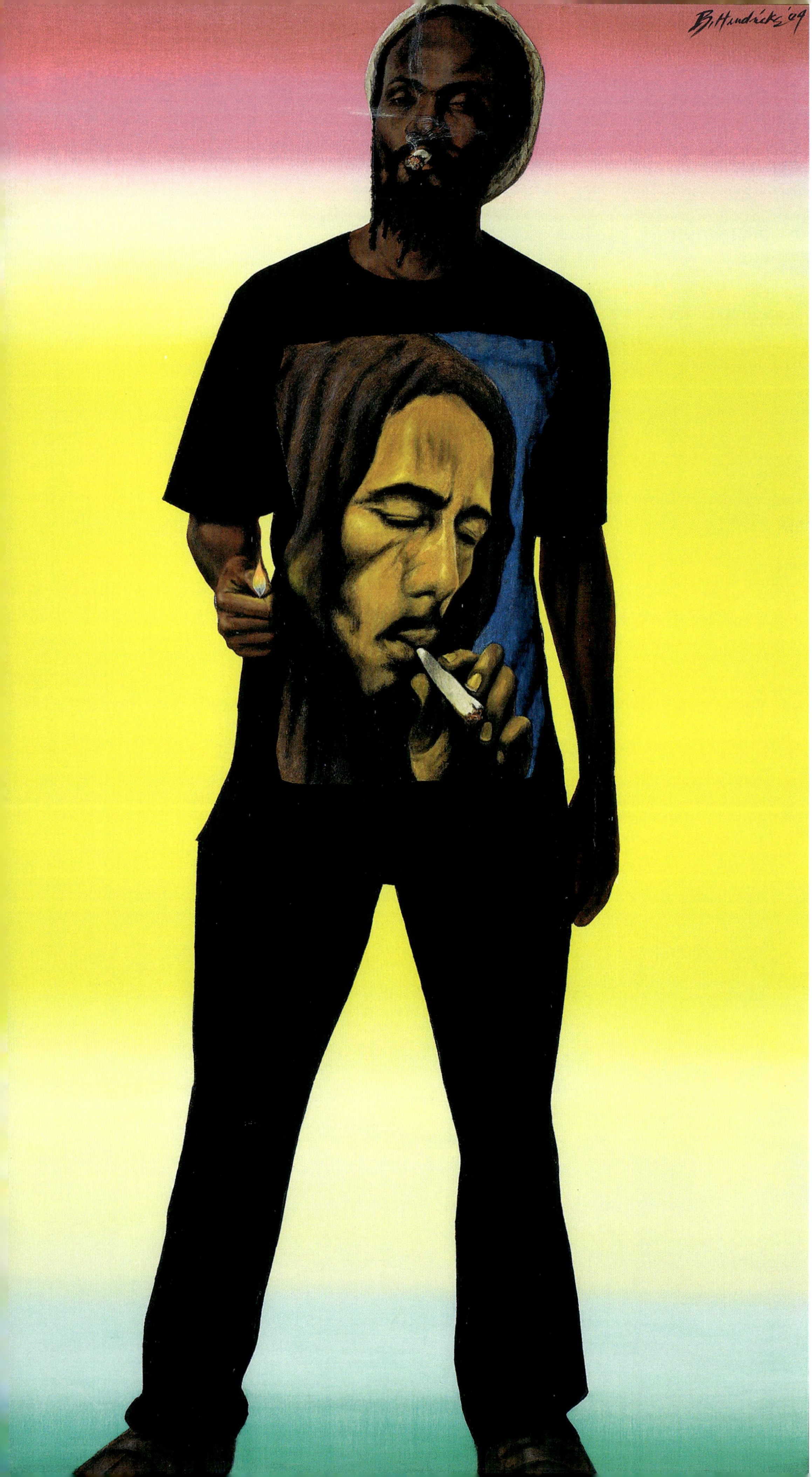

cat. 47
Roaring River Apostle (Serious Smoker Series), 2004
Oil on linen canvas, wooden frame
72 1/4 x 40 inches

cat. 23 (opposite page)
Bahsir (Robert Gowens), 1975
Oil and acrylic on linen canvas
83 1/2 x 66 inches

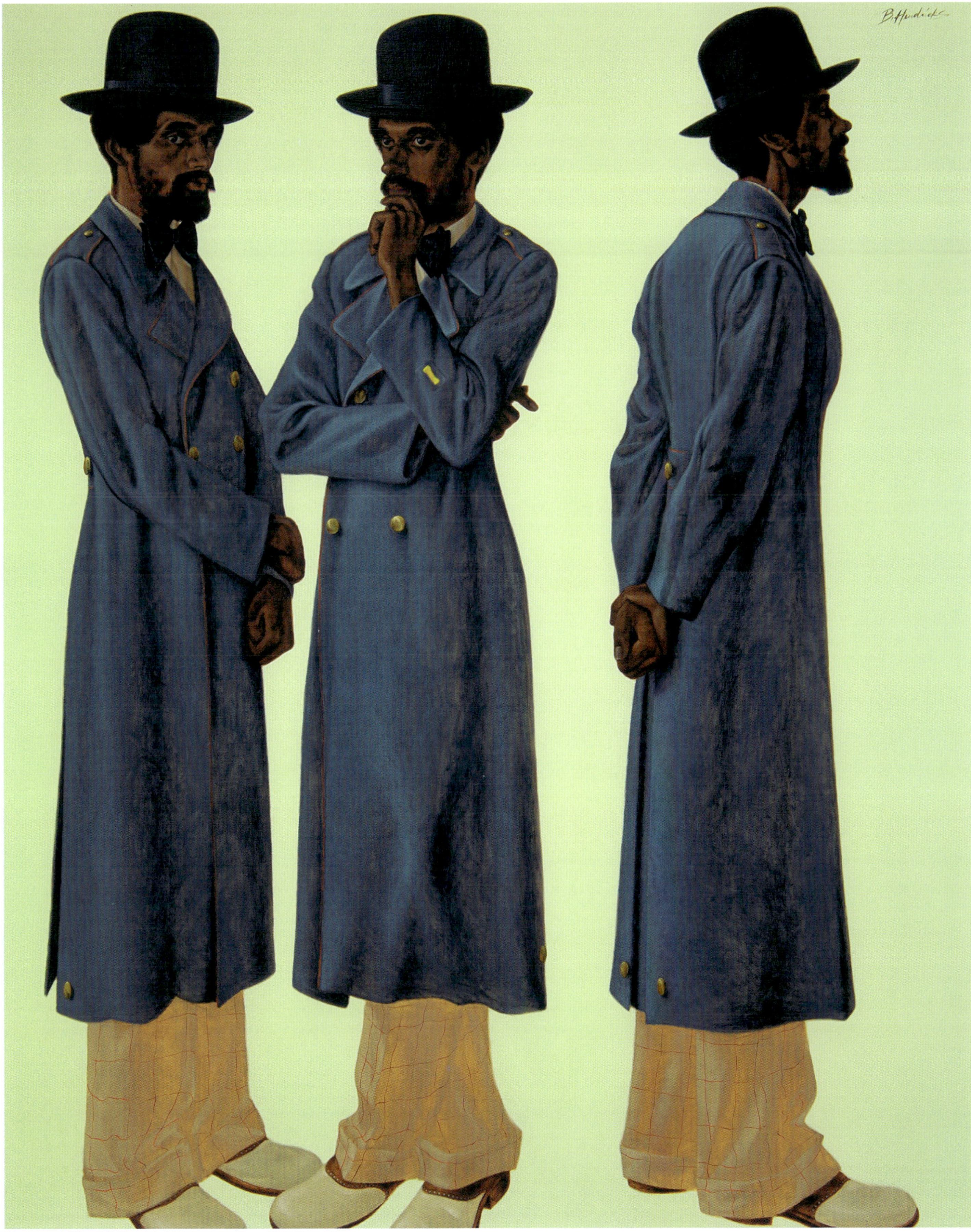

cat. 13
Down Home Taste, 1971
Oil and acrylic on
linen canvas
48 3/4 x 48 5/8 inches

fig. 12 (opposite page)
Jules, 1971
Oil and acrylic on linen
canvas
60 1/2 x 45 3/4 inches

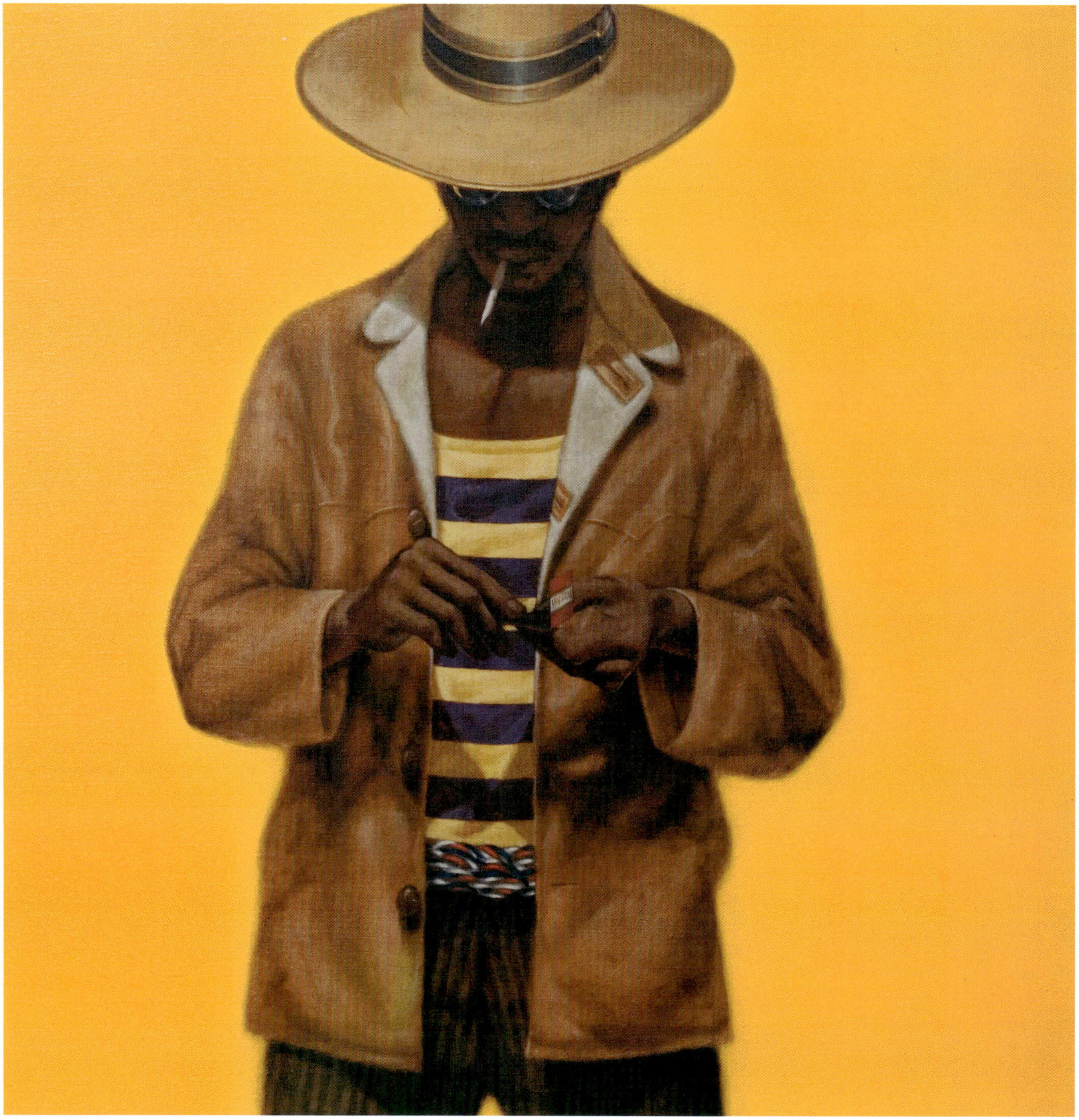

That chemistry in *Bahsir* invariably has to do with recognition of its visual basis: artistic matters both autobiographically familiar and aesthetically mind-boggling. For instance, consider Bahsir's fashion statement, which is part *Superfly*, part reminiscent of the male Hasidic uniform, entirely self-concocted, and assiduously assembled by Bahsir (né Robert Gowens) and Hendricks in concert. As knowledgeable as one might be of that superfluous, outrageous 1970s look, Hendricks's artistic enshrinement of it functions almost like Roland Barthe's *punctum*; details (such as the black fedora and two-toned platform shoes) and "powers of expansion" (as in the cultural accounts of when "black" became incontrovertibly "beautiful") that invest *Bahsir* with a subterranean, psychological dimension.[31] One of very few artists on the heels of the civil rights era brave enough to push black corporeality into the darker realm of psychoanalysis, Hendricks invites a reappraisal of how questions of identity in late twentieth-century art interface with, if not inadvertently undermine, the so-called politics of representation.

Sartorial excesses are juxtaposed in *Bahsir*, cleverly, with physical reserve and contemplation (i.e., folded arms, a hand-on-chin gesture, staring off into space, etc.). Yet viewers still sense, as in so many of Hendricks's paintings, that the self-absorbed figure, multiplied by three, is completely aware of his subjectivity and, as a result, willingly participates (on the receiving/brandishing side) in this game of spectatorship. Acknowledging Bahsir's tripled presence that day in New London sparked the realization that despite Hendricks's "place" in a specific historical era and cultural milieu, his art resonates especially with today's new figuration and joins its fundamental critique of the alleged "truths" in portraiture, albeit through a consummate academism and in other, subtly subversive ways. The visual dynamism in this silhouetted dandy—turned into an improvisatory pattern set against a white, neoconstructivist, painted field—is unlike anything I had ever seen before and makes the idea of a Barkley L. Hendricks retrospective beguiling, with the opportunity to encounter old friends, audacious strangers, and engrossing paintings, it seems, for the very first time.

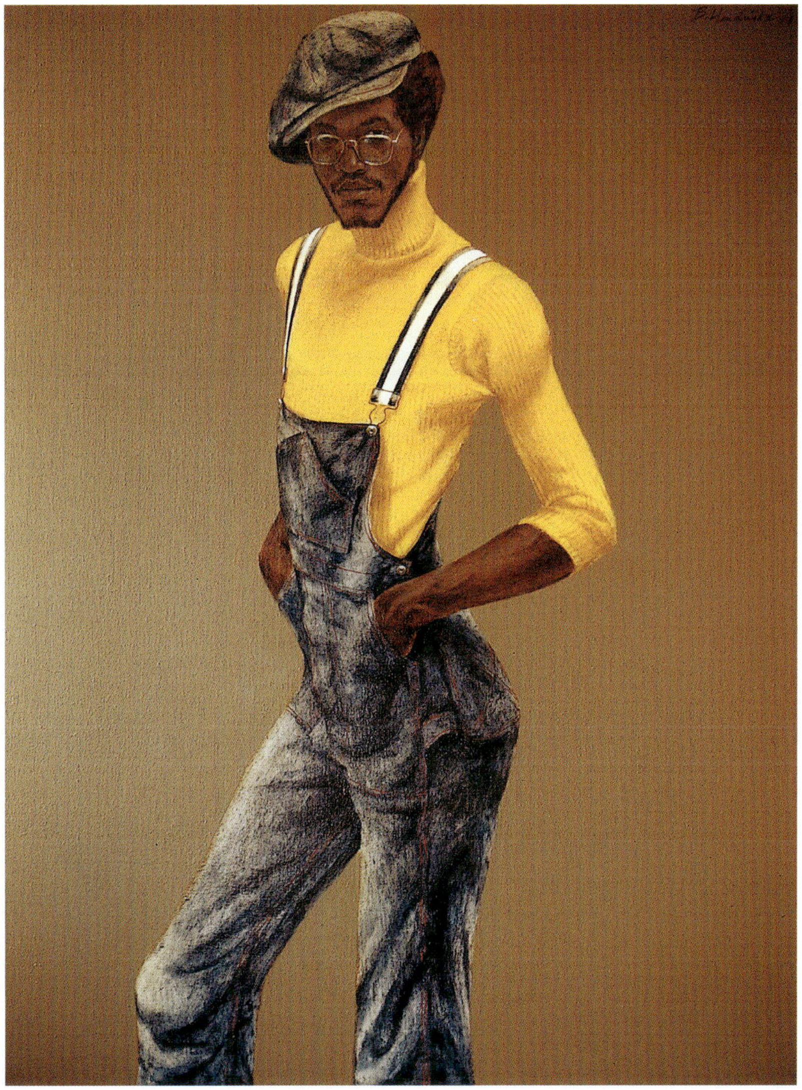

Paint a perfect picture,
bring to life a vision in
one's mind,
the beautiful ones
always smash the picture,
always everytime.

—Prince, "The Beautiful Ones"[32]

Notes

1. Thelma Golden, *Black Male: Representations of Masculinity in Contemporary American Art* (New York: Abrams, 1994). "Mr. Hendricks," writes *New York Times* art critic Michael Kimmelman of the *Black Male* exhibition, "is represented by three crisply realist portraits from the '70s, handsome images that can bring to mind Sargent in the dignity and scale they lend to their subjects." Michael Kimmelman, "Constructing Images of the Black Male," *New York Times*, 11 November 1994.

2. David H. Katzive, "Introduction," *Millenium* (Philadelphia: Philadelphia Museum of Art, 1973), n.p.

3. One early reviewer, perhaps acknowledging the need to take a second, third, and fourth look at Hendricks's portraiture, described his paintings as "straight-at-you realism" but immediately follows this observation with "Or are they?" Victorial Donohoe, "Philadelphia Art Scene: Art Alliance Solos, Groups," *Philadelphia Inquirer*, 5 January 1969.

4. Two *Artforum* articles in particular (both by artist/critic Sidney Tillim) convey the crisis in figurative realism of that era: Sidney Tillim, "The Reception of Figurative Art: Notes on a General Misunderstanding," *Artforum International* 7 (February 1969): 30–33; and Sidney Tillim, "A Variety of Realisms," *Artforum International* 7 (September 1969): 42–47.

5. Cindy Nemser, "An Interview with Chuck Close," *Artforum International* 8 (January 1970): 51–55.

6. Quotations and specific biographical citations were all culled from interviews with Barkley L. Hendricks (2001–2007), conducted in preparation for the author's forthcoming book: Richard J. Powell, *Cutting a Figure: Fashioning Black Portraiture* (Chicago: University of Chicago Press, 2008).

7. Dorothy Grafly, "Seasonal Imaginings and Timeless Realities," *Philadelphia Bulletin*, 19 April 1970.

8. Tillim, "A Variety of Realisms," 43–44, 47.

9. William Zimmer, "Private Visions Dare the Public Eye to See," *New York Times*, 28 February 1993.

10. I discuss this paradigm shift in African American culture, circa 1960s, in Richard J. Powell, "Black Is a Color," in *Black Art: A Cultural History* (London: Thames and Hudson, 2002), 121–160.

11. For an overview of this period, see Mary Schmidt Campbell, *Tradition and Conflict: Images of a Turbulent Decade, 1963–1973* (New York: Studio Museum in Harlem, 1985).

12. Allon Schoener, ed., *Harlem on My Mind: Cultural Capital of Black America, 1900–1968* (New York: Random House, 1968); and Edmund Barry Gaither, *Afro-American Artists, New York and Boston* (Boston: Museum of Fine Arts, 1970).

13. *Afro-American Artists, 1800–1969* (Philadelphia: School District of Philadelphia, Pennsylvania, 1969); and Lisa Gail Collins and Margo Natalie Crawford, eds., *New Thoughts on the Black Arts Movement* (New Brunswick, NJ: Rutgers University Press, 2006).

14. Jeff Donaldson, "10 in Search of a Nation," *Black World* 19 (October 1970): 80–89.

15. "Putting a basketball on a table with apples wasn't a satisfactory still life," Hendricks is quoted as saying. "I felt I had to put the basketball into an environment that I was comfortable with. So my studio became the basketball court, with myself as the referee." Barkley L. Hendricks, as quoted in Doreen Mangan, "Barkley Hendricks and His Figurative Drama," *American Artist* 40 (July 1976): 36.

16. The title *Black on Black in Black* was derived in part from the satirical monologues of 1960s black entertainers (like comedian Godfrey Cambridge and singer Lou Rawls) who regularly spoofed the zealous racialism of the more witless and reactionary members of the black power movement. Mel Watkins, "The New Comics," in *On the Real Side* (New York: Simon and Schuster, 1994), 508–511. In the Philadelphia Museum of Art's archives, curator Henry G. Gardiner wrote about visiting Hendricks's 1969 exhibition at Philadelphia's Kenmore Galleries. "It was a circular painting of a basketball goal ring casting an elliptical shadow" Gardiner noted about one of the basketball paintings he "really like[d]." "The interplay between the three circles was fascinating physically, in painterly terms and psychologically." Henry G. Gardiner, in a memorandum to Dr. Evan Turner, director of the Philadelphia Museum of Art, 5 February 1969. Curatorial Files, Philadelphia Museum of Art, Philadelphia, PA.

17. Donaldson, "10 in Search of a Nation."

18. For two perspectives on African American figural realism, see Elizabeth Mermin, "'Searing Portraits': The Persistence of Realism in Black Urban Cinema," *Third Text* 34 (Spring 1996): 3–14; and Thelma Golden, *Black Romantic: Figurative Impulse in Contemporary African American Art* (New York: Studio Museum in Harlem, 2002).

19. Floyd R. Thomas Jr., "A Personal Reflection on the Barkley L. Hendricks Experience—As I See It," in *The Barkley L. Hendricks Experience* (New London: Lyman Allyn Museum of Art, Connecticut College, 2001), 7.

20. I discuss the black arts movement at length in Richard J. Powell, "Racial Imaginaries, from Charles White's *Preacher* to Jean-Paul Goude and Grace Jones' *Nigger Arabesque*," in Petrine Archer-Straw, David Bailey, and Richard J. Powell, eds., *Back to Black: Art, Cinema and the Racial Imaginary* (London: Whitechapel Art Gallery, 2005), 9–27, 44–46.

21. For a brief but focused commentary on Hendricks's *Sweet Thang*, see Zimmer, "Private Visions Dare the Public Eye to See."

22. Roland L. Freeman, *Southern Roads/City Pavements: Photographs of Black Americans* (New York: International Center of Photography, 1981); James Crump, "Quasi Documentary: Evolution of a Photographic Style," *New Art Examiner* 23 (March 1996): 22–28; Barry Schwabsky, "Picturehood Is Powerful," *Art in America* 85 (December 1997): 80–85; and *Kerry James Marshall/One True Thing/Meditations on Black Aesthetics* (Chicago: Museum of Contemporary Art, 2003).

23. Terrie Sultan, "Contemporary Portraiture's Split Reference," *Art on Paper* 3 (March/April 1999): 38–42.

24. *New Michael* was first published in Doreen Mangan, "Barkley Hendricks and His Figurative Drama," *American Artist* 40 (July 1976): 38.

25. For a discussion of contemporary portraiture, see Pernilla Holmes, "In Your Face," *ArtNews* 106 (June 2007): 106–111.

26. Barkley L. Hendricks, "Rome Rendezvous: Rendezvous with Myself," in *The Barkley L. Hendricks Experience*, 45.

27. For Hendricks's perspective on the spiritual dimensions of people and their possessions, see Barkley L. Hendricks, "Head over Heels or Variations on a Seam," in *Barkley L. Hendricks Presents Barkley L. Hendricks, 1967–1987* (Bridgeport, CT: Housatonic Museum of Art, 1988), n.p.

28. Pavel Florensky, *Iconostasis* (1922; reprint, Crestwood, NY: St. Vladimir's Seminary Press, 1996); and Chris Ofili and Brice Marden, "Painters' Paintings," *Artforum International* 45 (October 2006): 218–225, 286, 288.

29. *The Barkley L. Hendricks Experience*.

30. Edmund Barry Gaither, *Jubilee: Afro-American Artists on Afro-America* (Boston: Museum of Fine Arts, Boston, 1975).

31. Roland Barthes, *Camera Lucida: Reflections on Photography* (New York: Hill and Wang, 1981), 38–59.

32. Prince, "The Beautiful Ones," from Prince and the Revolution, Music from *Purple Rain* (Warner Bros., 1984; 9 25110-2).

fig. 13
Michael BPP (Black Panther Party), 1971
Oil and acrylic on linen canvas
48 x 34 inches

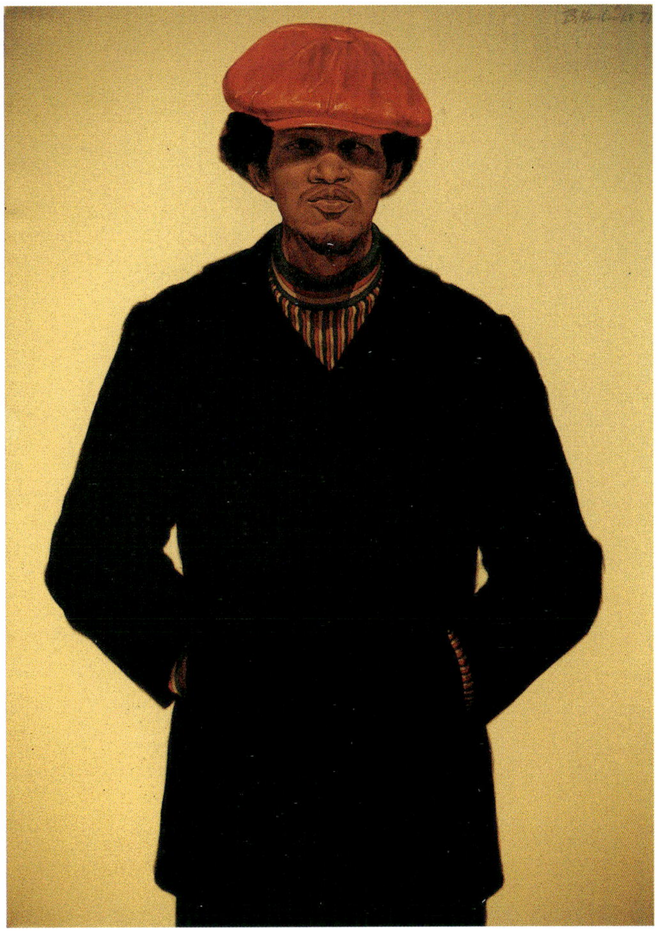

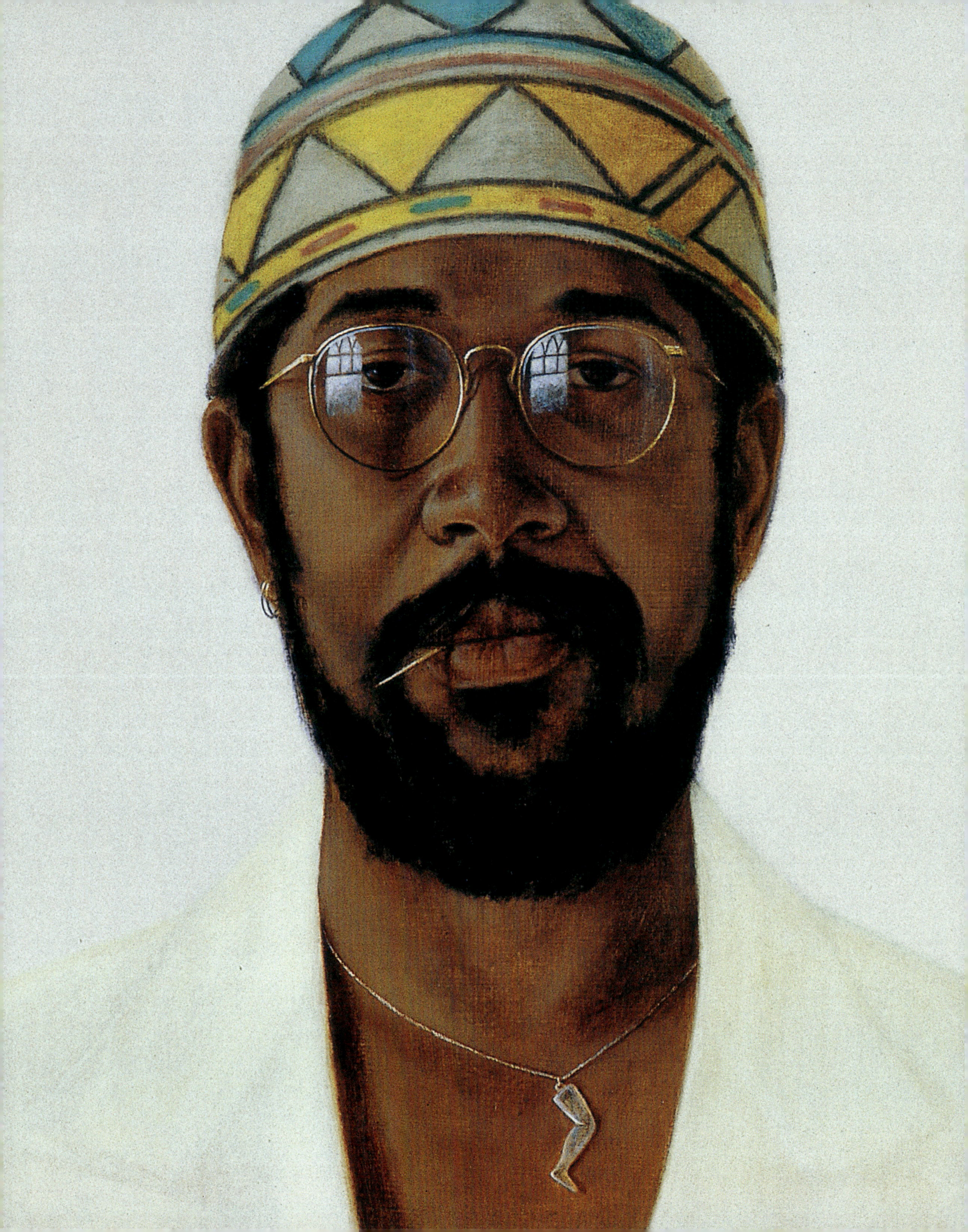

Conversation with Barkley Hendricks Thelma Golden

This interview took place via telephone on September 6, 2007. It was transcribed by Leslie Ava Shaw.

TG: Hello. I am thrilled that we are able to have this dialogue so that I would have the opportunity to talk to you again about your work. I wanted to ask you how you feel about the idea of a retrospective. This exhibition begins with work from 1965 and continues to the present with recent work. I'm just wondering what that feels like for you at this moment to look back at your production as an artist.

BH: Well, it's not really a retrospective in the classic sense of the word. A retrospective includes a whole body of one's creative activities, and this is just focusing on paintings.

TG: That's true. That brings me to one of the points that I wanted to discuss with you, and that is the fact that while this is a survey of paintings, you are and have been an artist who works across mediums and artistic styles. Painting, photography, portraiture, and landscape all are part of your work. Do you see any of these media or styles as primary, and more important, how do they feed off one another?

BH: Well, I like foods. If you're lucky enough, you don't have the same diet every day, and there are times when it's necessary by virtue of the media to go to a different medium to get a different perspective on the one waiting in the wings.

TG: So that for you, it's the ability to move across all of these different ways of working for their different qualities.

BH: There are certain things that mandate a particular approach. If I'm doing a figurative drawing for the most part, that would mandate another medium that wouldn't work for that particular subject matter, and the landscapes, for example, require a kind of immediacy that painting doesn't offer.

TG: How did you come to portraiture?

BH: The influence of looking at people, and that was a history that was a strong one where I went to school, but I was drawing people before I went to any of the established institutions.

TG: And most, perhaps all, of your portraits actually are of real people you know. How do you choose your subjects?

BH: There is sometimes a desire by virtue of fashion and personality. I think they play a large role in the selection of subject matter.

TG: In many ways, it seems that what your portraiture captures are not simply the details of the person or their facial features, but the sense of their aura or their particular and unique attitude. It seems that the intimacy of this exchange is very present in the paintings. I can remember when I was working on the exhibition that became *Black Male*, what was interesting to me is that your paintings very much exhibited something that refuted the kinds of images that some people were only willing to read and understand as stereotypes. In your paintings you offered a much more complex way of being. You captured in those portraits your subjects' sense of themselves and the way in which they look at the world, which is what made those paintings so critical in that exhibition. You really were able to capture not only the profound sense of looking at someone but also the someone else looking out into the world, and I found that very compelling.

BH: Thank you for seeing that aspect of them. It's not what everyone sees given where we are on the planet, as far as land of the free, home of the brave.

TG: Well, that's it. I think that's what makes portraiture and figurative painting and art that deals with the figure now so important. Because images are so potent and we are in a place in our culture where the reading of images can be so loaded. That's why, as I looked at the range of works being considered for this exhibition, I was reminded of all of the ways you have created portraits, all of the ways you see people: images of men, images of women, images that are single bodies, and the ones where several poses or people are featured. Seeing this range again it was interesting for me to think about—particularly in that early moment of your painting—how much photography influenced you and more important, how much looking at all the images in the world of film and photography that you were doing at the time.

BH: In the very beginning I didn't use the camera as much as I did later on. Much of my training had to do with using the eyes and as things got more active and I had to deal with work and scheduling, the camera came in as a very vital tool to record information that I didn't have the luxury of having the figure in front of me.

TG: Can you tell me a little bit about the difference between the paintings of women and the paintings of men? Is there a difference in the way you thought about the female form than the male form?

BH: Not especially. Certainly, there's an obvious difference between males and females to a certain extent unless you're dealing with drag queens or something like that, but the personalities kind of directed my focus.

TG: The landscapes that are in the exhibition begin in 2000. When did you begin landscape painting?

BH: While I was in art school. The works that I did in the city were cityscapes, blocks and neighborhoods, so being able to paint outdoors, on the spot, was something that originated there. As I got more involved with my figures, some of the activity there had to be put on hold until I found a particular locale that really intrigued me, that I really loved, and it just so happens working in the Caribbean was just beautiful. Jamaica was especially magnetic in a number of areas, and certainly the beauty of the land of wood and water was enough to have me coming back for twenty years or so.

TG: Tell me about *Sophisticated Lady*. I was drawn to the white ground and the white outfit, and then of course her as the figure coming out of that and that work along with some of the others that have a similar compositional style, including *Slick*, which is a self-portrait. *Steve* seemS to be about a way of looking at the background and the foreground.

BH: They're double whammies, if I may use that expression to a certain extent, the personality—she was part of a family, and I did a couple of paintings of her, and her sister Barbara. There was a technical focus that was also a part of what I call my limited palette series.

cat. 34 (page 58)
Slick (Self-Portrait), (detail) 1977
Oil, acrylic, and magna on linen canvas
67 x 48 1/2 inches

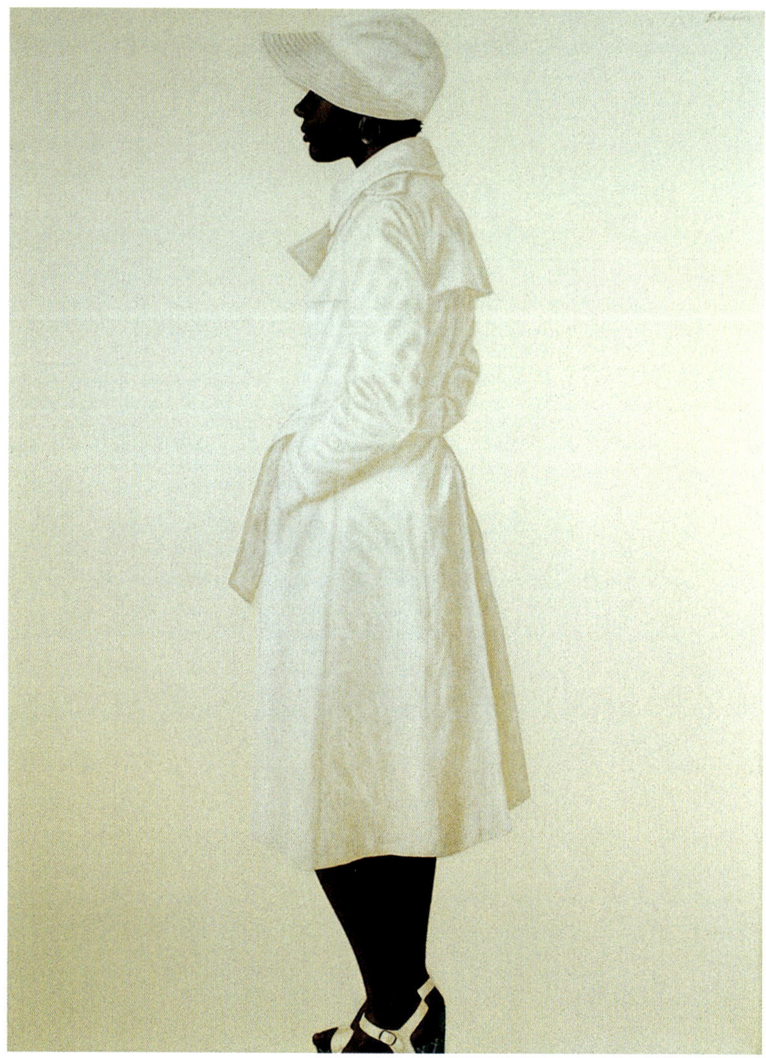

fig. 1
Sophisticated Lady (Barbara Perry), 1976
Oil, acrylic, and magna on linen canvas
60 x 48 inches

cat. 30 (opposite page)
Steve, 1976
Oil, acrylic, and magna on linen canvas
72 x 48 inches

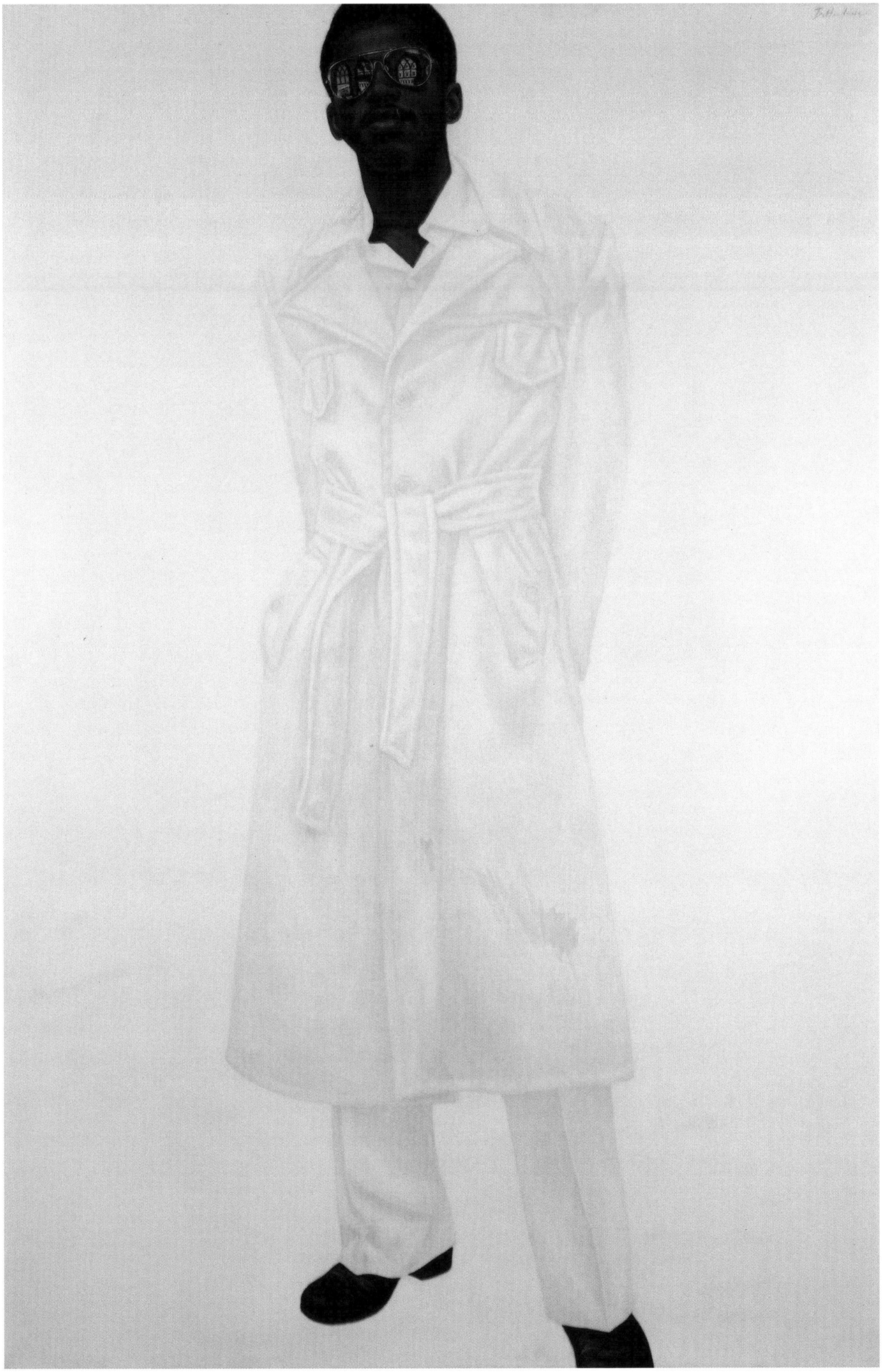

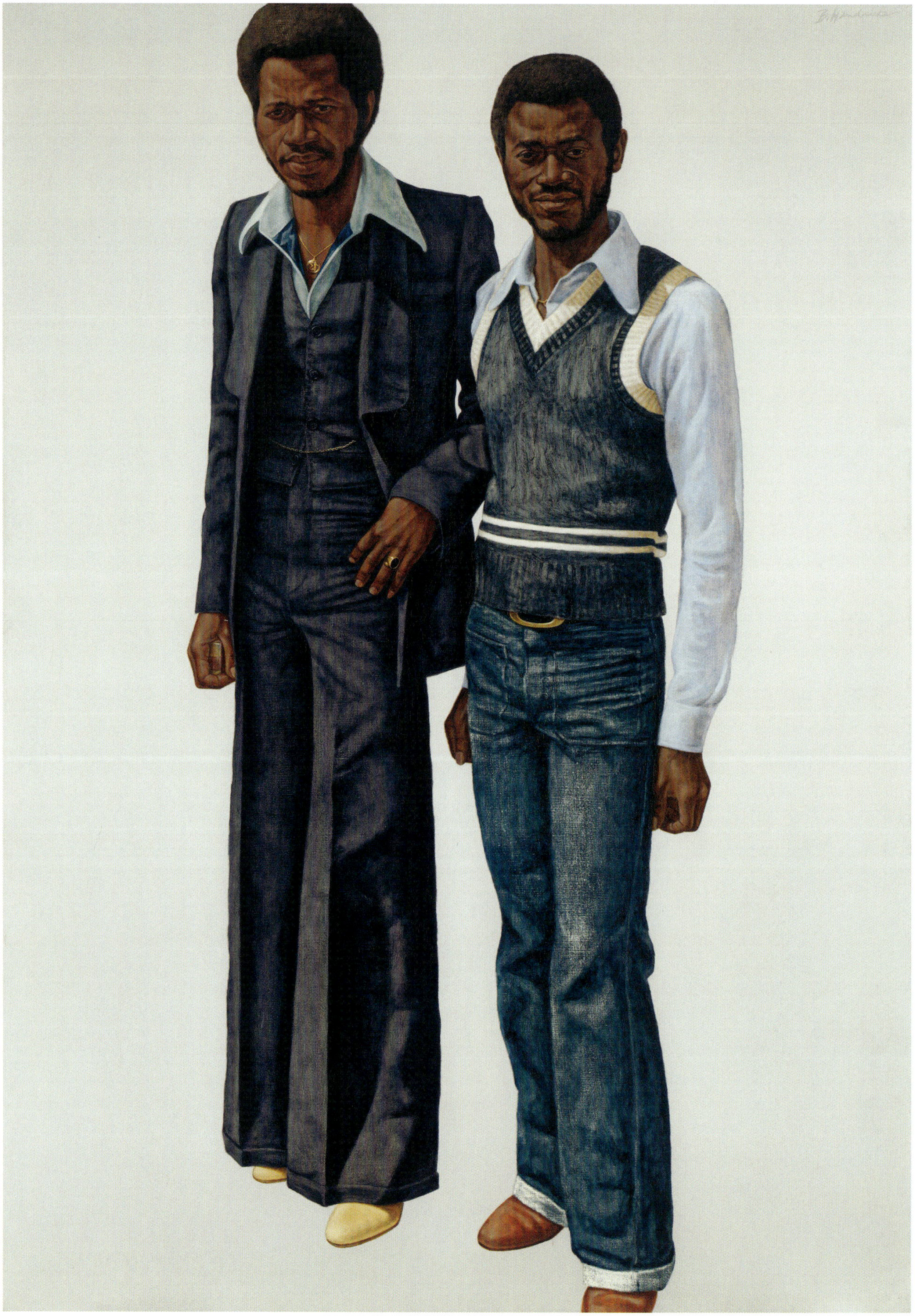

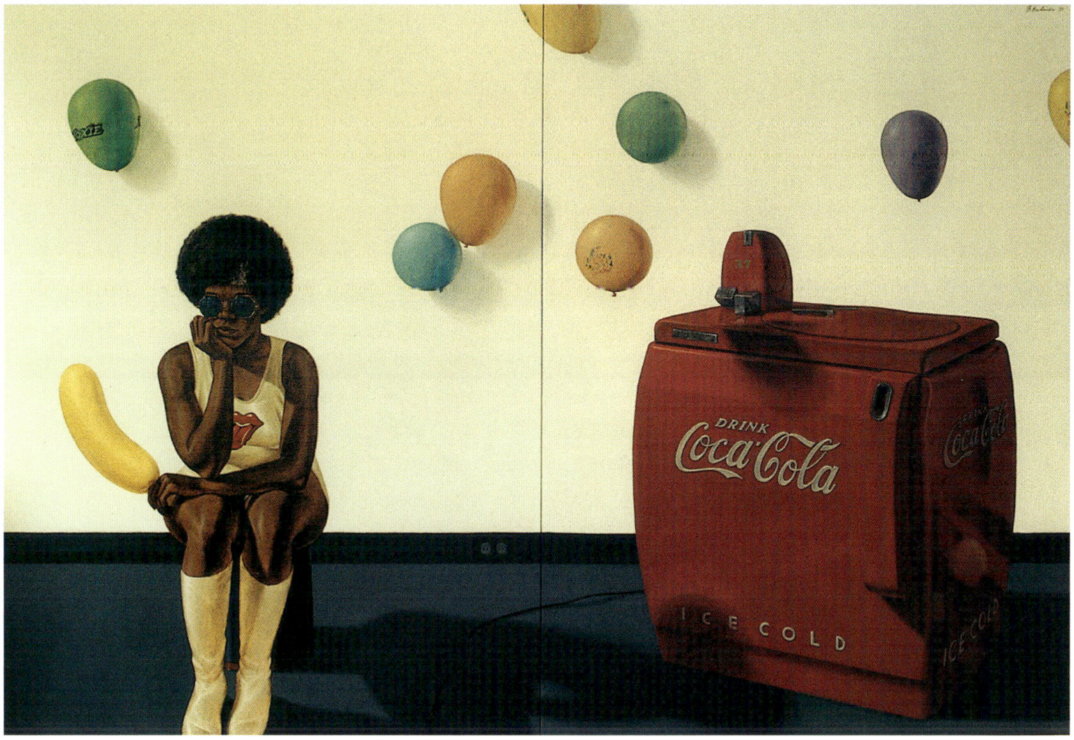

That was white on white, and I did several of the white-on-white images, and there was red on red, black on black, yellow and so on, so besides the individuals, that was part of my visual approach.

TG: *Afro-Parisian Brothers* . . . Where did you meet them?

BH: In Paris. There was a style at the time with the long, slit-back suits that you saw a lot of tall, graceful African brothers wearing, and these gentlemen were gracious enough to allow me to photograph them. Once I got back, I did a couple of paintings from them or at least one piece with one guy and then another painting with both of them.

TG: Both of them together. Wonderful. Who is *George Jules Taylor*?

BH: Jules was a former student that I had in a painting class at Yale. He was an Egyptologist with his studies, and Jules was a real character, and . . .

TG: You can see that.

BH: And I found myself doing four images of him; each time that he sat for me, there was a lively conversation that ensued. I found Jules to be a wonderful friend. Unfortunately, I think he's dead now. He used to work at the Brooklyn Museum.

TG: I'm interested in both *Arriving Soon* and *Sweet Thang* because in both of these paintings women are positioned within an interior landscape as opposed to a more neutral background.

BH: *Arriving Soon*, the title comes from an Eddie "Cleanhead" Vinson song, and the actual piece was inspired by a time when I had gone down to Philadelphia for something and I came back to my studio in New London and my girlfriend at the time had put balloons all over my studio because it was near my birthday, and when I walked in all these balloons were all over the place, and the painting was on the easel and I hadn't finished it yet, and I turned around and saw some balloons in front of the piece, it was kind of Eureka! That's it. The model was posing for another piece. Her name was Angie. She posed for three paintings in all, and she was taking a break during one of those sittings and I had a five-gallon can in my studio, and she sat down, and she looked compelling to the extent that I nailed the two large canvases together and did the drawing and started the piece from that. *Sweet Thang* was a student at

cat. 36 (opposite page)
APB's (Afro-Parisian Brothers), 1978
Oil and acrylic on linen canvas
72 x 50 inches

fig. 2
Arriving Soon, 1973
Oil on linen canvas
72 x 104 1/2 inches

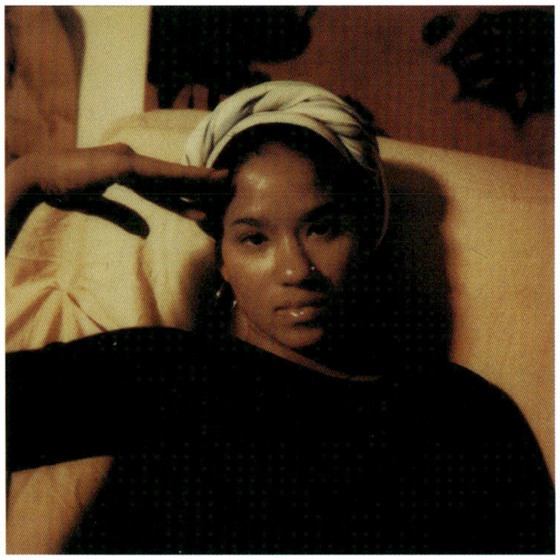

Connecticut College, and I wanted to have a piece with a bit more of a pattern situation, and there's a pattern that goes across the back that is a configuration of some mosaic tiles from when I was in Morocco. The floor is a composite of a rug that I saw somewhere and photographed.

TG: Then her dress becomes the third pattern.

BH: Yeah. She was also, well, quite compelling in the conversation that we were having and it was an intense conversation, and all of a sudden she blew this bubble and it just made us both laugh. It changed the whole mood from one of being very, very serious to a rather lighthearted view, and I had to include the bubble.

TG: It sounds like from the way you describe some of these works that there's an important aspect of what happens in the studio between you and your sitter that really determines the final image of the painting.

BH: I could think I'm reasonably astute in hopefully recognizing things that can help make the piece interesting, but then again, when you're working with live folks, you never can tell what's gonna happen. In fact, you said you saw the *Black President* show and my contribution to that exhibition.

TG: Yes I did.

BH: That was only a partial presentation there. I'm working on the other part of it as we speak, because you're familiar with Fela Kuti and his involvement with his singers and dancers, and that particular piece had an altarpiece concept to it, but it also has twenty-seven pairs of high heels that I've painted that represent the women that he married, and that's going be a part of the presentation at the Nasher and hopefully at the Studio Museum and the other venues. I painted each pair of shoes in a different pattern and color, not only making them a fashion statement but representing the various patterns and makeup the women apply prior to performing. There's a number of different patterns, as you know, used by the Yoruba, and the women would paint certain patterns on their face and body and I've incorporated some of that. Some of the shoes have a Ndebele kind of patterning. Spray paint and other additives go into giving them a kind of focus that's not, how can one say, Manolo Blahniks. Not that I don't like Manolo Blahniks or Jimmy Choos and some of the others, but there is that paint element that could be associated with Mama Africa.

TG: There's another painting I want to ask you about. It is *My Black Nun*.

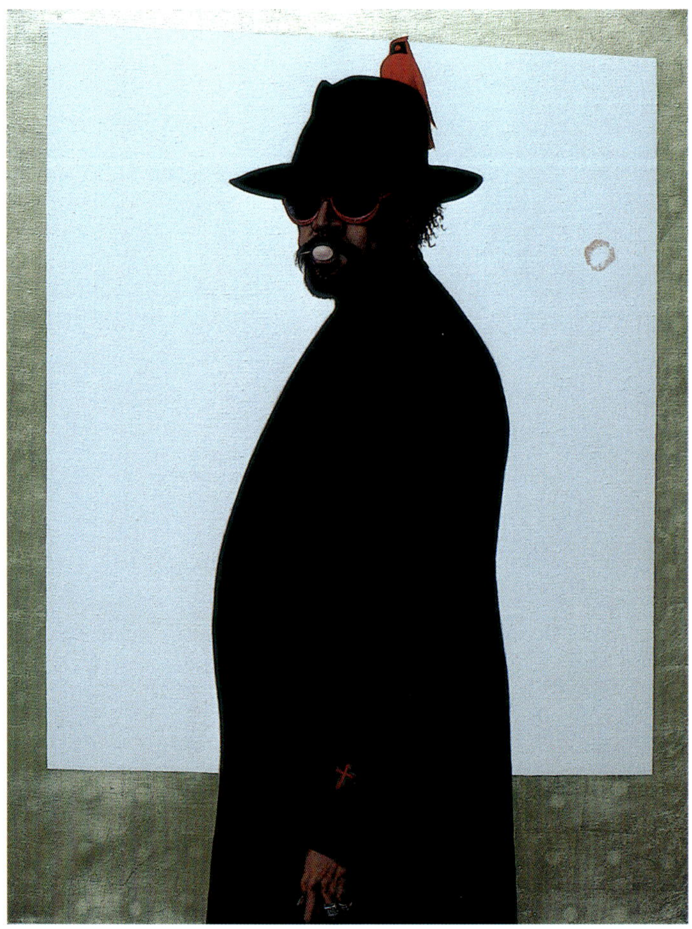

fig. 3
Lynn Jenkins, Connecticut College student, 1976
Subject of *Sweet Thang*

fig. 4
The Way You Look Tonight / Diagonal Graciousness (Self-Portrait), 1981
Oil, acrylic, and white gold leaf on linen canvas
48 x 36 inches

cat. 34 (opposite page)
Slick (Self-Portrait), 1977
Oil, acrylic, and magna on linen canvas
67 x 48 1/2 inches

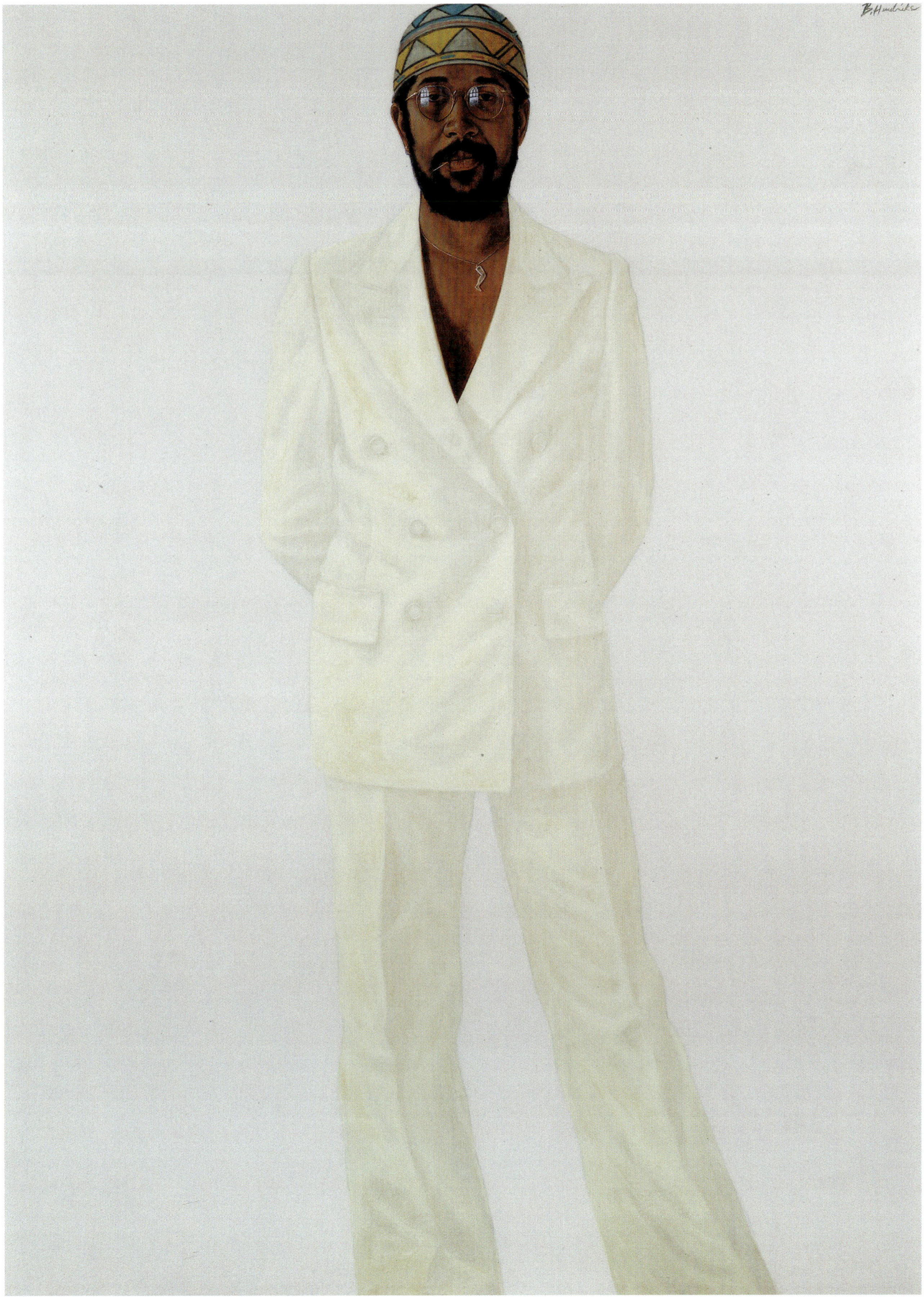

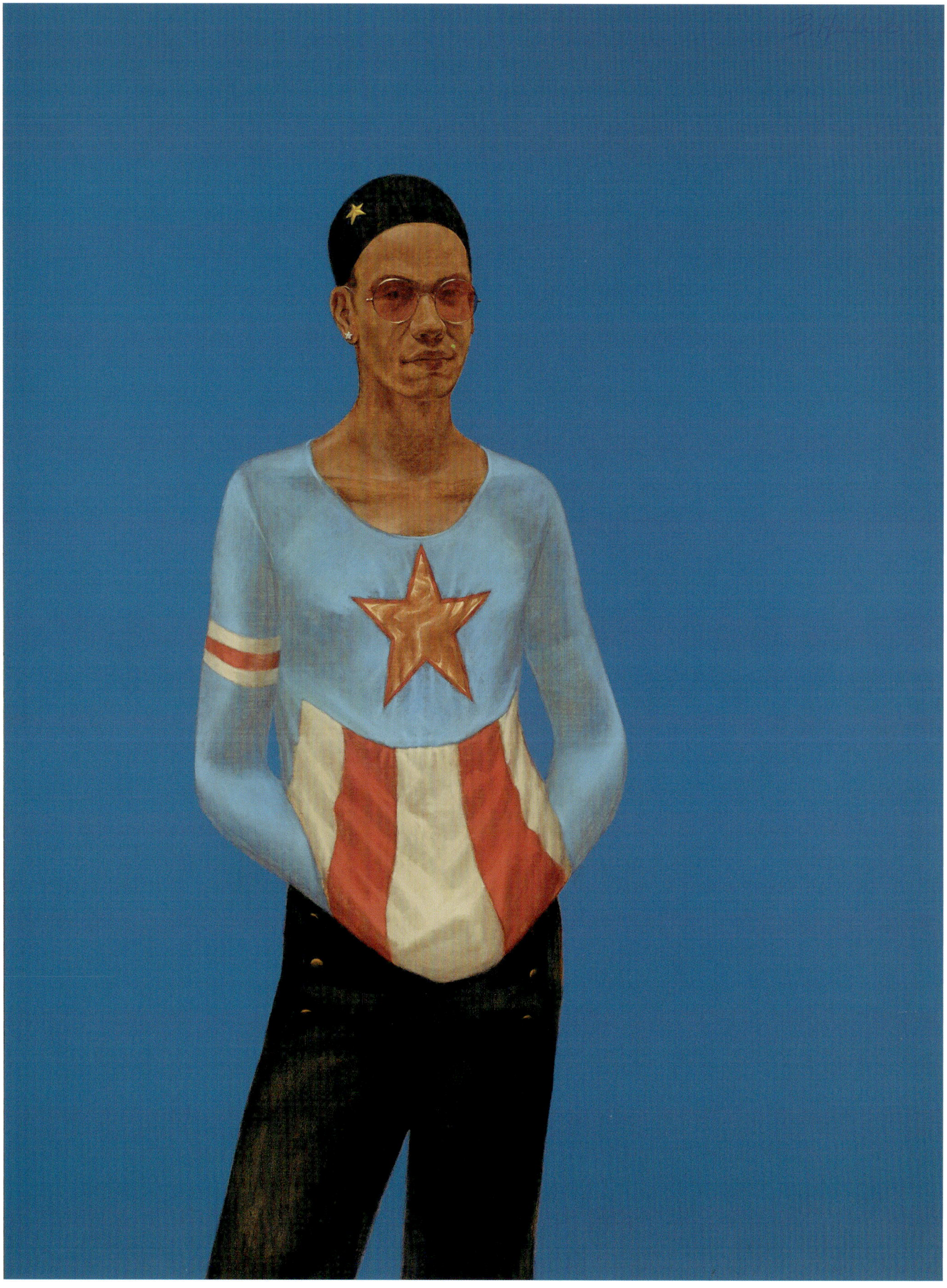

BH: Growing up in Philadelphia, there was a Catholic school that I had to pass every day going to school, and as I got older, I started to wonder about the whole area of religion and never seeing any black nuns, and these are all white figures that got me to thinking, and I decided to create my own little black nun. Later I saw some [black nuns] that were part of the Catholic Church when I was in Rome and in Florence, but I've never seen any in Philadelphia. I suppose there are some there now, but not when I was growing up.

TG: There are a group of works that span your career chronologically that are self-portraits. How long and how often have you used yourself as a subject?

BH: That depends. The first piece that I showed in New York was at the Whitney in the *Contemporary Black Artists* in America exhibition. Do you remember that show? That was a self-portrait where the Icelandic hat that I had bought on one of my trips to Europe and the sunglasses made a kind of focus that made me laugh. I've always liked playing around with hiding eyes and using the sunglasses as a fashion statement as well as protecting my eyes, so that became the major prop [in the painting]. There are several other pieces that are reasonably, I will say profound, and some that were part of an experiment. For example, the gold leaf in *Lawdy Mama* had to be tested first, and I did a self-portrait so that I could learn how to use the gold leaf process, and that gave me some experience before I started doing *Lawdy Mama*. Also, there's that association with icons, and I just liked shiny stuff.

TG: Right. And that interest in shine and reflection, does that affect the sense of how you treat your surfaces?

BH: I learned that you can't depend on getting a particular visual effect by using one single medium and the technical handling of that medium. For example, the drying rate of oil doesn't necessarily allow you to finish rapidly. The visual illusion that I wanted to create was as though the person was coming off the canvas, and the flatness to create that illusion would take forever to dry if I used oil. At the time, I was introduced to using acrylics. I could roll my colors on in a day with acrylic and be finished and that way, I could see where I was going with the other part of the canvas. For me, one medium does not fit all illusions and concepts.

TG: When you began working in the late 1960s, photorealism was a mode that many artists were working with and experimenting with. You are credited for a certain engaged reinvention of the form. How do you see the use of the figure in art today? What's your feeling about the commitment to investigate figuration right now?

BH: Since I'm not in the hot bed of activities in the city, I'm not quite sure what's going on other than what I see or read in the papers, and

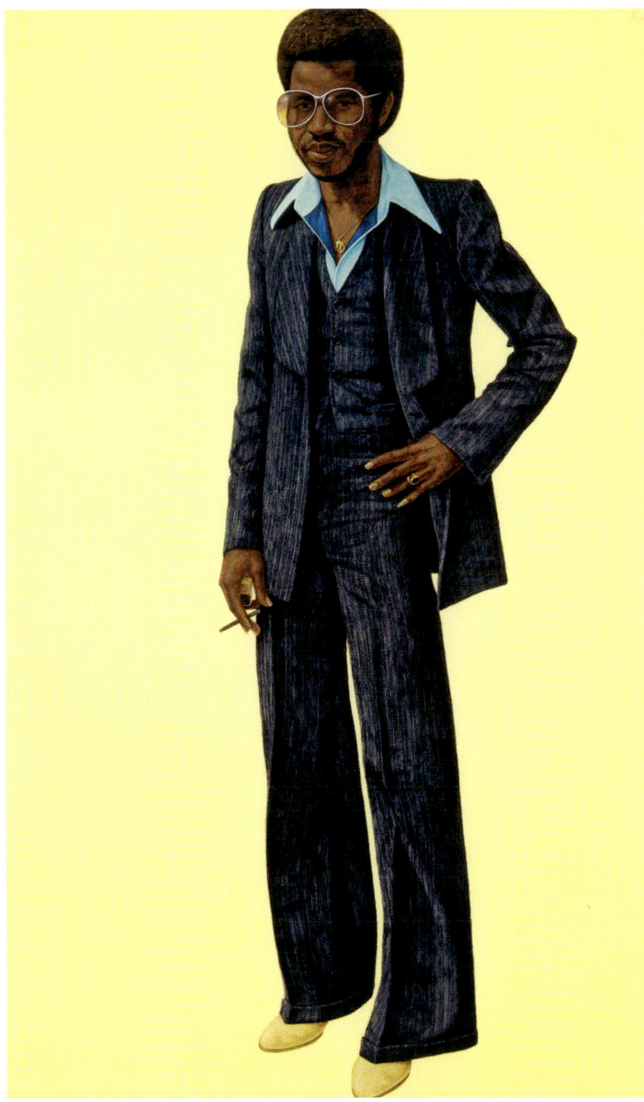

cat. 16 (opposite page)
Sergio, 1972
Oil and acrylic on linen canvas
60 x 44 inches

fig. 5
Noir, 1978
Oil and acrylic on canvas
72 x 48 inches

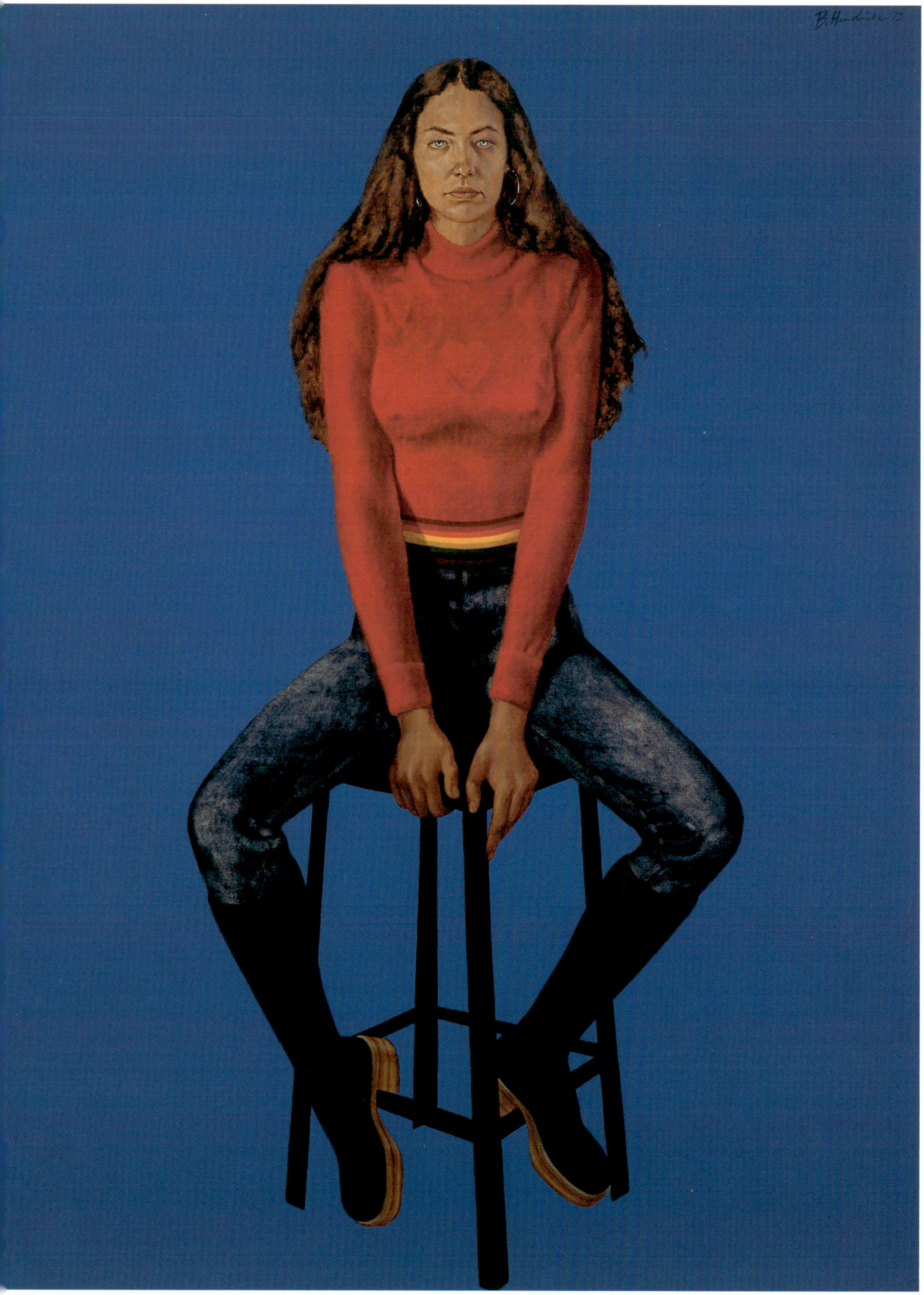

cat. 20
Mayreh (Mary Sheehan), 1973
Oil and acrylic on linen canvas
72 1/4 x 52 inches

I don't get a chance to see the variety that may be happening, given what I've read, so I have to just sort of go on the written word and some photos, and that will only educate you to a certain extent.

TG: What work do you look at that inspires you?

BH: I would say I love the work of Caravaggio, Rembrandt . . . There was a teacher that I had in school named Ben Kamihira. I don't see too many contemporary painters I get inspiration from.

TG: That's interesting, because many of them get a lot of inspiration from you. The resonance of your work in the contemporary realm is profound. I see it in artists who are working not just in painting and in photography but in video as well. What I think is interesting about your work and particularly being able to see it again in these recent group exhibitions and your exhibition at The Project, is seeing that your work feels of its moment and of the present as well. That is, your concerns and your particular way of expressing these concerns span several artistic eras and conversations. Looking at the early work—it very much feeds you and gives you a lot of information about the moment. I think in many ways, my visual sense of the era of the 1970s comes almost entirely from your work. At the same time, the works also feel very new. They feel somewhat timeless, and I think it is that quality, the way in which you exist as someone who documented very precisely in a way that allows for very specific information to come from the works, but also they don't feel like a relic. They feel as if they can sit within the present moment and still speak visually to their past. I think in many ways that's probably what defines work that has a significant role in its era, its ability to be of its moment but also to continue to speak beyond that. I know that there is a way that the influence of your aesthetic has seeped out as a mode of thinking of how art can picture a culture and think about a moment. This exhibition is going to be a wonderful opportunity because many will be reintroduced to your work, and others will get to see some of these works for the first time, which also then gives one the opportunity not only to be introduced to your subjects but also to understand and see your painting technique. You talked a little bit before about making the switch from oil to acrylic. Is there anything else about your technique that has transformed over time as it was needed by this body of work you've made?

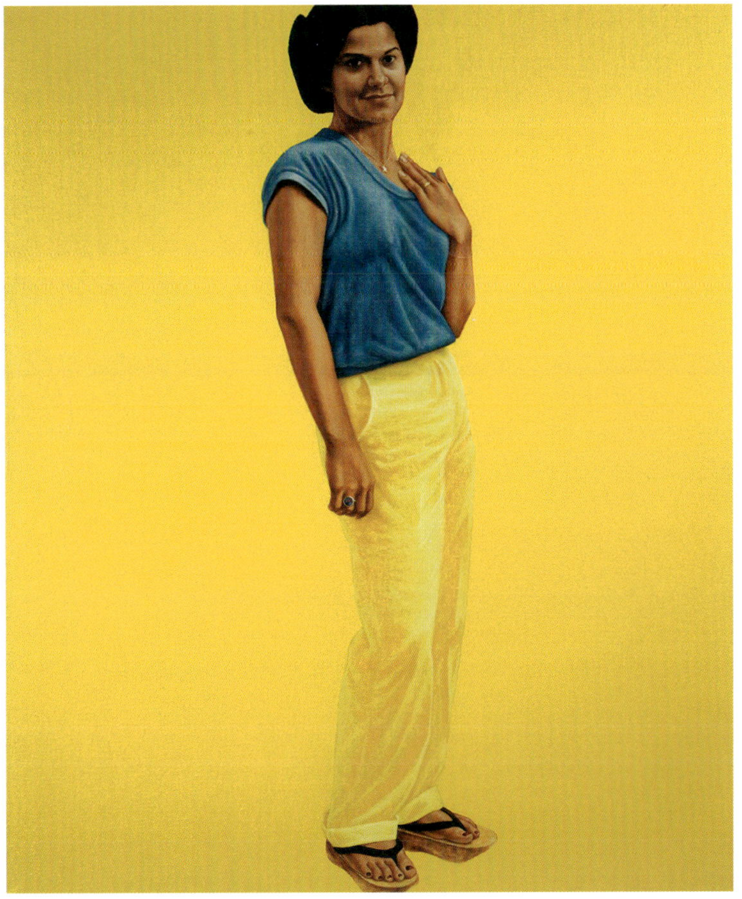

fig. 6
Salina/Star, 1975
Oil and acrylic on linen canvas
60 x 50 inches

BH: There are a number of experiments like working with magna paint. That was a paint that was invented, and was a cross between oil and acrylic. It had the workability that was close to oil and a drying rate that was close to acrylics, so it was supposed to be a medium that would yellow less than oil, and I worked with that for several years. Of course in terms of what I learned with watercolor, I feel my landscape pieces are more akin to watercolor than the impasto element of oil. There's a rapid area of comprehension required for working on the spot [in nature]. I had an instructor many years ago that made a comment that nature didn't give a shit whether you painted it or not, so one would have to be reasonably tuned in and open to the changes of nature, and I like to think that helped refine the colorist approach that I've developed.

TG: It seems that you have always worked on a scale that is at once intimate, but at the same time monumental.

BH: There's an area of illusion that if you work with the figure—work pretty close to life scale—it moves you a little bit closer to the feel that there's an interaction between the spectator and the work. If you get too large, if you get too billboardish, it becomes something that dwarfs the spectator who's looking, and if you get too small, you get into a kind of miniature feel, and you really dwarf that. So there's an interaction that I want to have with the spectator, and using the human scale I think makes that point a little bit better for me.

TG: The most recent work on the checklist that was shared with me is a painting called *Roaring River Apostle*. Can you tell me about that work?

BH: Actually, I just got finished writing about that, because as I said, I'm working on the timeline and stuff for the catalogue. While I was in Jamaica, I saw this man with this Bob Marley T-shirt on getting ready to light a spliff, and I thought it was a wonderful interplay between the T-shirt with the spliff and the man with the spliff. There's a posterization situation that you may be aware of in terms of musical posters where there's a kind of rainbow effect, and I wanted to incorporate that along with again the illusion of volume with a flat black because there's a similar approach that I started years ago. Take, for example, the painting *Miss T* that's in the Philadelphia Museum. That's a rather limited piece, black and white basically, and her skin color. So there is black, white, brown, and the gold of her jewelry and glasses, and the figure is completely flat and the chain changes as far as light is concerned

fig. 7
October's Gone... Goodnight, 1973
Oil, acrylic, and magna on linen canvas
72 x 72 inches

cat. 33 (opposite page)
Sisters (Susan and Toni), 1977
Oil and acrylic on linen canvas
66 x 48 1/4 inches

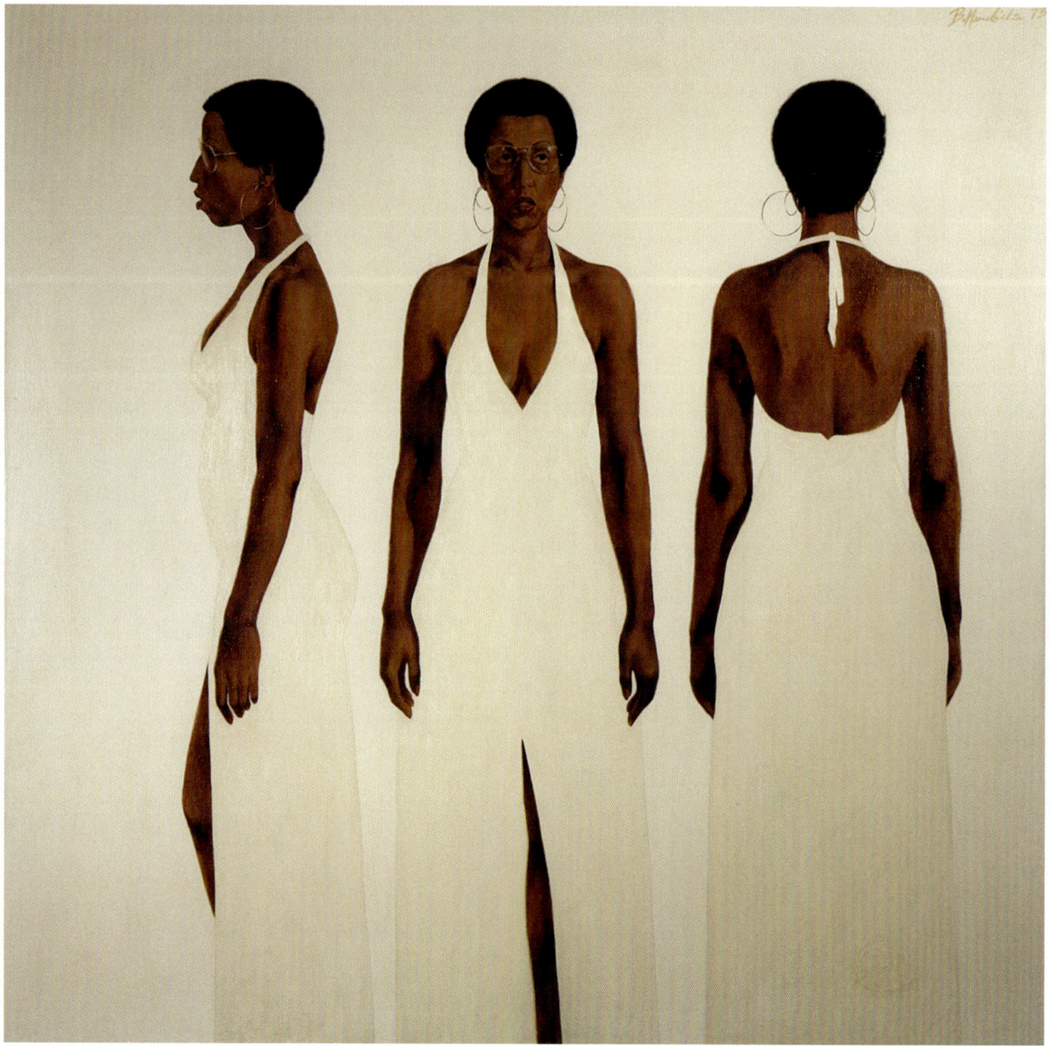

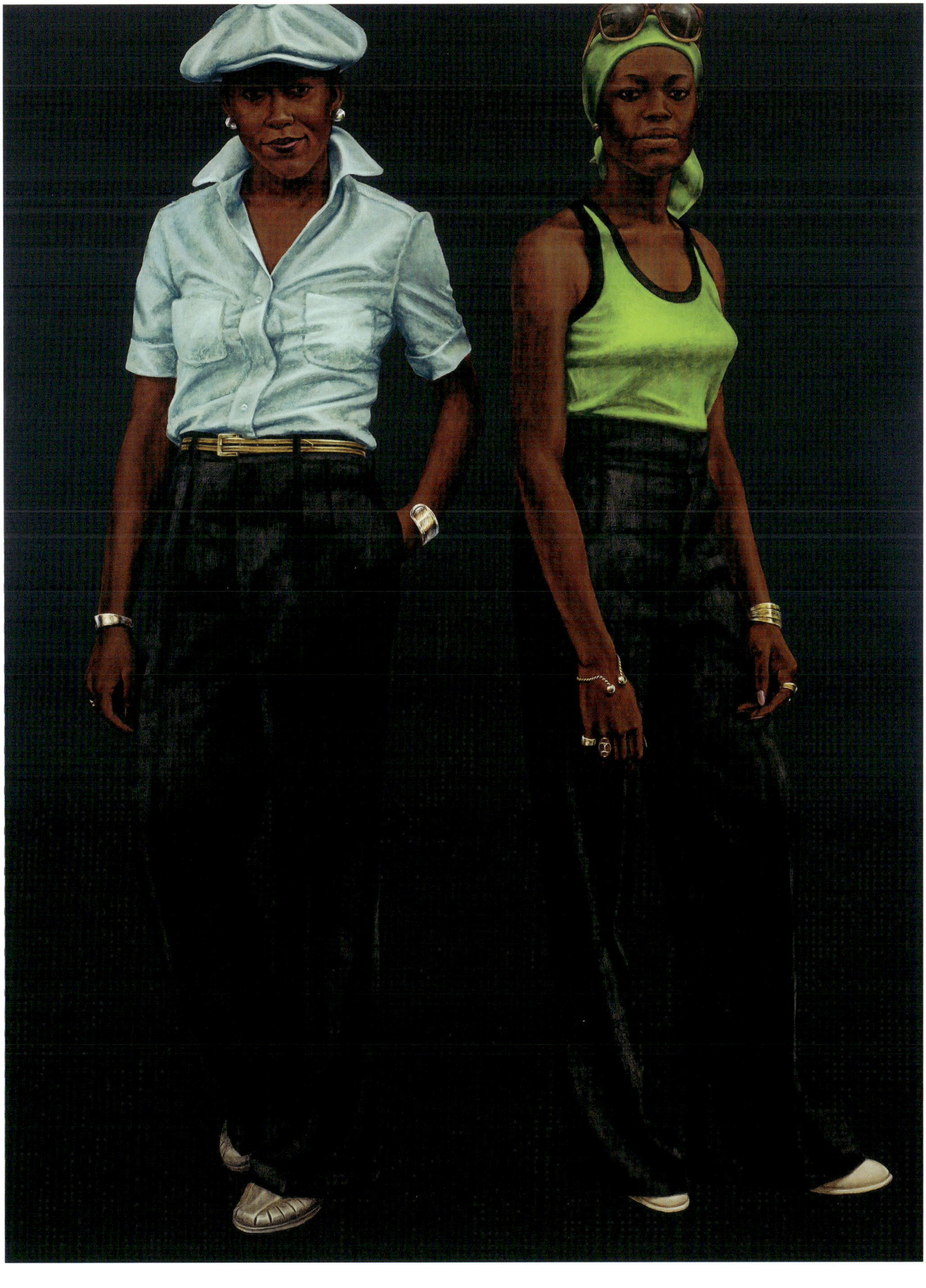

cat. 42
View from Behind the School, 2000
Oil on linen canvas
22 inch diameter

Opposite page:

cat. 51 (upper left)
Lyrical View from the Villa, 2005
Oil on linen canvas
12 x 21 inches

cat. 55 (center left)
Boxing Day in the Quarry (Marl Hole), 2006
Oil on linen canvas
18 3/4 x 26 1/2 inches

cat. 44 (lower left)
Mustard YS Falls, 2002
Oil on linen canvas
12 x 21 inches

cat. 43 (upper right)
View from Red Banks School, 2000
Oil on cotton canvas
12 x 21 inches

cat. 52 (center right)
New Year's Day in the Quarry (Marl Hole), 2006
Oil on linen canvas
18 3/4 x 26 1/2 inches

cat. 54 (lower right)
Cold Day on the Mountain, 2006
Oil on linen canvas
17 1/2 x 27 3/4 inches

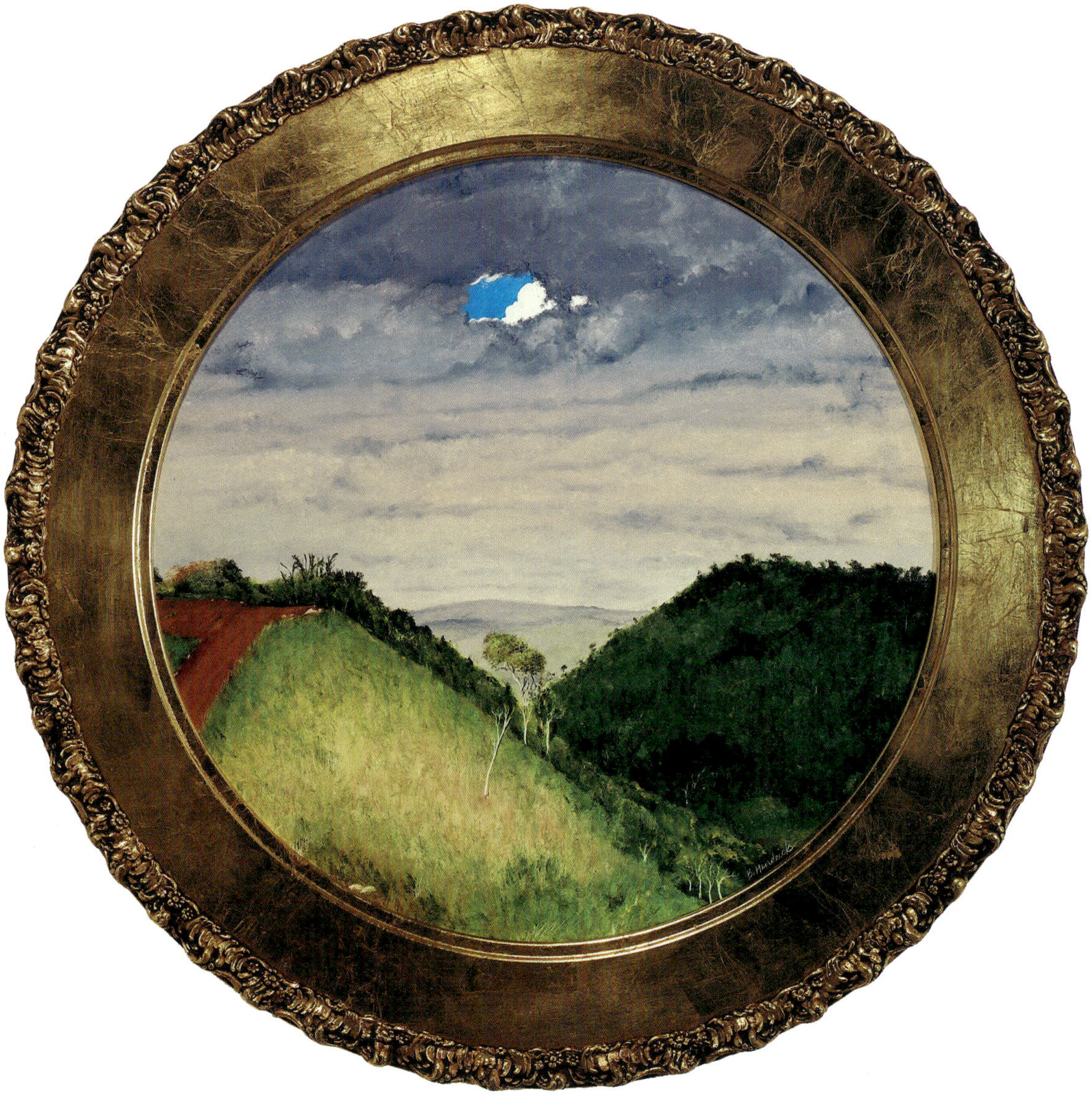

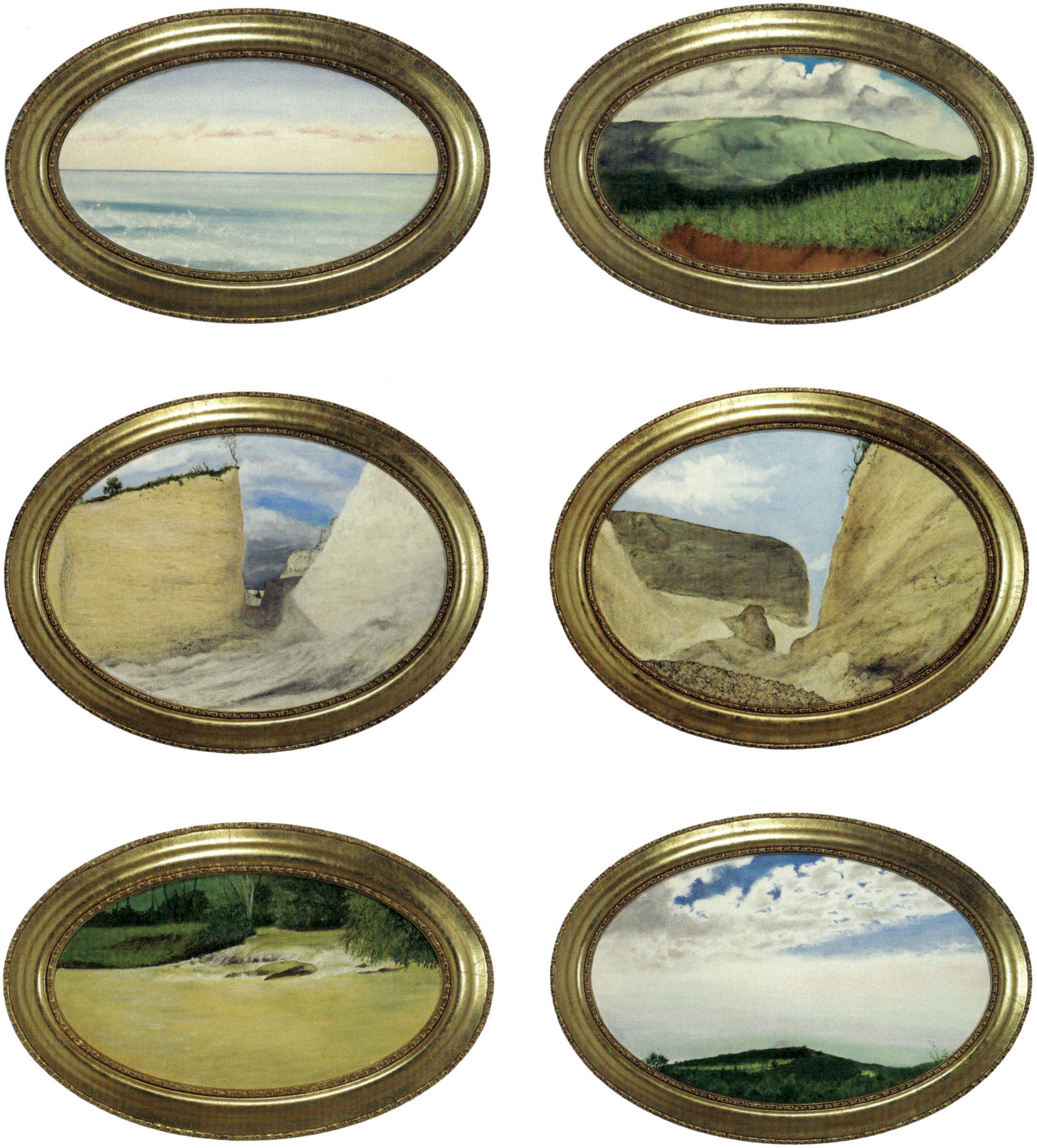

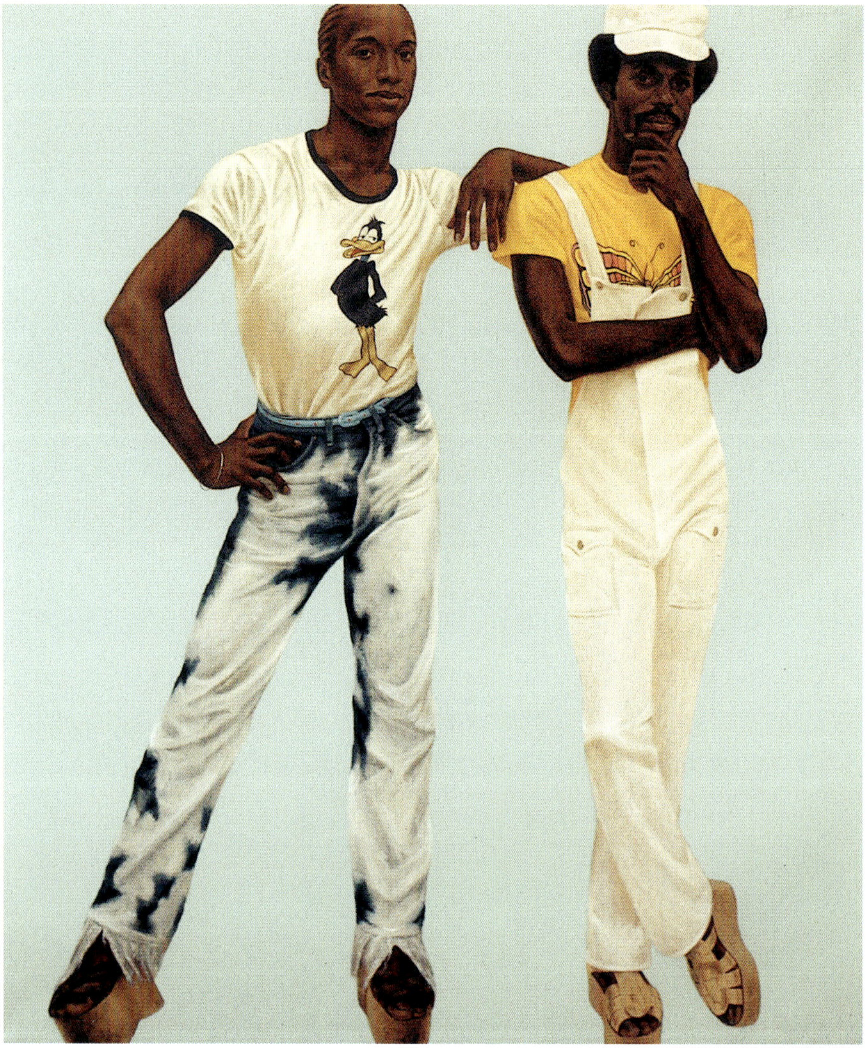

fig. 8
Ralph and Alvin–Sikkayou, 1974
Oil and acrylic on linen canvas
72 x 60 inches

on a volumetric body. Well, for *Roaring River Apostle*, I did the same thing, only there's a bit of change that recognizes his body underneath the image that says not everything is completely flat. So between the flat black, the rainbow effect of the yellow, red, and green, and the spliff and the scale, and plus it was handmade frame, so [it explores] that aspect of completing the entire piece from the stretcher bar to the frames. I've been kind of influenced by Dutch presentation with black framing, so I have several of those that I've made.

TG: These are unique, handmade frames.

BH: I have a background that deals with construction. My father was a contractor. I'm reasonably tool-savvy, and I'm able to negotiate certain power tools.

TG: So you actually made this frame yourself?

BH: Oh, yeah, from scratch. The first life was certainly a tree, but then once it was turned into a two-by-four, I introduced it to a table saw and routers to get what configuration I wanted. Actually, I just put one of the self-portraits in one of the frames that I built this summer.

TG: Just hearing you talk about *Roaring River Apostle* from 2004 and *Miss T* from 1969, works separated by over thirty years, makes me want to ask you if you think about the progression of your subjects and themes chronologically or if you think about them in a more circular relationship, moving back and forth between certain ideas, subjects, and themes?

BH: Everything is up for grabs in the creative arena, and I think it's only a limited artist that limits his or her approach to using what's available.

TG: Looking forward, what are you most excited about in your work? What are you thinking about in the studio now?

BH: As I said, there's a time in my life now where there's an area of immediacy. The landscapes offer that immediacy, working outdoors. With a figure, you have to plan and you can't necessarily finish it in one full sweep. Not mine. Whereas the paintings, I try to finish them in a setting and the only time within the context of the hunches that I have that I had to stop is when nature makes itself. Whereas between two, three, four, five hours, if I'm lucky, I can finish a piece and at least get it to the place where it's ready to be glazed and framed.

TG: That's what you have been working on?

BH: Part of it. The thoughts of what potentially are other figures are on the drawing board. But the landscapes do require a tender touch after they've been done so that they can be presented, because I don't do any framing in Jamaica. All of that happens here. I have the frames custom made in Canada. The company that I use has allowed me to put a finishing touch on them that I love, on all of the images in terms of the oil works, ovals and circles and lunettes, so there isn't a square or rectangular piece in the bunch.

TG: In most cases, they also seem of a fairly similar scale and size . . .

BH: Yeah, well, given what time I may start . . . around that time of year, December/January in Jamaica, it's usually light from six to six, and if you don't get it at six, you're in the dark!

TG: Does seeing your work in different exhibition contexts change your experience with your work?

fig. 9
Something Like a Bird: Double Barbara, 1982
Oil, acrylic, and variegation leaf on cotton canvas
66 x 72 inches

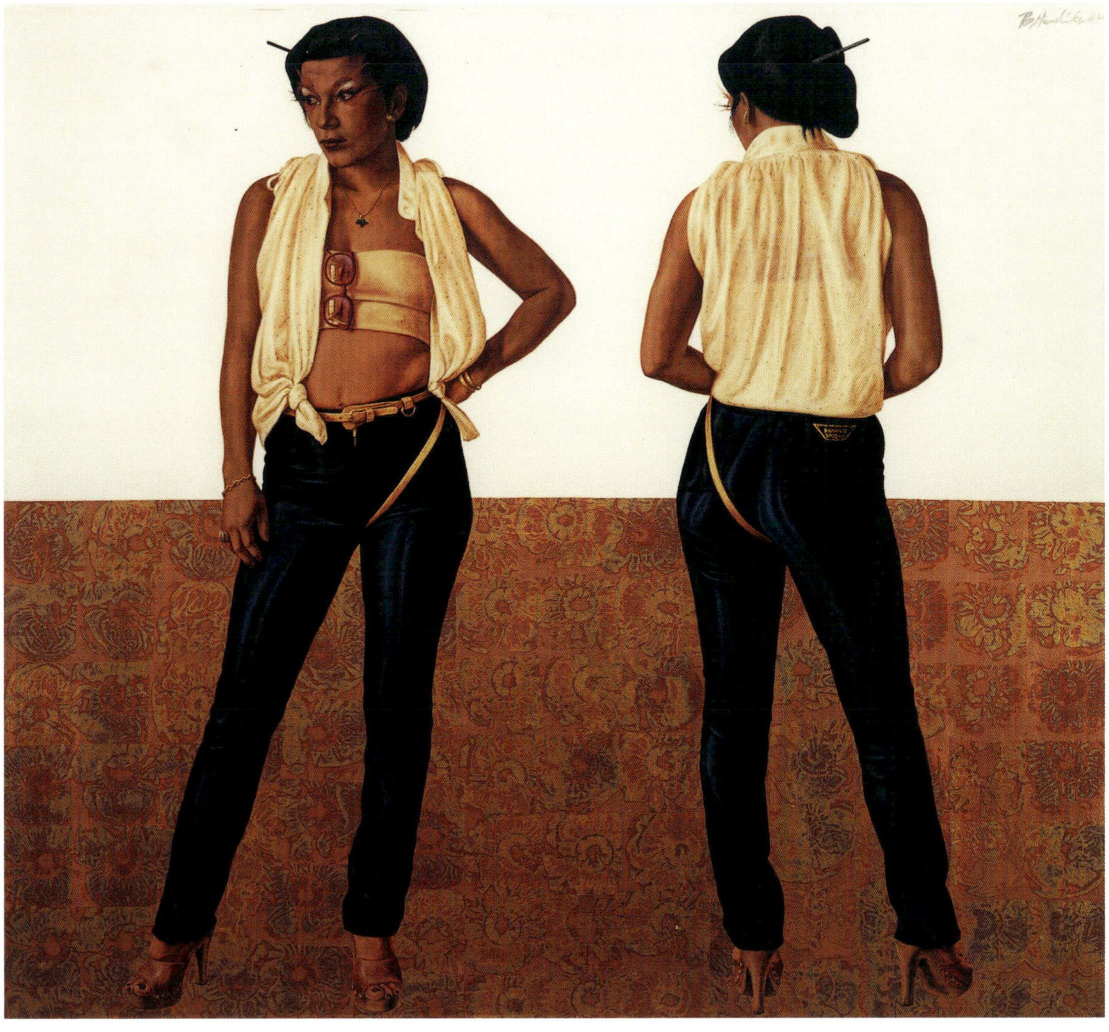

BH: Well, there are some works that I hadn't seen in a while. For example, the work that you mentioned in London I hadn't seen, *Sir Charles, Alias Willie Harris*, for twenty years.

TG: What was that like to see it again?

BH: It brought back a number of memories, and say, damn, that's a good painting, and, again, being reacquainted with *Lawdy Mama*, it kind of makes me think of the ordeal I went through in putting the gold leaf down. It worked the hell out of me.

TG: So generally it allows you to kind of reexperience the moment the painting was made.

BH: Sure.

TG: You know, I was thinking about the fact that in many ways, your titles seem to give information a name, but a lot of them incorporate a level of humor, and I'm wondering how much you wanted your viewers to read the sort of double meanings in some of the titles.

BH: Given the way that we deal with titling, at times I want to play with your head. I did have a reviewer from the *New York Times* once who made a comment about Barkley Hendricks's unhelpful titles, and I was wondering, what the hell does she want from me, you know? But I think it was enough, the titles, to get your attention, because in our culture, as I tell my students, we have maybe four or five seconds to get folks' attention and if you don't, they're off somewhere else, and I like to think that in certain situations, if you go to an exhibition, a group show, you don't remember everything. There are certain things that get your attention, certain things that you like, certain things that get your visual attention, or things that might piss you off, or things that might endear you. I like to feel that once you leave a show you remember my work either through what I've done with the paint or something that may have intrigued you or something that got your attention, so right there, there are three things that are potentially something that would make you memorable, and if you're gonna do it, you might as well be memorable.

fig. 10
Father, Son, and..., 1969
Oil and acrylic on canvas
Triptych, each canvas
64 x 49 7/8 inches

cat. 17 (opposite page)
Sir Charles, Alias Willie Harris, 1972
Oil and acrylic on linen canvas
84 1/8 x 72 inches

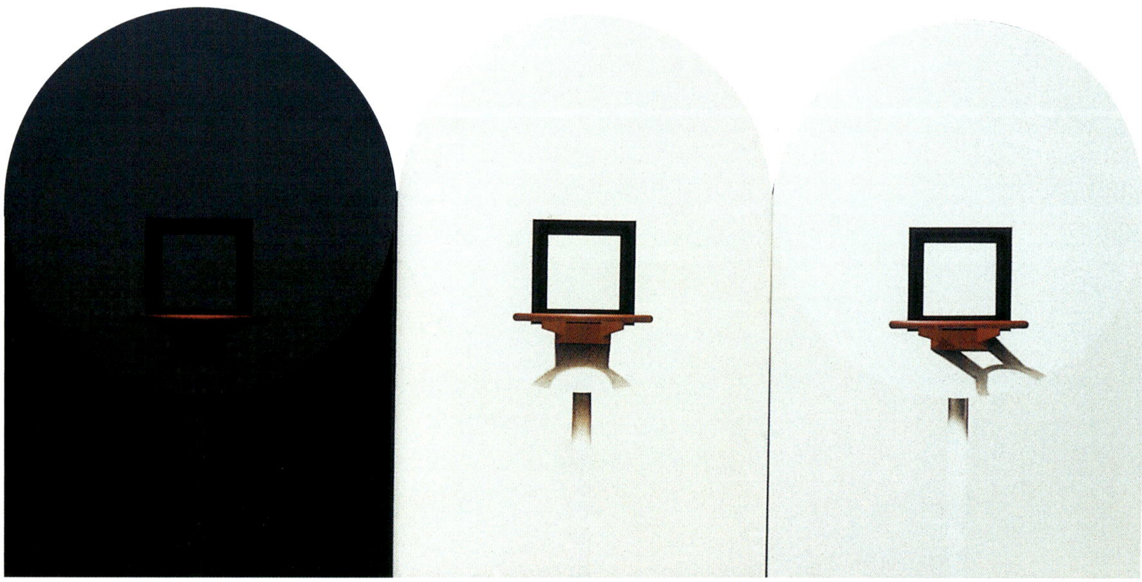

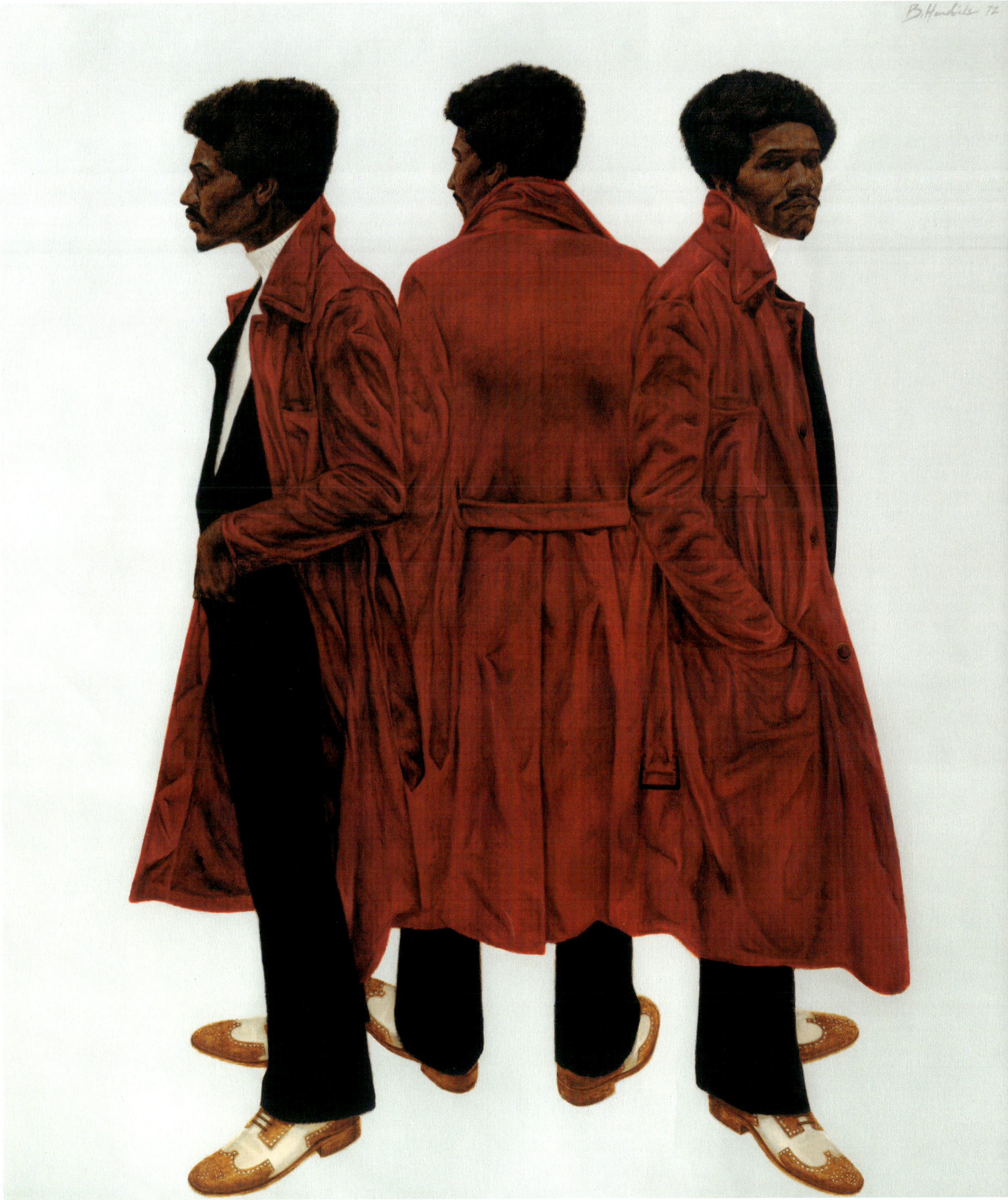

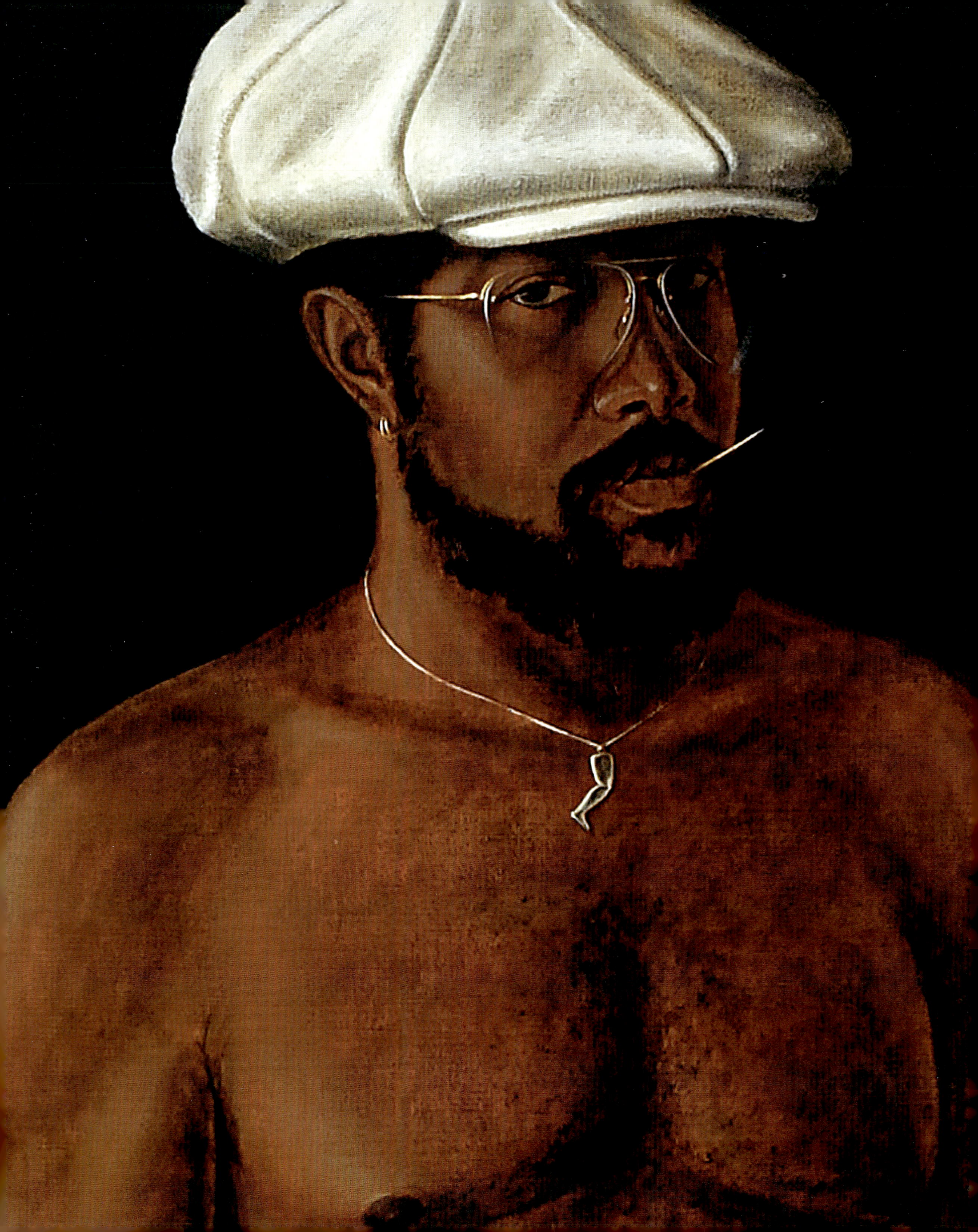

Barkley Hendricks: Ordinary People Franklin Sirmans

"In his self-published pamphlet, *Black Is a Color* (c. 1968), the artist Raymond Saunders lashed out at the 'uptown critics' and 'politico-sociologists' who, in that era of heightened black conscience, burdened African American artists with civil rights battles, an eternal pessimism, and narrow inquiries that led nowhere."[1] Though Saunders made these comments in light of late 1960s calls to black nationalism and "image management" via art, the sentiment goes back to the Harlem Renaissance. In light of these words, let us consider Barkley Hendricks and his influence.

Accused of being a modern-day Jekyll and Hyde or a bit of a two-faced character, Hendricks's embrace of two very different formal styles offers insight into the proverbial black painter's burden of representation versus abstraction—the spook who continues to sit by the door. Hendricks may not have gone the route of opportunity and stuck to making only his well-known figurative portraits, but younger artists have found sustenance in those paintings, as opposed to his diligent landscapes, or his equally delicate, small black and white photographs of still lifes. Artists like Kerry James Marshall, Kehinde Wiley, Mickalene Thomas, and Jeff Sonhouse recall Hendricks's use of black figures in portraiture, and a look at the passage of time from the late 1960s to the present offers some clues as to how we look at black bodies in paint and how we view portraiture in art history.

The early painting of Barkley Hendricks, a second-generation pop artist, offers something in common with early pop artists and the realist painters of the 1970s, for instance, Mel Ramos. The common type or image of things in the work of many of the pop artists is transferred to people. In Hendricks's art, these are the black people who are rarely glimpsed outside their community (not art galleries), but within these communities they can be seen just as easily as common symbols of vibrant everyday life. In some ways, Hendricks's early work synthesized the societal concerns of Larry Rivers with the commercial products of Ramos or Warhol. As in the 1970s sitcom *Good Times*, whose opening credits are interestingly illustrated by painter Ernie Barnes, Hendricks's figures conjure types: superfly dudes, black power fighters, proud, afroed sistahs, and super-sexy women with their hands on hips—that 1963–64 painting of a fully clothed nun very much included in the sexy category. Like Barnes, Hendricks paints black folk in liberating moments of, if not joy then unadulterated comfort. Here there is no need to wear the mask or assume your double-consciousness. They both traffic in kitsch as popularized by the young Clement Greenberg, who cited kitsch as an opiate of the masses in contrast to the "complexity" of the avant-garde. Hendricks's paintings actually affirm qualities of the vernacular culture and, as Greenberg would allow, kitsch, "now and then, produces something of merit, something that has something that has an authentic folk flavor."[2] The figures seemingly care less about a so-called white gaze—explored in much of the art theory since Hendricks started making his mark in the late 1960s—than you could possibly imagine. Heck, *what* white gaze (or black for that matter)? By enacting representative tropes with unabashed theatricality, his figures take on the language of fashion in a way that limns the possibilities of kitsch as a strategy. In Hendricks's paintings, the gaze is but one complex confrontation mediated by what the viewer brings to the picture. As Kobena Mercer has recently theorized, "The unique photo-realist depictions of vernacular style produced by painter Barkley Hendricks participate in the self-conscious 'superficialism' that pop artists had utilized as a strategy to explore the visual seduction of the viewer's gaze." He goes on to note,

> Where the politics of sexuality were seen as mutually exclusive to the identity politics of "race" in the either/or universe of black cultural nationalism, the erotic and libidinal investment in the gaze that Hendricks lays bare with such "cool" analytical precision had to wait until Thelma Golden's acclaimed *Black Male* exhibition before it could be recognized as revealing the ways in which clothes function in the construction of subaltern masculinities as ambivalent signs that both attract the gaze of others and defend the subject from the unconscious projection of primitivist fantasies.[3]

The inviting vernacular of Hendricks's work updated realist portraiture in the 1970s, a subject that had already been dealt a second-class citizenship by the invention of the camera, subsequent death in the midst of abstract expressionism, and a further blow amid the popularity of minimal and conceptual strategies that often sought the dematerialization of the art object—painting being enemy number one. That said, the young Hendricks set himself into a challenging field of inquiry by focusing on realist depictions of characters. It is a testament of his strength and gifts that the work continues to play such a vital role. Like his peer David Hammons, who is often cited by young sculptors and practitioners of conceptual art forms, Hendricks's work frequently offers younger painters an important historical precedent for their own work.

I first saw a Barkley Hendricks painting in the early 1980s. The bodies were not abstracted like those of Basquiat, X-rayed, flayed, and filleted. They were not just "black is beautiful" type of portraits either. A five-by-four-foot painting of a black man, naked save shoes and socks and a fly hat, called *Brilliantly Endowed*, is beautiful to some and really complicated to others, as it verges closely on the erotic. In fact, young conceptual artist Rashid Johnson has reenacted the painting as a photograph starring himself. Thanks in part to Hendricks's work having been included in a broad range of exhibitions since 2000, it has become ever more

cat. 31 (page 78)
Brilliantly Endowed (Self-Portrait), (detail) 1977
Oil and acrylic on linen canvas
66 x 48 1/4 inches

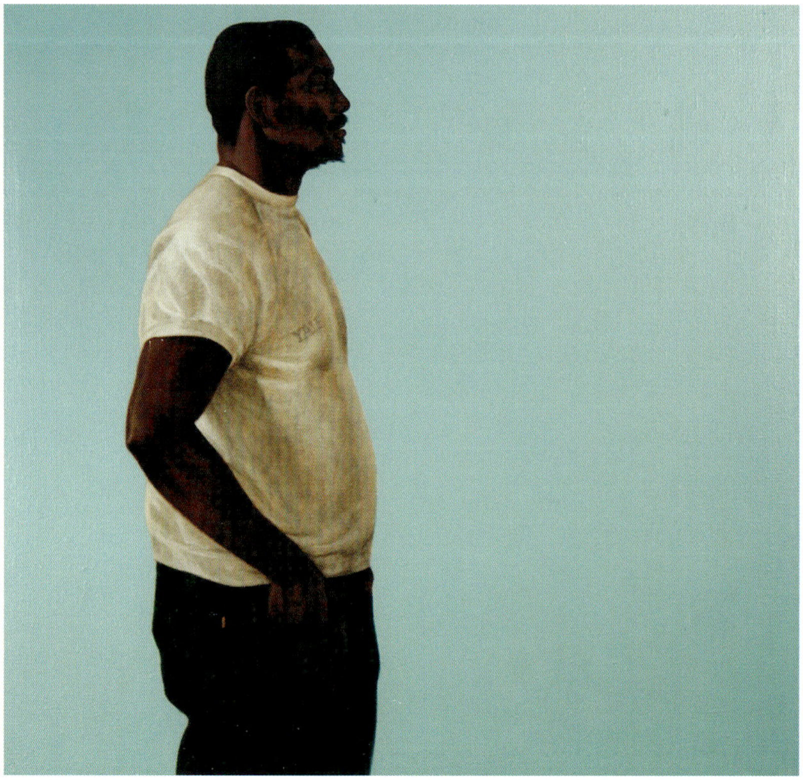

fig. 1
New London Niggah/ Big Chuck (Charles Harvey), 1975
Oil and acrylic on linen canvas
48 x 48 inches

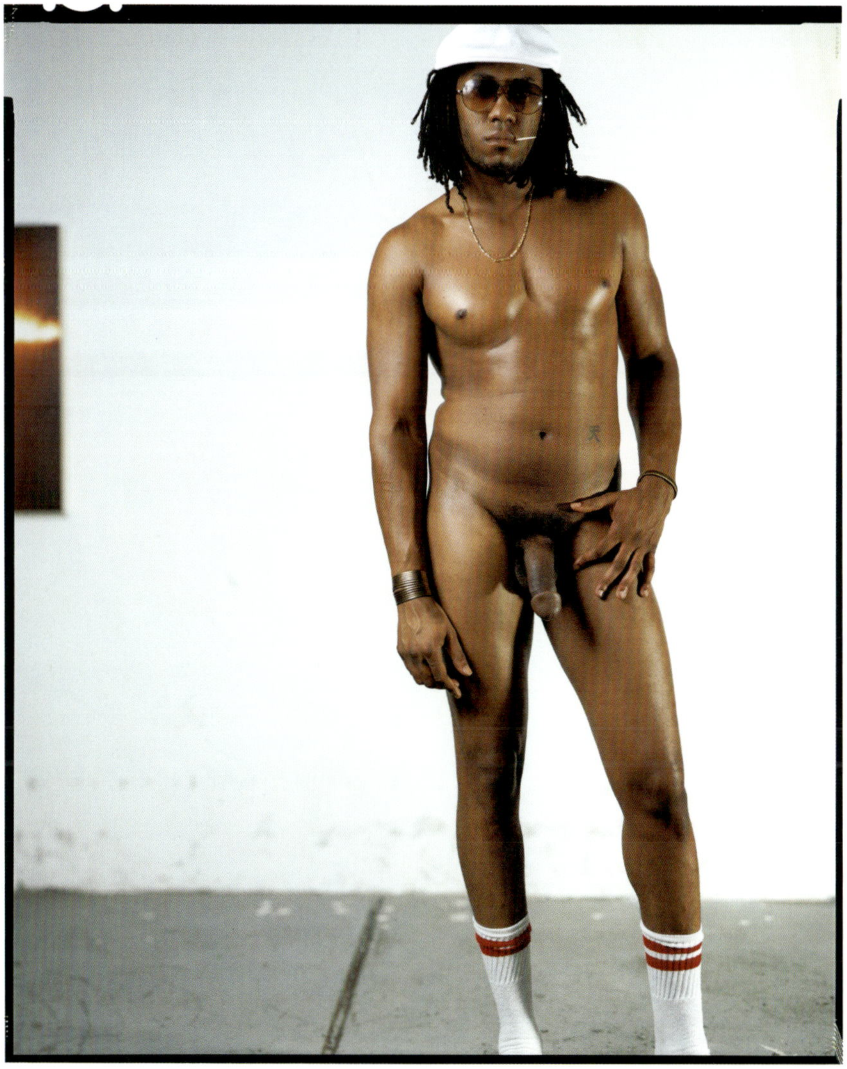

fig. 2
Rashid Johnson
Self-portrait in homage to Barkley Hendricks, 2005
Ink jet print on white PolyFilm, with Luster laminate

a topic of discussion. Hendricks has enjoyed a bit of a renaissance not so much driven by his own output as by the contemporary art viewer's maturation and the quality of presentation at galleries like Brent Sikkema and The Project, where diverse groups of artists are seen on equal footing. Luckier than many black artists of his generation, Hendricks has gotten out of the ghetto that pits black art for black people against art for art's sake. As Mercer alludes to when he cites Thelma Golden's *Black Male* exhibition, Hendricks has also benefited from society's ability to see the image of the black in more complex ways, even in the face of MTV. In addition to that, in looking at the work of several younger artists, particularly painters, we can see that Hendricks has become an important part of art history and has recently influenced some talented young artists.

Neither responsive to the calls of the black arts movement nor seemingly concerned with the opposite black artist approach of embracing color in the form of abstraction, Hendricks's work in the late 1960s and 1970s updates the concerns of pop art while anticipating the 1980s return to the figure in the form of neo-expressionism. His first mature paintings dovetail with the height of Bob Thompson's popularity. Unlike that beat generation artist, Hendricks didn't color his figures in primary colors as symbols in landscapes highly inflected by religion. As Michael Brenson has pointed out, "There is the memory of Bob Thompson, who seemed in the 1960s to be trying to paint all the history of art into one whole."[4] No, Hendricks wasn't trying to do that. He was not driven by Thompson's demons to paint the whole of art history or surrounded by

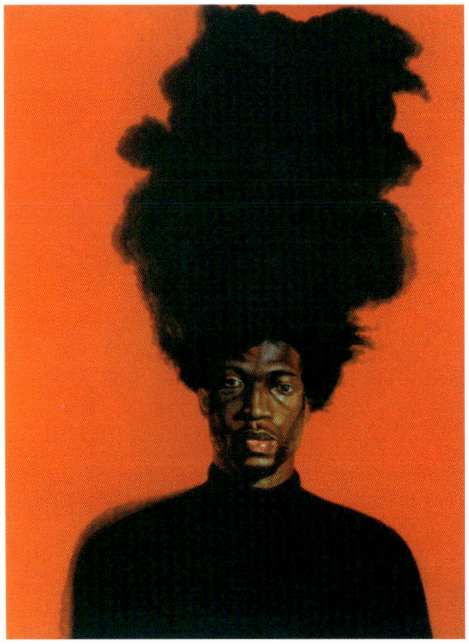

the ghosts that undoubtedly come with such aspirations. Unfettered by the figure as symbol, Hendricks was also unconcerned with dry, unemotional likenesses or the psychically charged glimpse of well-known figures. His figures, though often named in titles—including the numerous self-portraits—are composites (or at least act as such) of many different people in one role.

If you think of black artists in the United States in the early 1970s, you might find it difficult to name a figurative painter. Since then, there has been a steady stream of black bodies in visual art, albeit largely in conceptual frameworks and more often using photography. If there is any zeroing in on the body of work of the most popular black artist, Jean-Michel Basquiat, we would decidedly hit the bull's-eye in pointing to his extensive exploration of the black male body. In some way Basquiat may be the link between Hendricks's old school and the new in the form of Kehinde Wiley's contemporary beautiful black boys.

Titian and Tiepolo provide art historical junkies with the visual precedent and conceptual framework for referentially viewing Wiley's work within the continuum of Western art history, but there is also the ornamentation of Versace, Gucci, and throwback jerseys. The work of Hendricks figures greatly in Wiley's artistic genealogy. Wiley's work—with its full frontal concentration on black bodies—is by default socially engaged. His portraits are also evidence of a social engagement that is perhaps more thoroughly of the moment, hinting at an artistic project bigger than painting. In Wiley's paintings, the gaze of young black boys in popular garb is sometimes filled with cunning desire, though usually the gaze is more the projection of the mask, covering their inner lives. Like the paintings of Hendricks, Wiley's work has found a home in the consciousness of a black familiar by intertwining the classical and the contemporary.

Where Hendricks's male figures often take the aggressive posture of the pre–B-boy stance players and pimps, Wiley's standers mimic similar postures that are however more heavily known in the mass marketplace, post–hip hop.[5] Though his early paintings of 1999 and 2000 captured his posers on predominantly monochromatic backgrounds in primary colors (not unlike the open swaths of color that characterize most of Hendricks's paintings), Wiley's more recent works allow for readings outside the sitter or the subject. Their neo-baroque backgrounds of opulent color and detail shift the gaze off and on for the viewer. A right hand pointed to the sky in several paintings, both

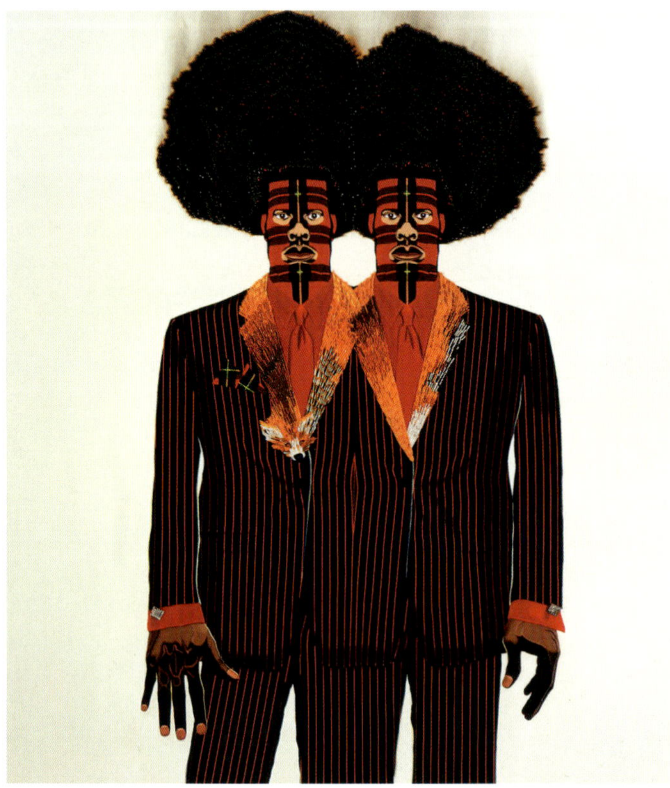

fig. 3 (left)
Kehinde Wiley
Conspicuous Fraud (Portrait Study), 2001
Oil on canvas
18 x 24 inches

fig. 4
Jeff Sonhouse
Meeting at the Crossroads, 2003
Oil and mixed media on canvas
75 x 65 inches

cat. 5 (opposite page)
J.S.B. III (James Sherman Brantley), 1968
Oil on linen canvas
48 x 34 3/8 inches

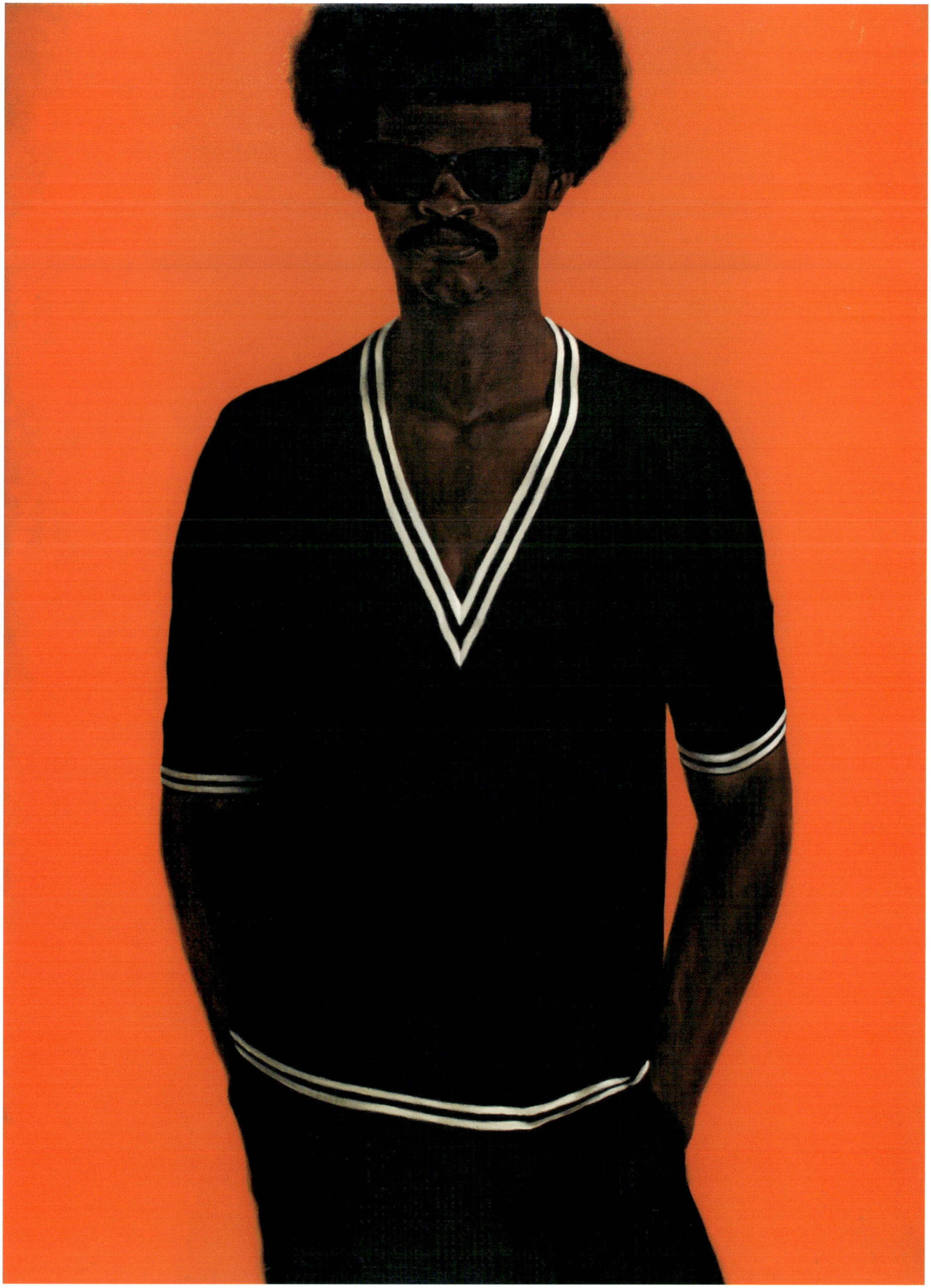

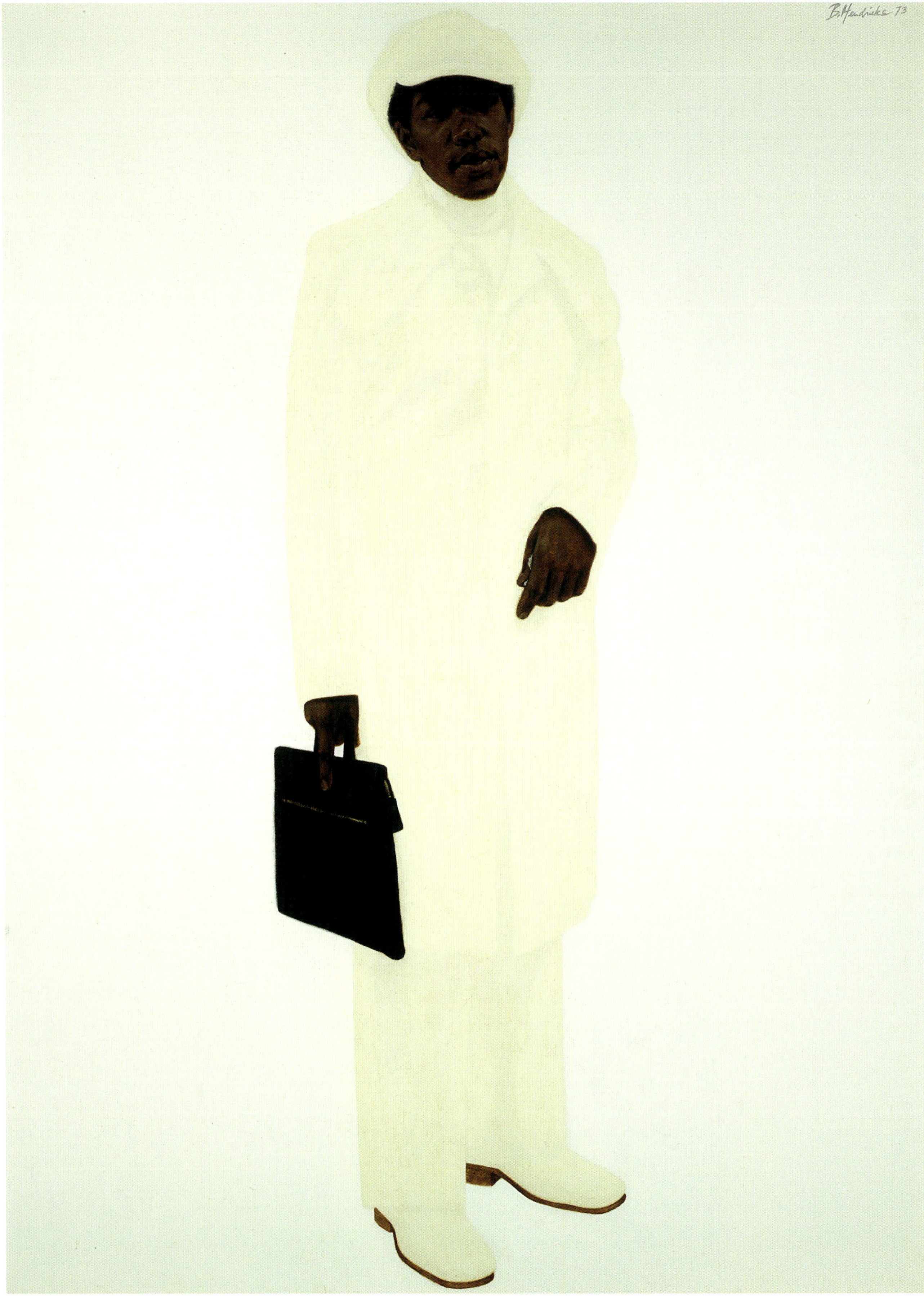
B.Hendricks 73

cat. 19 (opposite page)
Dr. Kool, 1973
Oil and acrylic on
linen canvas
72 3/4 x 52 3/4 inches

cat. 35
Vendetta, 1977
Oil, acrylic, and magna
on linen canvas
36 x 48 1/8 inches

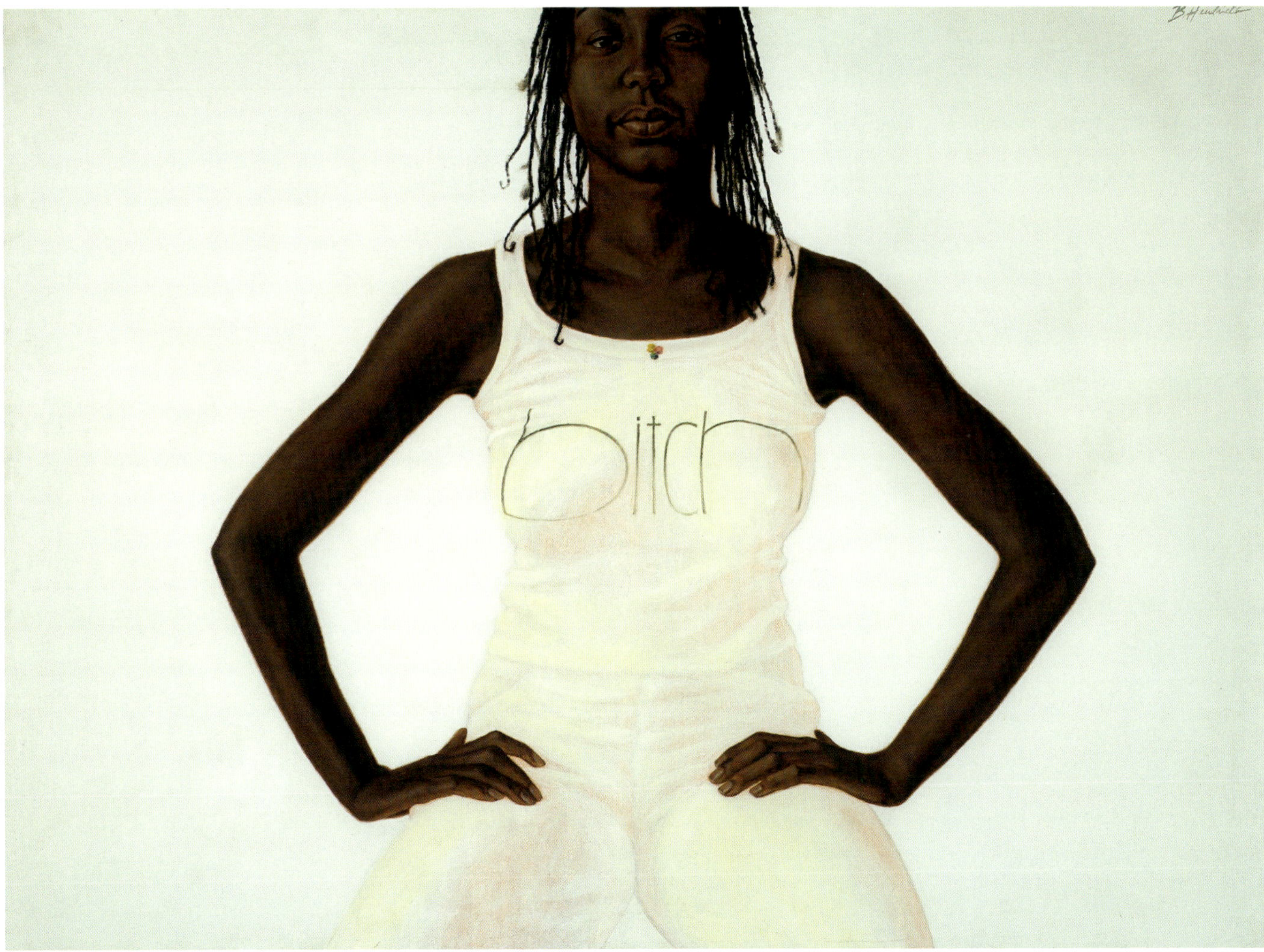

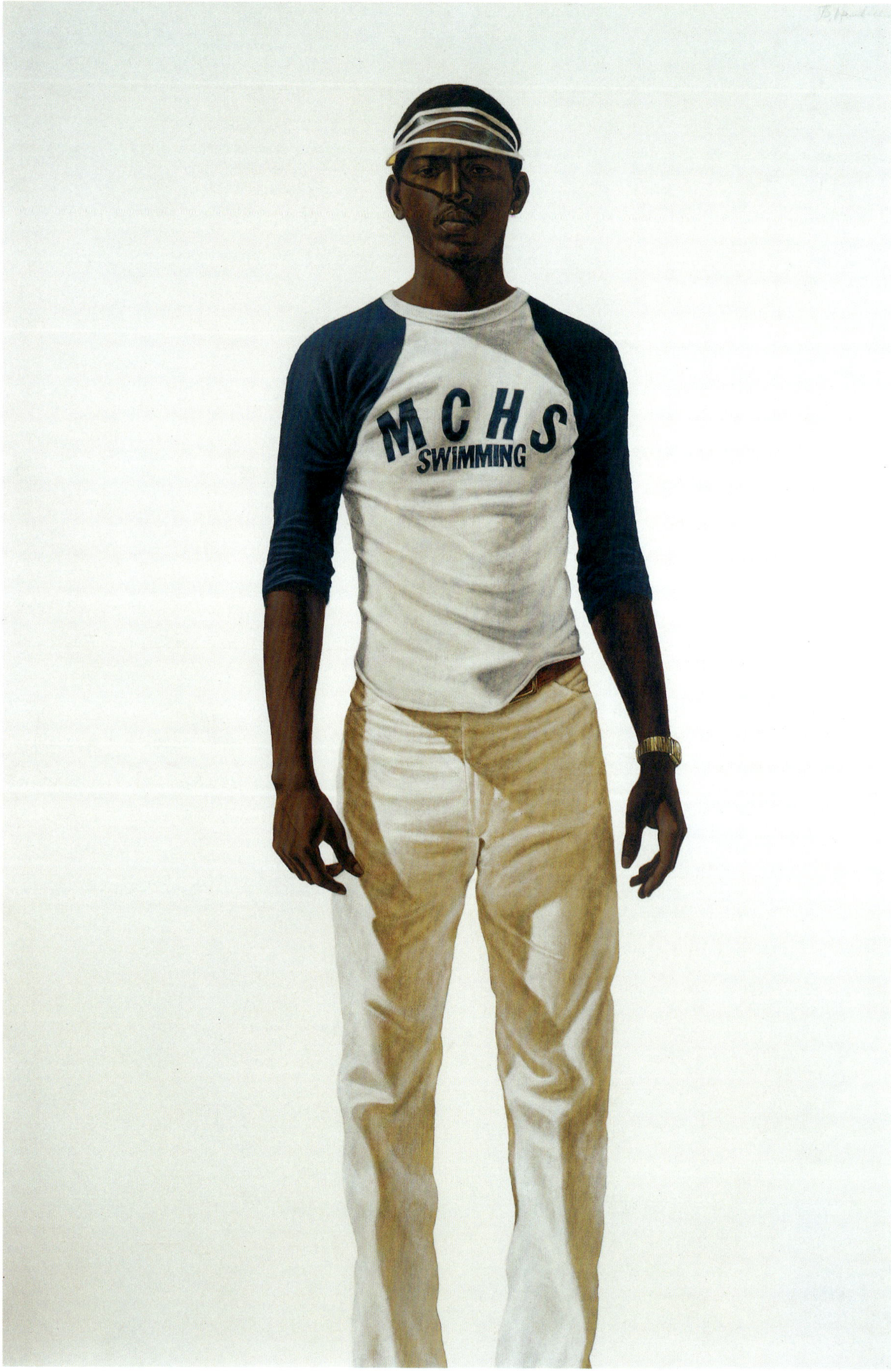

cat. 38
Tuff Tony, 1978
Oil and acrylic on linen canvas
72 x 48 inches

fig. 5 (opposite page)
Kehinde Wiley
St. John the Baptist II, 2006
Oil on canvas
72 x 96 inches

arms raised and palms open in others, or the sign of prayer in the hands of another—all of Wiley's figures share an open, confident stare. Their thoughts and feelings as living subjects are hard to grasp from simply their gaze; they project to the world a coat of arms that is mental and spiritual rather than physical. Is it the posture of the figure selected (by the sitter) from a book of classical painting, or is it the outstretched arms and raised palms of a B-boy "mugging" for the camera, proud in his sartorial splendor? This ambiguity is further heightened in Wiley's painting by the ethereal backgrounds filled with ornate spermatozoa, flowers, and blueprints from rococo architecture. There is no floor on which these boys stand, just shifting ground. In a recent series of paintings made for a 2006 solo exhibition at the Columbus Museum of Art, the comparisons with Hendricks are most apparent. Monumental figures are presented at the center of the painting. Though everyday people, their swagger suggests they are more than the tropes or stereotypes that society allows on first perception—extending the narrative possibilities that underlie any great realist portrait.

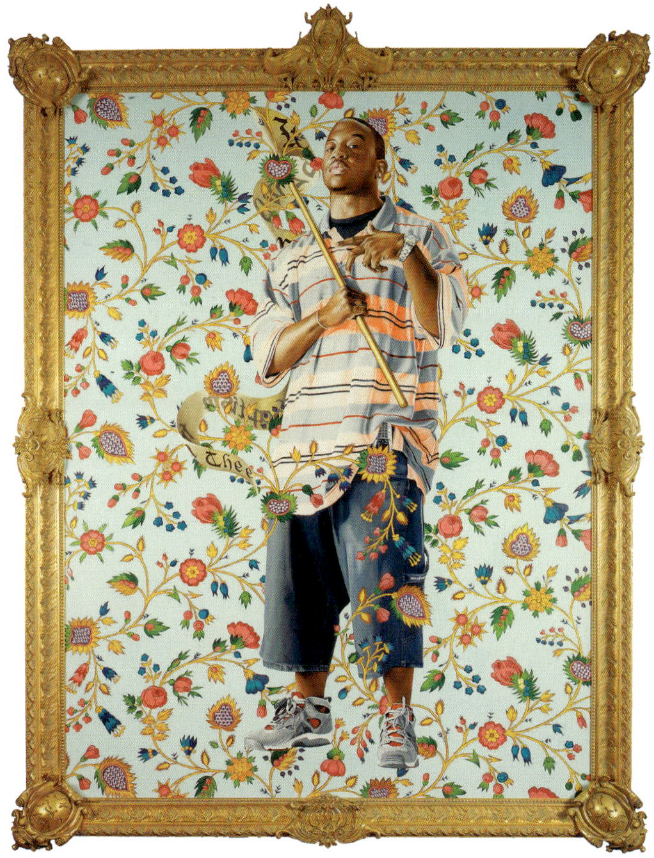

For Jeff Sonhouse, seeing *Tuff Tony* in the *Black Male* exhibition was his first and crucial visitation with a Hendricks painting. He realized that Hendricks's figures carried the political import of figurative works by the likes of Leon Golub without being explicitly about politics. "He allowed me to understand how the black body alone is loaded with meaning and how the artist can choose to play with people's preconceptions."[6] For Sonhouse, an artist who came to the fore with his first New York solo exhibition in 2002 at the Jack Tilton Gallery, Hendricks's work provided a prime example from close to home to go along with his interests in a revitalized painting scene. While looking at works by artists like John Currin, Richard Phillips, and Lisa Yuskavage, the presence of Hendricks's work helped allow Sonhouse to get at the heart of what he wanted to do with painting. In Hendricks's extreme and complex attention to detail, Sonhouse found an artist interested in "masking" in a way similar to his own explicit renderings. Sonhouse literally masks his figures with materials and an emphasis on eyes staring out from the canvas. His portraits of masked figures allude to classical and modern portraiture and illustrate a strand of thought and rhythm that runs throughout the work of the three artists—music. In the same way that Wiley's and Sonhouse's figures recall contemporary hip hop icons, there is no doubt that James Brown, the Godfather of Soul, provides the soundtrack to many a Hendricks painting.

Though the soundtrack changes with time, Hendricks' paintings retain the aura and power of beauty created by the human hand for visual pleasure. That his paintings do so much more, as alluded to here, is a bonus. There are the older paintings and the newer ones in the same style, such as his brilliant orange-drenched canvas in homage to Fela Kuti, that demonstrate the unstinting effort of an artist who has never missed a beat. The paintings are also evidence of things unseen—an artist in his studio, undaunted and unencumbered by the world outside—through the turmoil of the 1960s or the global wars of 2007, Hendricks remains undeterred. In the process, he confronts the universal issues of making art with more than success, but valiant beauty.

Notes

1. Richard J. Powell, *Black Art and Culture in the 20th Century* (New York: Thames & Hudson, 1996), p. 125.

2. See Clement Greenberg, "Avant-Garde and Kitsch," in his *Art and Culture: Critical Essays* (Boston: Beacon Press, 1971).

3. Kobena Mercer, ed., *Pop Art and Vernacular Cultures* (Cambridge, MA: MIT Press, 2007), pp. 30–32.

4. Michael Brenson, "Black Artists: A Place in the Sun," *New York Times* (March 12, 1989).

5. A "B-boy" or "break-boy" is a male devoted to hip-hop culture, and specifically the art of breakdancing. Females are commonly referred to as "B-girls."

6. Jeff Sonhouse in conversation with Franklin Sirmans, November 12, 2007.

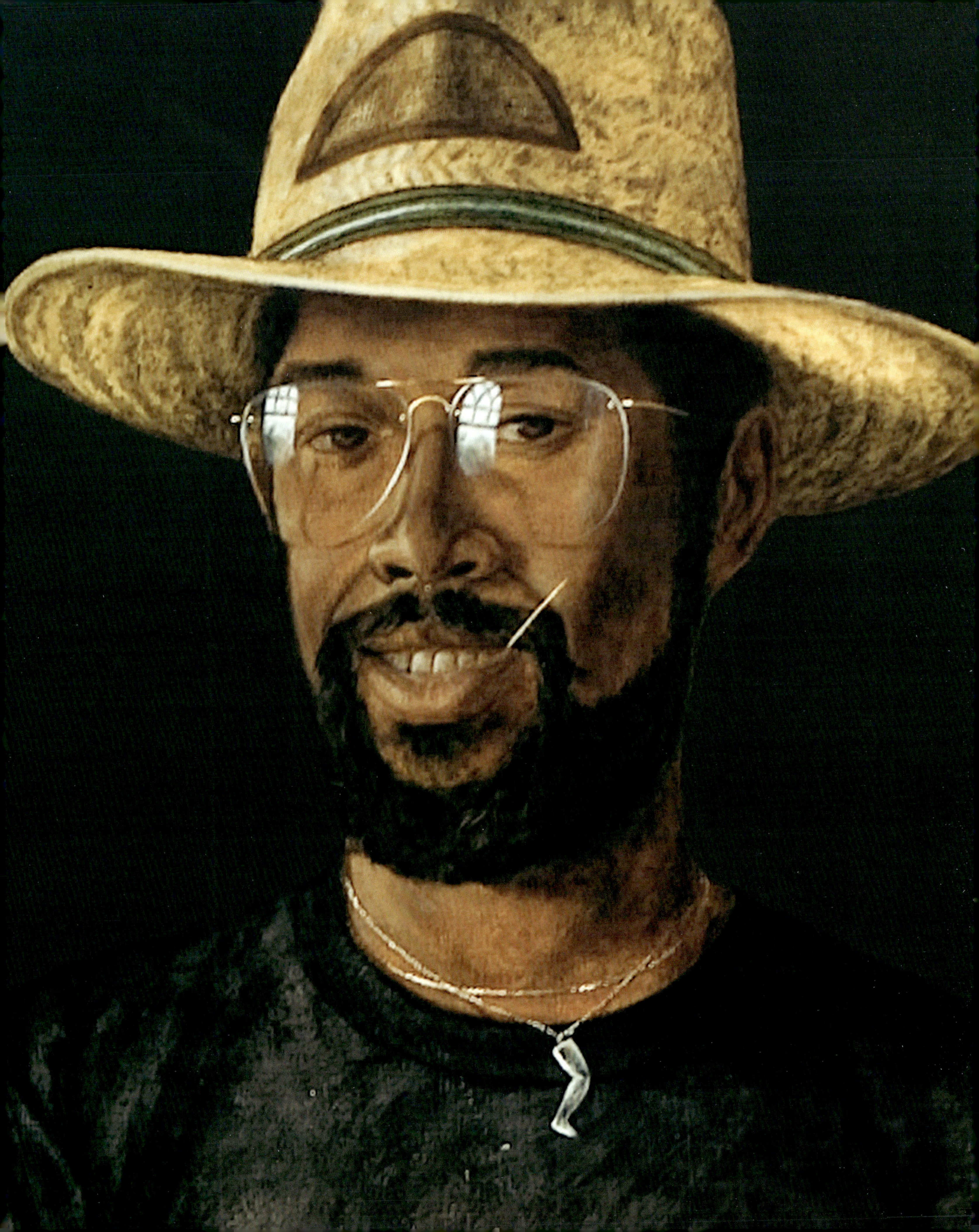

Palette Scrapings Barkley L. Hendricks

1. How cool is that? Find your spot and sit like Carlos Castaneda did when he wrote several decades ago. Like Cézanne did when he painted his beloved Mont Sainte-Victoire. December and January are perhaps Jamaica's coolest months. It most certainly can be in several of its mountaintop vistas and its "marl holes," otherwise known as the rock quarries. As the winter winds whip through and threaten to take my hat, painting, umbrella, and everything that is not locked down, it's quite cool. I'm almost certain that wasn't the cool curator Trevor Schoonmaker had in mind when he ran the title for this exhibition past me. On several occasions, I've had my people portraits referred to as "cool realism" or "cool representationalism." I certainly can live with being associated with anything having to cozy up to being called cool. So much so, it is always a cool thing to find a place in the heat of the Jamaican countryside to sit and paint for several hours. It's a meditative event with oil and watercolor pigments. There are rapid dictations from Mother Nature where you have to pay attention. Actually some days are quite hot. How cool is that?! That is if tropical downpours do not chase me away from my chosen task and topics or bombarding bugs don't crash land in my wet paint or ants and other insects are not dining on me or my palette's cadmium and titanium colors.

The three-, four-, five-, or six-hour joust with the elements leaves me in an exhausted and refreshed state of mind. To have nature program a course of study that one follows makes for authentic and challenging subject matter. To respond with a material (oil that can be called a miracle material) helps shape the outcome and directions, thus formulating a thought process and making a sharper perception for the panoramic vistas as well as the pinpoint perspectives. And how cool is that?!

Being a staunch, dyed-in-the-wool jazz fan, I was very much aware of the origins of

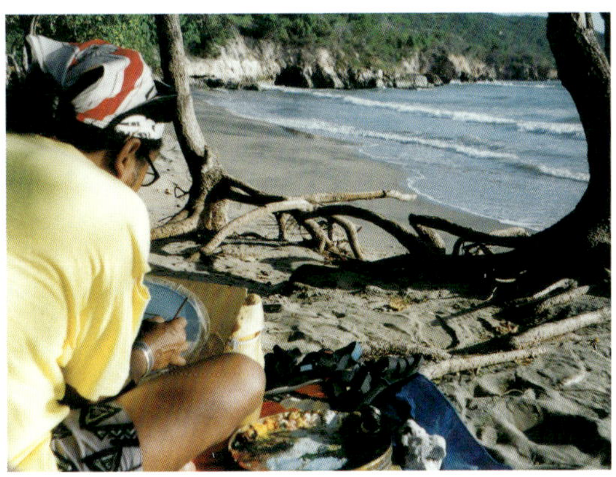

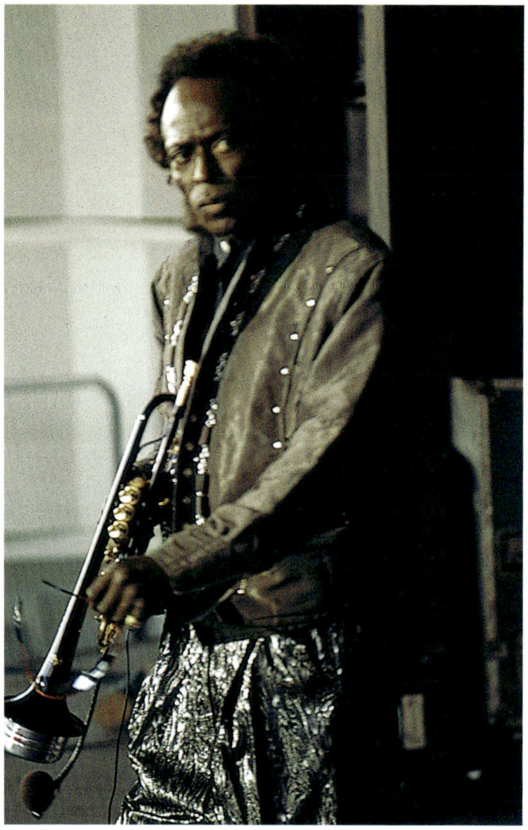

"Birth of the Cool." There was a pride in keeping up with all things cool in North Philly around the late 1950s, 1960s, and 1970s. Musical taste, dress, and dialogue were all a reflection of the prevailing school of thought. Coolness and hipness went hand in hand; to be unhip was to be uncool. Needless to say, Miles Davis was the epitome of being cool. It was monkey see, monkey do concerning Miles. One had to constantly set one's dial to cool winds of change. If you fancied yourself a record collector (33 1/3 platters), you always had to have the latest Miles. I remember when "Bitches Brew" came out and caused the ripple in the world of cool. As of 2007, I have all the formats that the classic was recorded in except eight-track (if it was even ever recorded in that format).

My hipness later obligated me to seek out my favorite musicians with my developing photographic skills. Julian "Cannonball" Adderley, a sideman of Miles, was the initial inspiration. I won't list the number of artists I have had before my lens. Miles, however, provides one of the best stories and most poignant experiences. I was backstage at the Canandaigua Jazz Festival in upstate New York. Miles was the major headliner. In his usual style of playing, he had his back to the audience. Being backstage, I was able to shoot through several rolls of film before one of the roadies came to me and said "Miles says to get off the stage." By that time, I had quite a few images of the master with his black trumpet and gold shirt. He later invited me back to his dressing room for some close-up photographs. At that time, I gave him one of my catalogues and told him I painted as well as he played, and he painted as well as I played the trumpet. Miles smiled. How cool was that?!

2. "Summertime and the Livin' Was Easy . . ."

Indeed, indeed. I spent far too many summers in Virginia to recollect them all. Meadville in Halifax County, Virginia, is sixty or so miles up the road apiece from Durham, North Carolina. "Fish were jumpin' and the tobacco was high." We looked forward to our escapes from the streets of Philadelphia to the green pastures of Meadville, to home-churned butter from contented cows, free-range fried chicken, smokehouse-cured ham, and chitlins from slop-fed hogs. For us kids, life was good. We all cried when it was time to head North and go back to school. At least I did.

Perhaps it is poignant that my largest exhibition to date is so near to the place I loved deeply. As a child, I would have traded my eye teeth to stay in Meadville. Many years later, one of my first cousins confided in me how much he envied me because his parents stayed in the South instead of moving North like my father and mother did. He, too, was interested in art and felt his creativity was squelched because there was nowhere he could follow his dreams on the farm, like his family. All eight of my father's siblings left the farm, and five of the six of my mother's brothers and sister "beat feet" North. Farm life was not a part of the adult life calculations. One of my mother's brothers put it succinctly when a local white country farmer and general store owner said to him during one of his visits "down home": "I guess you boys will be back here on the farm when Ike gets in the White House." Uncle Lacy's reply was, "I don't give a damn who gets in the White House, I ain't coming back down here to the farm."

cat. 32 (page 88)
Doc and Ruby's Oldest Boy (Self-Portrait), (detail) 1977
Oil and acrylic on linen canvas
72 x 48 inches

fig. 1 (page 89)
Hendricks painting beach scene in Jamaica, c. late 1990s

fig. 2
Hendricks's photograph of Miles Davis at Canandaigua Jazz Festival, Canandaigua, NY, July 1988

cat. 32
Doc and Ruby's Oldest Boy (Self-Portrait), 1977
Oil and acrylic on linen canvas
72 x 48 inches

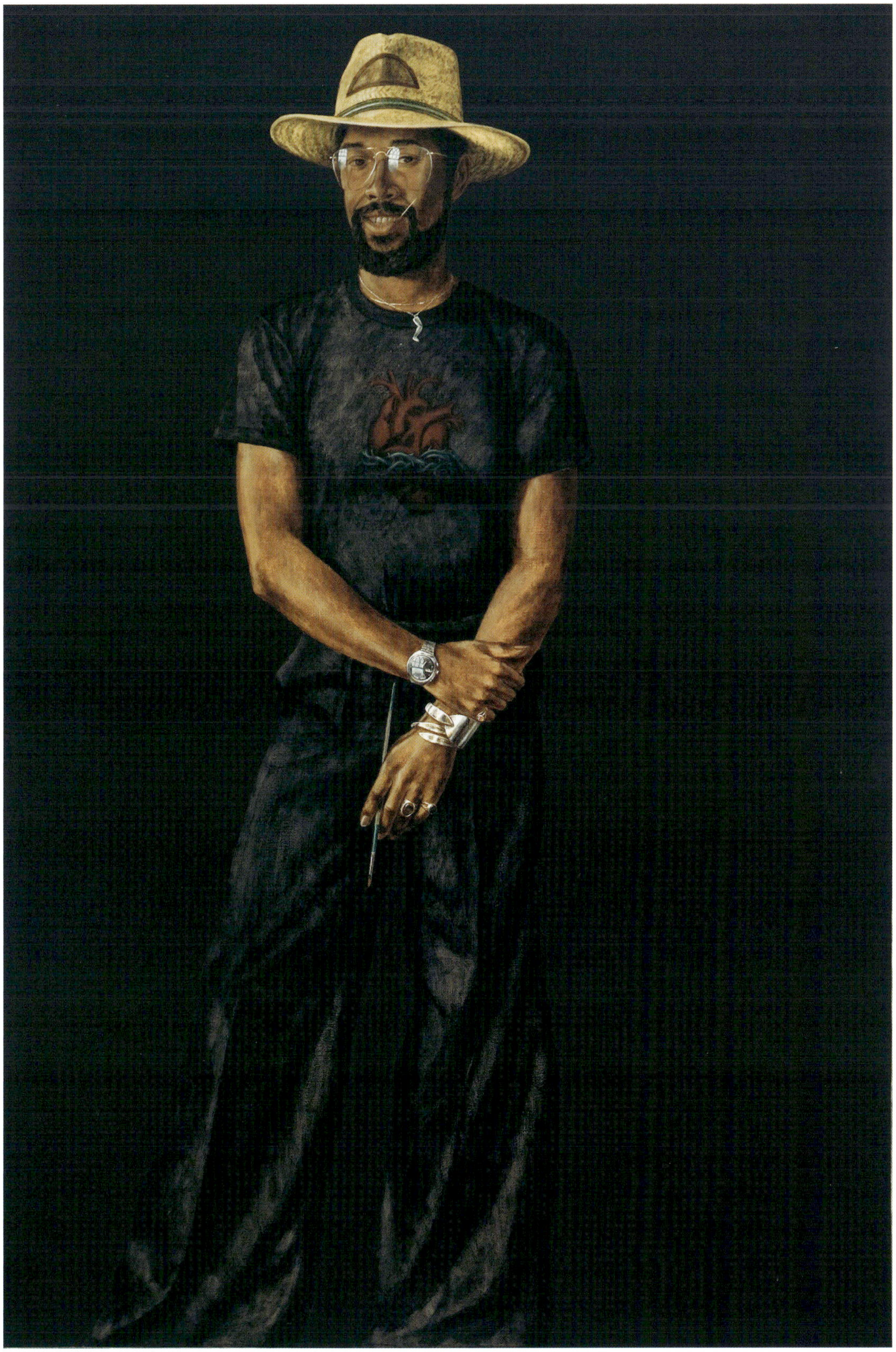

cat. 4
FTA, 1968
Oil on linen canvas
32 x 30 inches

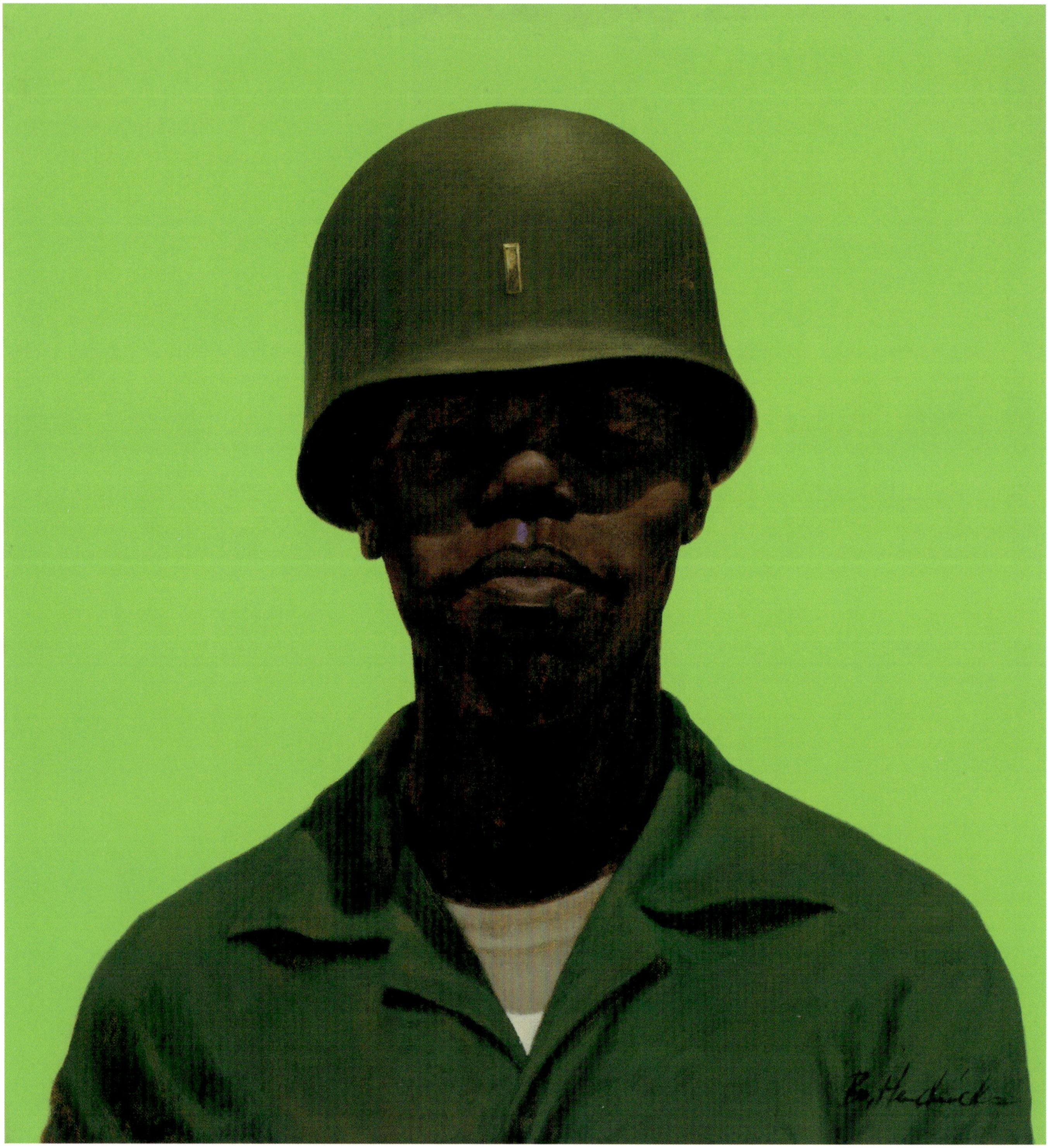

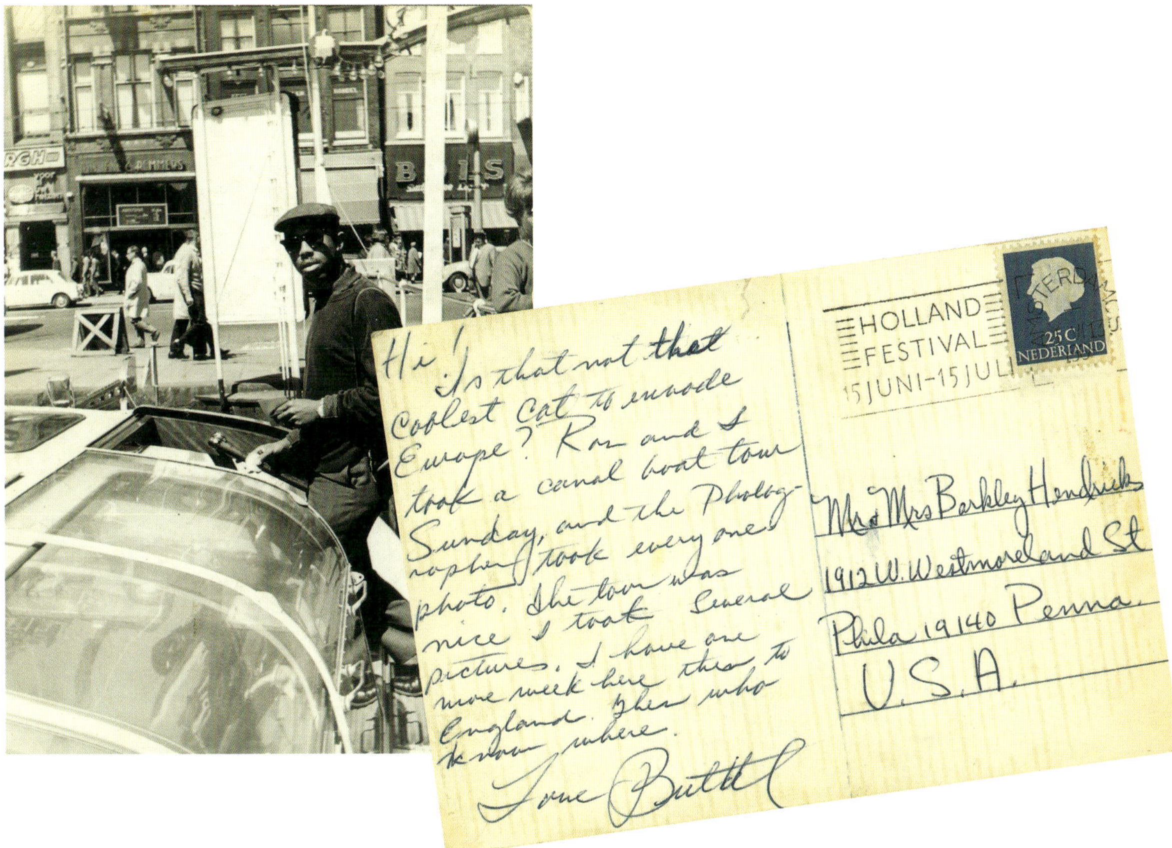

fig. 3
Hendricks postcard from Amsterdam, while traveling on Cresson Scholarship from the Pennsylvania Academy of the Fine Arts, 1966

As I got older, I learned the living was not all that easy. During one of the conversations with my mother's father, whom we called Papa, I asked him if he liked farming. His answer was no. Farming was hard work, and he had a family to support and feed. However it was better than the life he led as a single man. He worked in the coal mines of West Virginia where he did not see the light of day for weeks at a stretch. I suppose sharecropping had its advantages over the darkness and danger of the underground. Papa did say he loved the great outdoors. His way with his crop yields, edible and nonedible, was a testimony to his farm husbandry. My mother's remarks about the Depression were, "They had zero dollars but a storehouse full of food they raised themselves."

Both grandfathers were good with rifles and shotguns when they supplemented the family diet with food from the hunt. My father was good, too. When the various seasons opened up North, he would grace the table with rabbits, turkeys, and a pheasant or two. I never went hunting with my father. My dead-eye aim was sharpened on the weapons ranges during army basic training and the six years I spent in the New Jersey National Guard where I shot marksman, sharpshooter, and expert. No food there. However, after my stint with the ammo section, I was inducted into the cook section where I became head chef and kitchen leader in command of a cook squad. As a homeowner, I did battle with the squirrels with my trusty BB gun. I did bag several critters for the table. That defense kept some of them from getting into my living quarters and studio and doing major damage, munching on my drawings and high-heel art projects.

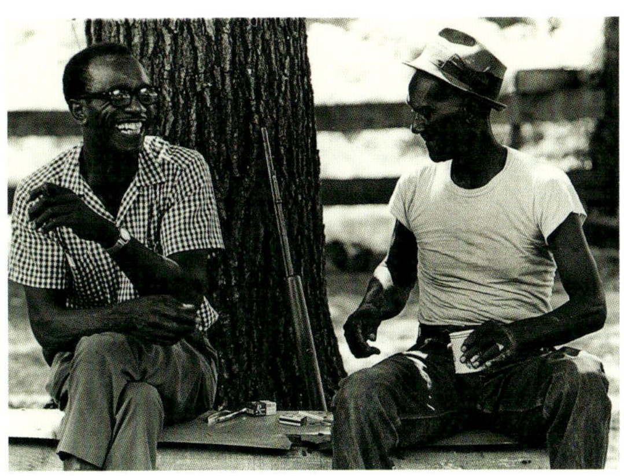

fig. 4
Barkley Herbert Hendricks (father) and James Hendricks (grandfather) in Virginia c.1971

After winning the Cresson Travel Scholarship from the Pennsylvania Academy, and upon my return from three months of traipsing around Western Europe, a neighbor asked me why I came back. He was aware of the treatment of many artists of color who stayed in Holland, France, Denmark, Sweden, and several other countries in Europe. "The hell brothers were catching in the States was enough to create many an expatriate across the pond," he said. As much as I loved my travels and reception abroad at that time, when I gave his question some thought, I felt if I were to establish any creative creds, it had to start on the turf of my birth. I have since grown to adore more and cherish more deeply my visits and residencies in several places on the planet. "Just because you were born and raised in one place doesn't mean that you have to stay and die there," was my reply to a question just last week about leaving Philadelphia.

Having multiple passports expire after putting them to good use and collecting a variety of entry and exit stamps, I can now say there are quite a number of countries I could spend a spell in: the twenty plus times I've visited Jamaica, the almost dozen trips to Western Europe, the half dozen trips to Mama Africa, where one trip alone shuttled me for two months between Morocco and Egypt. Another short excursion from Nigeria to Ghana in 1978 was inspired by a two-week stay in Lagos the previous year for FESTAC '77. I then spent five months in Ghana in 1996 on a study abroad program with a group of students. Italy and Holland have been the magnet for a diet of oil paintings, pasta, and pastries. The same can be said of London with its local and global cuisine offerings. Philadelphia has a hometown edge because of a work ethic origin. The City of Brotherly Love provided a survival indoctrination with skills that I will never forget. They haunt me daily. To this day, I have a dubious relationship with tools and manual labor—especially plumbing and roofing jobs.

Parts of Brooklyn and Manhattan have been neighborhoods to escape to; ninety miles up the New Jersey turnpike from Philly or just over a hundred miles down I-95 from New London, Connecticut. And of course, there is Connecticut itself. Actually my move North, despite my disdain for the cold weather, was a move to save my ass from the corruptness of the Vietnam War. I joined the New Jersey National Guard in 1968 when my student deferment expired and changed my status from 2S to 1A. Going to Yale made more sense than going to the other two schools to which I was accepted for graduate school. Both the Maryland Art Institute in Baltimore and the San Francisco Art Institute had given me the green light and open door. Yale had a two-tiered entry program that made me stall California and Maryland until I got the final word from New Haven.

All three institutions' cities had the National Guard on active duty assignments. Police actions for the riots in those towns made me develop a strategy that would keep me out of uniform while attending school. The Black Panther trials in New Haven, the riots in California, and Bobby Seale in Maryland made me rethink changing my Guard unit to any of those places. My New Jersey Guard unit was in Camden and Cherry Hill. I thought it wise to commute from New Haven to Cherry Hill and avoid the chance of being called up for army obligations in addition to the two weeks (actually seventeen days) for Guard summer camp plus the one weekend each month for six years. That plan worked out fine when I got the final

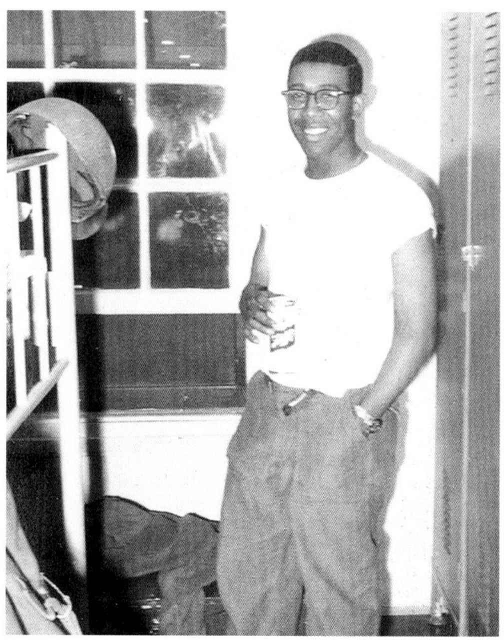

fig. 5
Hendricks in U.S. Army barracks, National Guard Summer Camp training in New Jersey
c. 1968

cat. 21 (opposite page)
New Orleans Niggah, 1973
Oil and acrylic on cotton canvas
72 x 52 inches

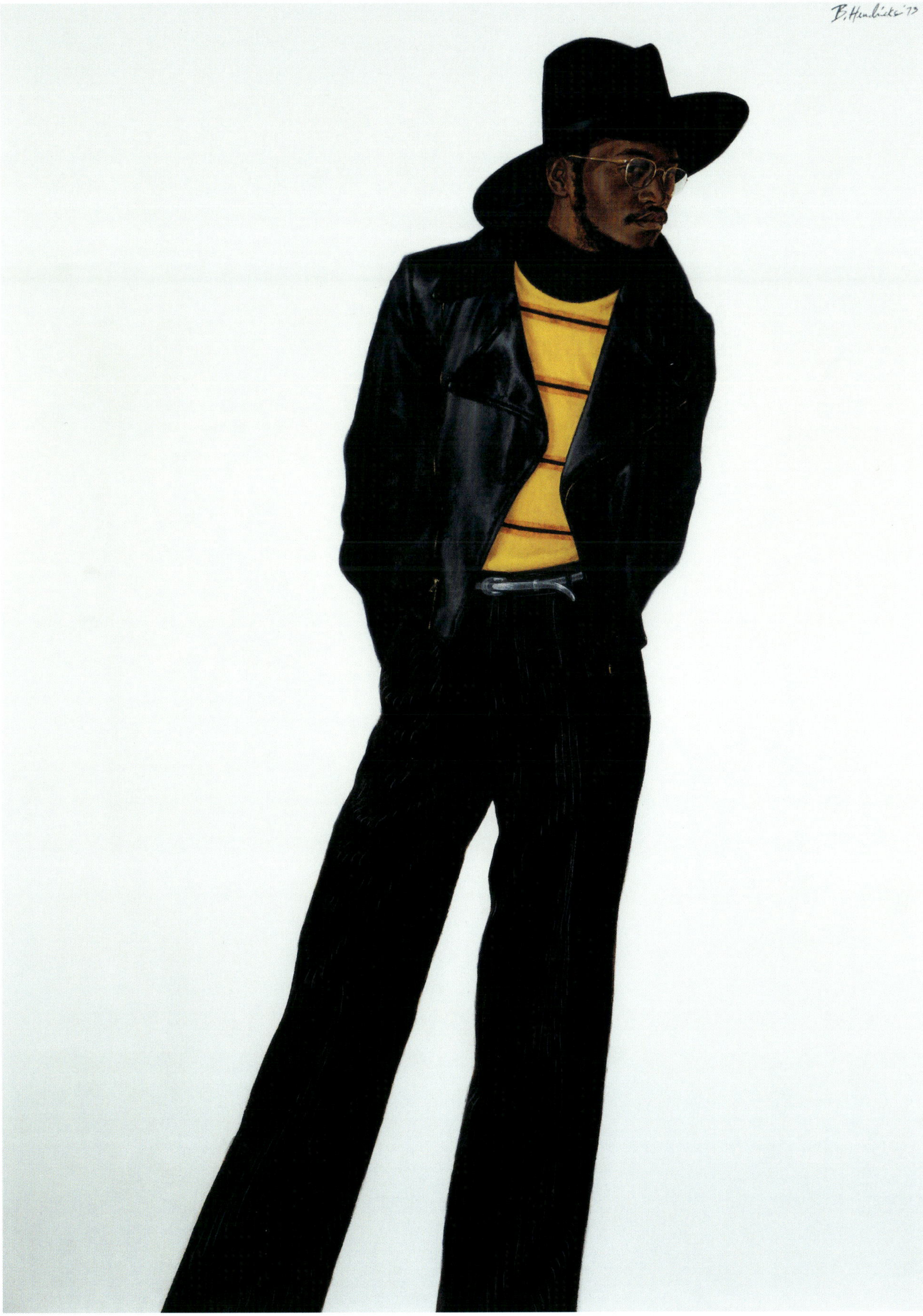

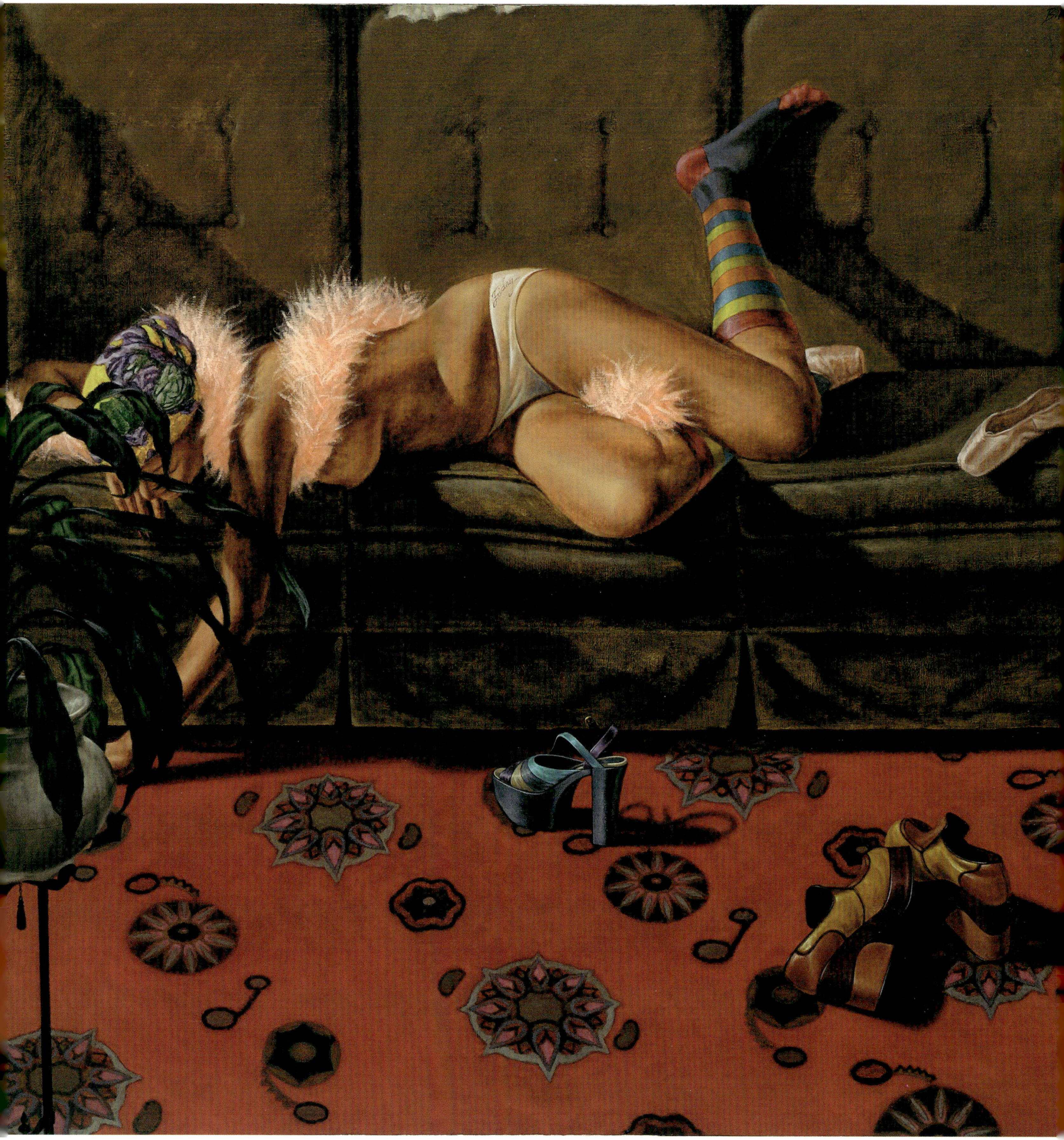

entry from Yale. New Jersey made the National Guard a trial experiment for African Americans after the Newark riots.

These various events and thoughts represent a timeline without being a timeline. In no way could any document cover all the situations and happenings of my life. The death of my father and the murder of my brother mark real low points for me. My marriage to Susan proves to be a significant and positive event that keeps paying rewards that defy description. Then there is the personal health reminder on a daily basis. Thank goodness there are those other reminders like the adventure this exhibition promises to start. Cool, cool, *cool*! Right on time.

Right on!

3. Art Pays

Art pays. My first commission was an erotic expression. An act that was purely from the minds of virgin adolescent young boys. For five cents, I was paid to draw a man and woman "doin' it." Never having "done it," I had to rely on Nick Ramos, the commissioner. The crude image was enough to ensure satisfaction, payment, and a suspension for Nick and Barry, since it was Barry's homework book in which the pencil illustration was inscribed. Easiest cash I ever made. Our teacher, Mrs. Payne, never was told who the artist was.

4. Musical Inspirations

For me, Nina Simone was a cause for inspiration and celebration. There were quite a number of artists who influence me in a variety of ways. Cannonball (Julian) Adderley was the reason I started to photograph musicians. At the start, I wanted to put together images as tightly composed as the works of the Jazz Quartet. Percy Heath, the remarkable bassist for the group, called me "home boy" when I told him that I, too, was from Philly.

Backstage privileges to a variety of performances added significantly to my visual archives and shoulder-rubbing with some of the greats of modern music commonly called jazz. Then there were the various clubs and nightspots where I would nurse a drink for hours because I was there to dig the music. One evening I caught Dexter Gordon at the Jazz Workshop in Boston. When he was in a solitary several minutes with his horn in the back of the basement, I saw a great photo op. I passed it up because I did not want my camera's shutter noise to create a distraction. When I told him that, he thanked me and invited me back to his dressing room for any photos I desired after he finished the gig for the night. I have yet to print one of the best images of him holding his tenor sax up like the sacred object that it most certainly was.

On many occasions, I've helped close the place down. Especially when Mingus was performing. Slugs was a small, *very* small place to see and hear Charles put his band through their paces. Being that close there were many images which made me proud to be a photographer/artist. I once took a date to see Roland Kirk at Manhattan's Village Vanguard. A mistake. I spent the entire night transfixed on Mr. K. That was our first and last date. A lesson I learned about whom you share your musical fixations with.

While in London, England, I had an illuminating conversation about family roots. Jon Hendricks also had family in the South. It was either North or South Carolina. He remarked that the chances of our being related were possible when I said my folks were from Virginia, close to the Carolina border. That meeting and conversation at Ronnie Scott's in London was before I started my photographic adventures.

The jazz program I had on WCNI radio at Connecticut College allowed me up-close-and-personal moments with George Russell. He got on my case for not having his latest CD. All I had for that interview was his collector's classic *New York, New York* vinyl album that still is one of my treasures. I got a light lecture from George about living in the past and resting on one's laurels.

When Harry Kulkowitz, my former agent and dear friend, told me the line-up for the Cape May, New Jersey Jazz Festival, I rejoiced! The great Oscar Brown Jr. was coming to town! Being the wonderful man he is, Harry set up a lunch date with Oscar at his Mad Batter restaurant. So I had a wonderful birthday lunch with Oscar before his performance. Lucky me again!

cat. 27 (opposite page)
Take All the Time You Need (Adrienne Hawkins), 1975
Oil on linen canvas
72 1/4 x 72 1/4 inches

5. Women as Inspiration

Several paintings come with good color besides what's on their canvases. Robin (*Miss T*) scared the shit out of my mother when she told her "if she couldn't have me, no one would." Fear for my life was Ruby's sense about that crazy woman who called and left that message. The portrait of Claire (*Claire*), not in the show, also was a cause for fear in both my mother and grandmother. A young blonde English woman meeting me in the former capital of the Confederacy, Danville, Virginia, made them quake a bit. However, my feisty grandpop James said, "Nobody better think about starting any stuff on his property." That was in 1971. Perhaps we were a new generation and it was the new South we were visiting.

Kim (*Vitamin K for Fun*) made a comment about "being up here in your little Barkley Hendricks world" that still makes me laugh when I think about her. I guess I do have my own unique perspective on things that others may not always share or understand. Part of the title in *Something Like a Bird: Double Barbara* is borrowed from the Charles Mingus LP title, *Something Like a Bird*. When I first met Barbara, almost thirty years ago, she told me that her birds had died the night before. As I write about painting her portrait, I remember looking out the window of my studio at the rainbowed, shiny necks of a flock of pigeons perched on the roof. I used the iridescence of their feathers as reference material for the tight blue-black stretch pants. I added feathers around her eyes that mimicked the pageantry of the disco fashions of the day. The bird reference is poignant and prophetic all these years later as *Double Barbara* is raising her exotic feathered friends in Delaware. Something like a bird, indeed.

Adrienne Hawkins was my model for several paintings. Her beautiful hazel eyes and muscular, smooth, tight dancer's body gave birth to *Frog* and *Take All the Time You Need*, and she was the body double, so to speak, for the lone nude in *What's Goin' On*.

Anderson Williams, whom I painted shortly after we became friends, was a wonderful cook and a knowledgeable gentleman with superb artistic tastes and an art collection to match. One day, he presented me with some little orange fruit I had only heard about in jokes. He said they were plentiful in his native Florida. Much of his Southern mannerism had evaporated, all but a select few words that he would sprinkle in his conversations like the seasonings in his cooking, which he used very sparsely. At the time he gave me the fruit, I was working on the portrait of Susan, and I needed an additional warm color. So that little piece of citrus, which necessitated an acquired taste attraction, gave the painting just what it needed as well as its name: *Ma Petite Kumquat.* Sho' nuff!

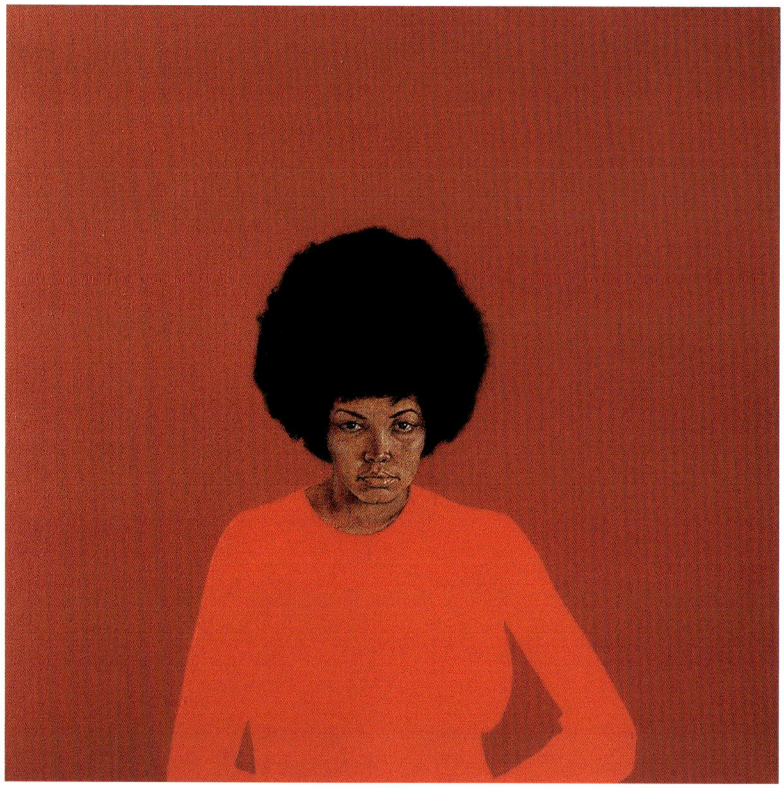

fig. 6
Miss Brown to You, 1970
Oil and acrylic on linen canvas
48 x 48 inches

cat. 6 (opposite page, top)
Dippy's Delight, 1969
Oil and acrylic on cotton canvas
46 inch diameter

cat. 3 (opposite page, bottom)
Vertical Hold, 1967
Oil, acrylic, and metallic silver on cotton canvas
47 x 44 inches

6. Basketball Series

Besides having a love for the game of basketball, I remember my father pointing out while we were at work with him that we seemed tired all the time. Then when he was done with us for the day we had energy enough to head to the basketball court. I was a recreation leader with the Philadelphia Department of Recreation, where I was made an Arts and Crafts specialist, a new position that was made for me because of my art background. Because much of the program was geared to spring and

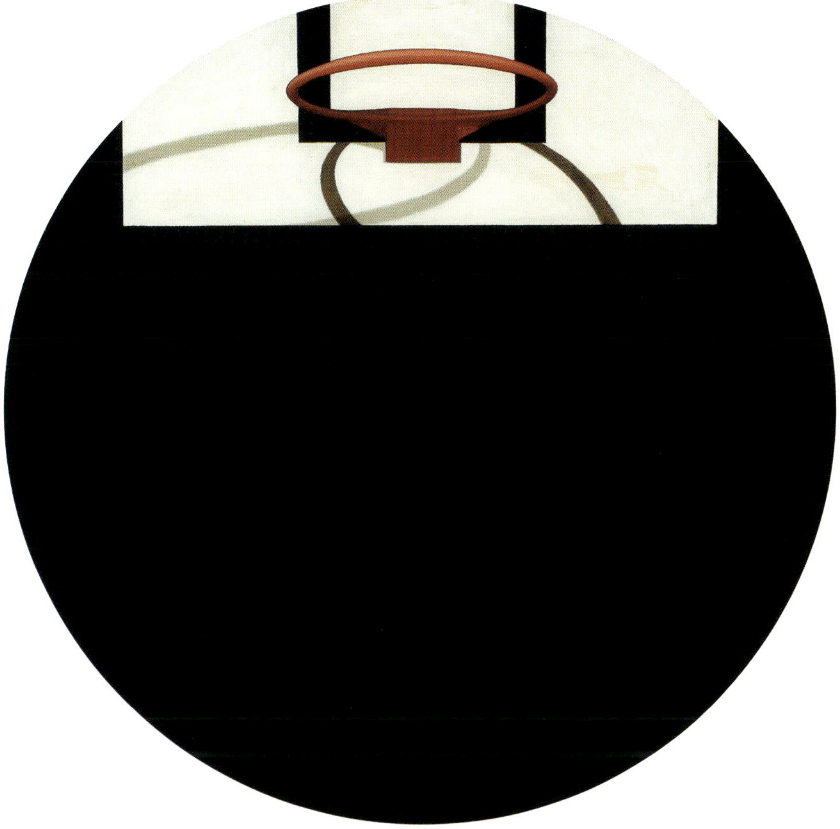

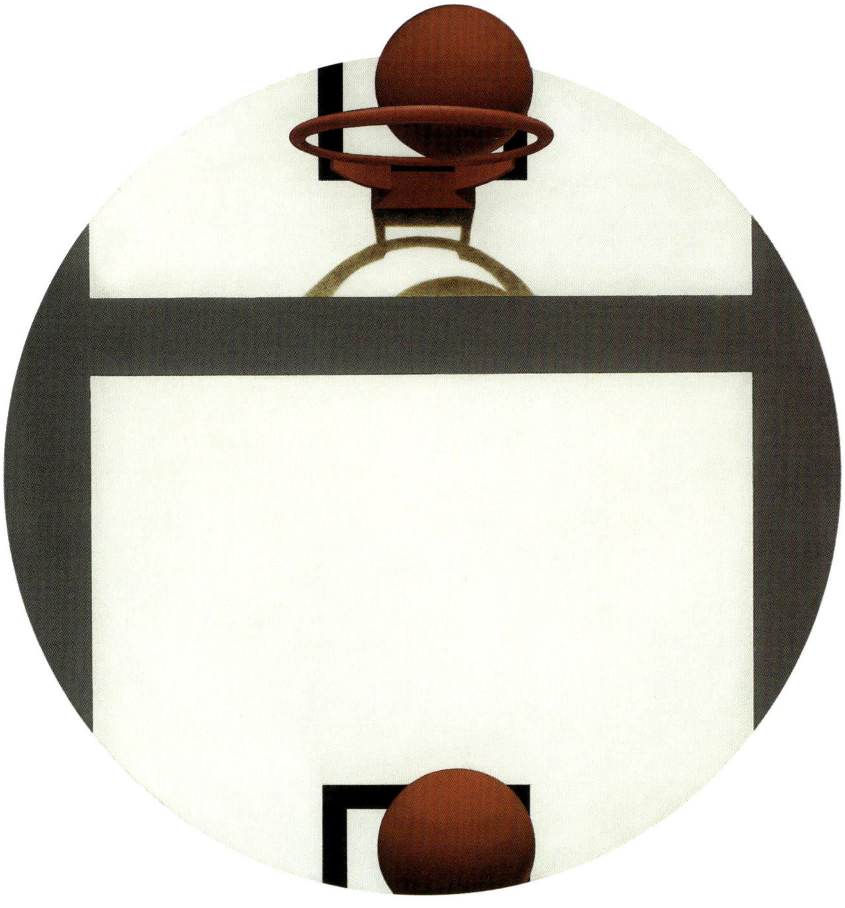

cat. 22
What's Going On, 1974
Oil, acrylic, and magna on
cotton canvas
65 3/4 x 83 3/4 inches

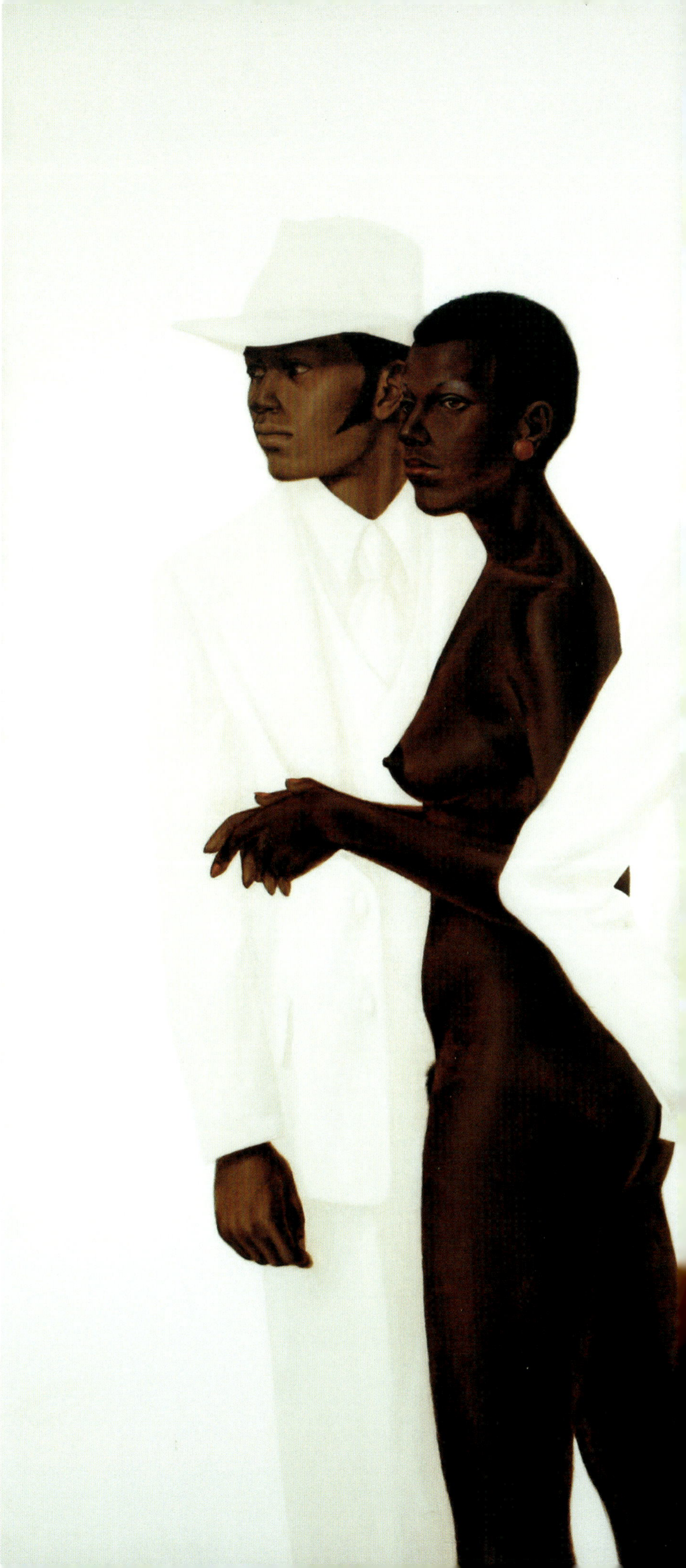

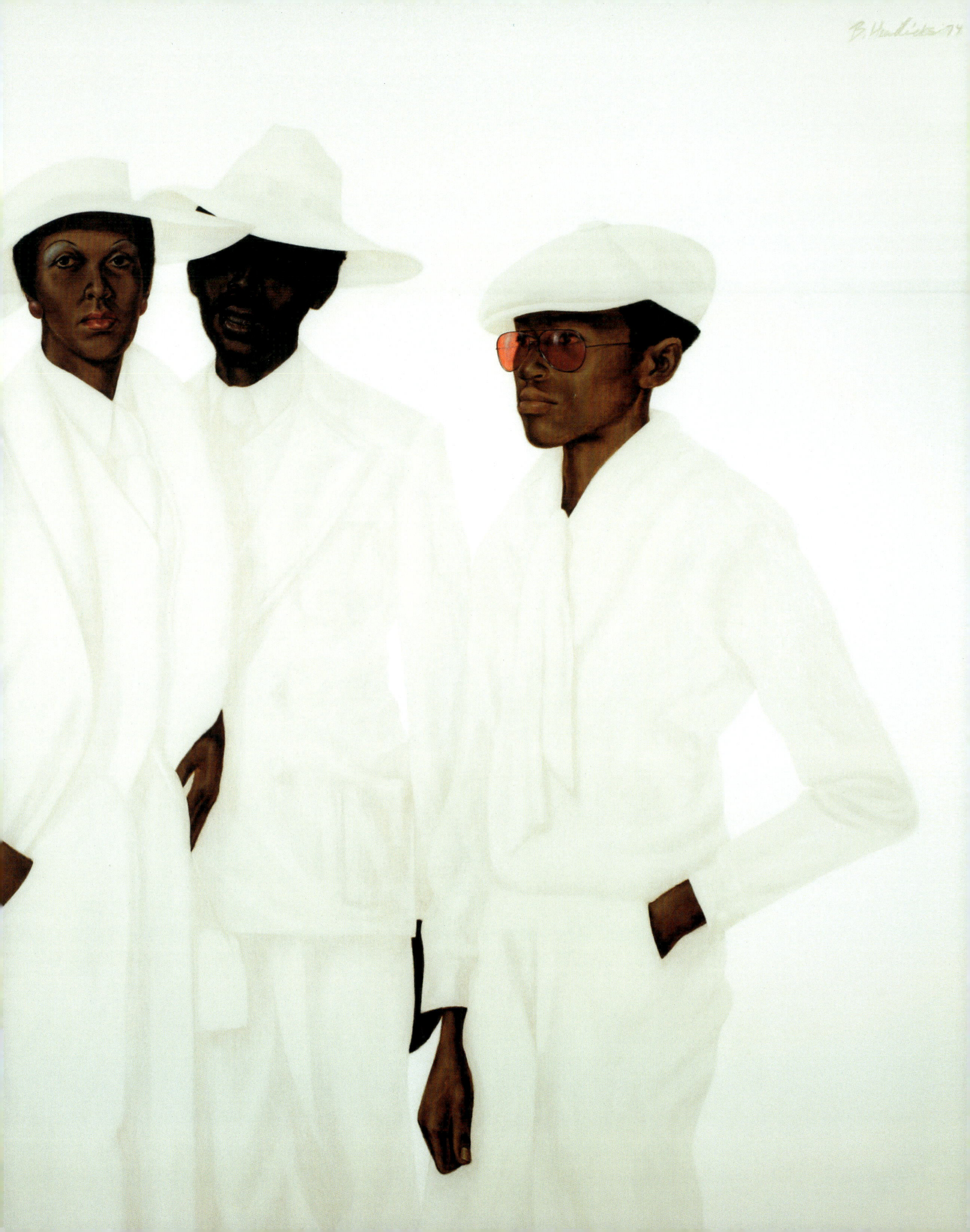
B. Hendricks '74

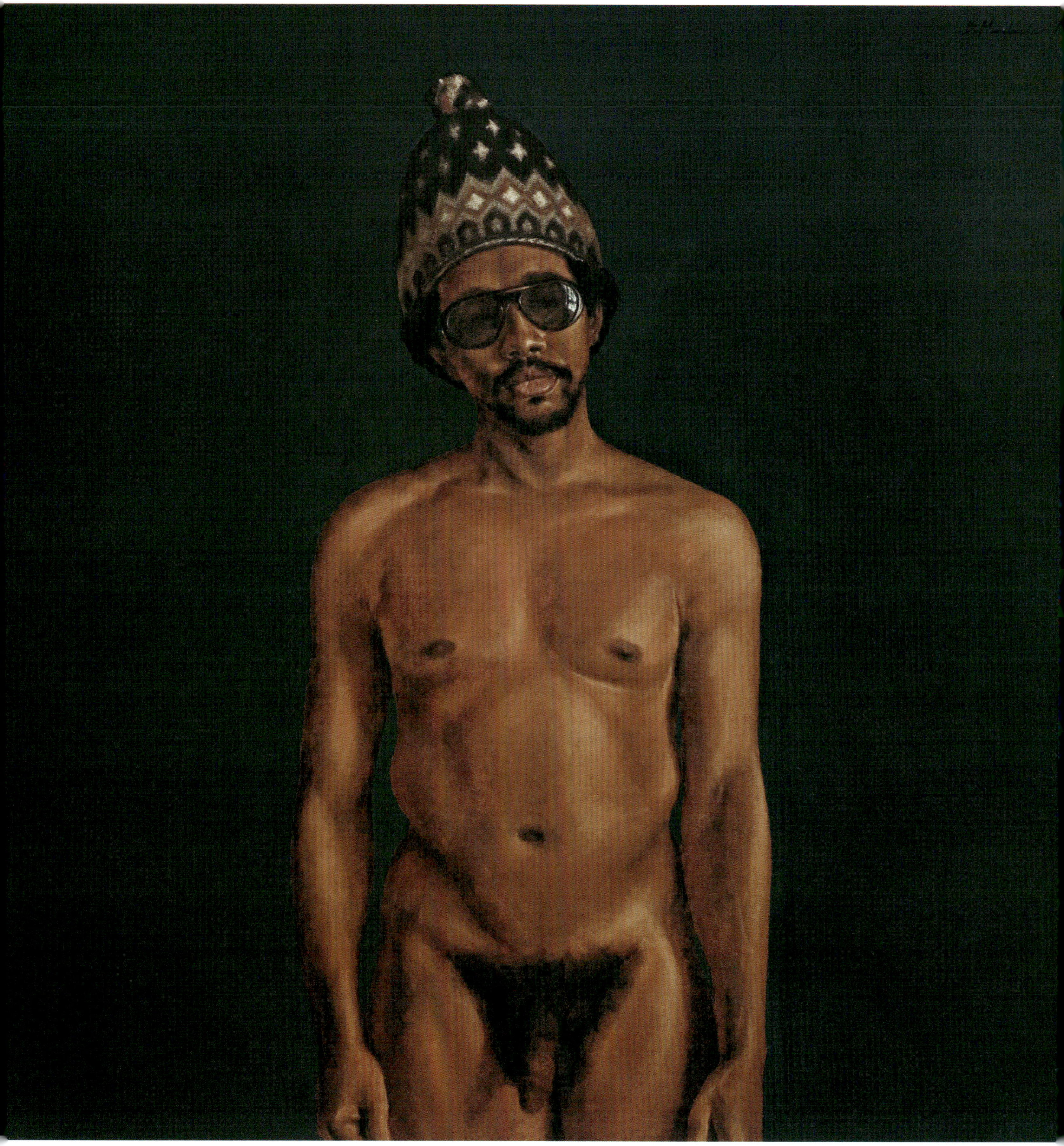

cat. 10 (opposite page)
Brown Sugar Vine, 1970
Oil and acrylic on
linen canvas
50 x 48 inches

cat. 15
Ms. Johnson (Estelle), 1972
Oil and acrylic on
linen canvas
73 1/4 x 50 3/4 inches

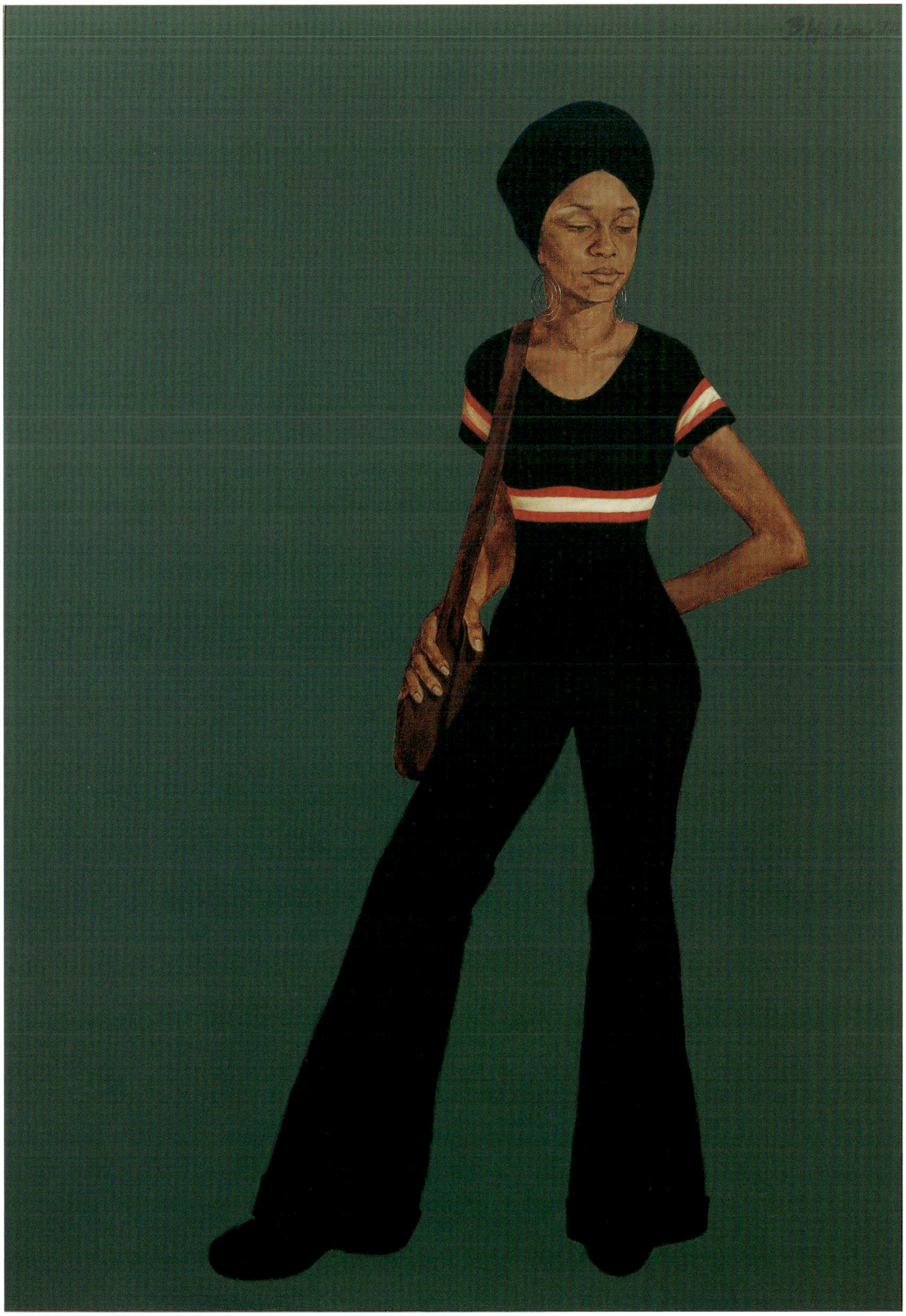

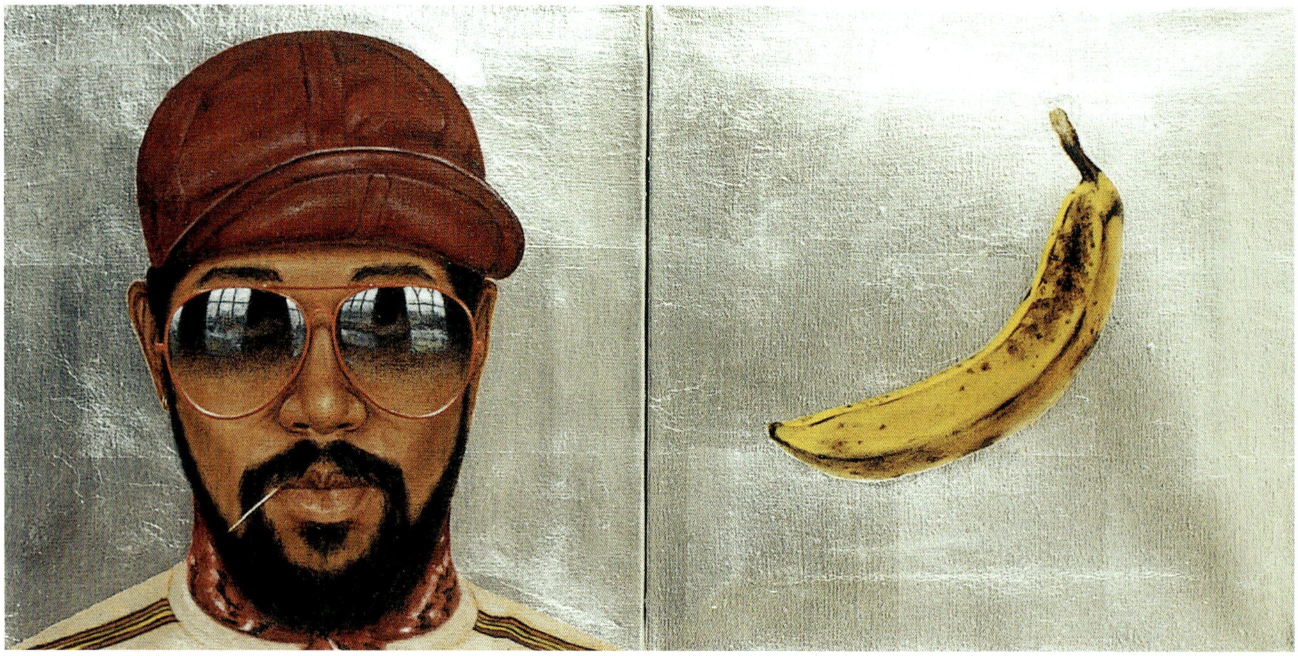

summer activities, I had time during the winter months to do drawings of the basketball court right outside the window. Besides the game that provided color and geometry for many of my compositions, there were the playground regulars who always provided attention-getting behavior besides their faces, fashions, and attitudes. *Two* was the first composition I completed. The courts were just barely marked, and the rims never had nets or chains that lasted more than a week or two (that is, if the entire rim was not bent or broken off from the backboard).

The street balls rarely had distinguishing lines on them to say, "I'm a basketball." When the large orange ball was launched from the shooter's hand, there would follow a confident cry of "Two!" which could often be heard in the next block. At times, which were many, the ball would hit the rim or backboard and soar in directions away from where the game was played. That was a call to shame the shooter, which was very much a part of the sport of "humiliation basketball," widely practiced on all the courts in all the neighborhoods I played on in Philadelphia. Scrugs, tremblers, and slop were just a few of the names labeling players of dubious skills.

There were a variety of street games that required sharp eyes and geometric aptitude. Besides basketball, there were dead box, half ball, and dodge ball when you wanted to be violent and aggressive.

While I was at Yale, one of the professors remarked about my basketball images having a Joseph Albers influence. I had to be very honest with my ignorance concerning my lack of knowledge about Mr. Albers's art and color theories. I did however take the color course given by Richard Lytle. Most of his curriculum was based on Albers's principle of color interaction. The class added to my deeper love and understanding of color in all of my art. However painting in the tropics *en plein air* proved to be the best teacher of all, for which I am one grateful and loving student.

7. Self-Portraits

"Since you are always around" was one of the descriptions I heard to define self-portraiture. I was not fascinated with myself as much as Rembrandt or depressed to the extent of Van Gogh. However at times, I could not resist myself as a subject. I used my head as the subject for a test canvas to enhance my skills with gold leaf and iridescent paints. My sister said to me one day, "You think you're slick, just wait, one a day a woman is going to straighten you out." Ah, a great title for a painting, which is now a part of the Chrysler

fig. 7
Innocence (Self-Portrait), 1977
Oil and aluminum leaf on linen canvas
12 x 24 inches

fig. 8 (opposite page)
BLH (Self-Portrait), 1968
Oil on linen canvas
12 x 12 inches

Museum's collection. There were several other quotes from various women I've known. *Innocence, Brown Sugar Vine*, and "How does Hilton Kramer know you're *Brilliantly Endowed*?" Another *New York Times* critic who was less observant said my figures were "all purpose brown." Ray Charles could tell you my colorist approach would not allow a "one color fits all" for my "peeps."

When Bobby Seale said, "Superman never saved any black folks" and I found a cheap Superman T-shirt, ta da! Another self-portrait op.

With both parents coming from small Virginia towns with Baptist upbringings, children were seen and not heard. Even just being seen did not mean they knew your name. *Doc and Ruby's Oldest Boy* got its name from that situation because that's who I was to most adults that knew our family. As a child, my father was asked what he wanted to be when he grew up. He said doctor. It stuck and to this day, many people never knew his first name. They only knew him as Doc. Just as many people, old and young, where I grew up in Philadelphia and Virginia only knew me as Butch. It seemed Barkley was a challenge to remember for both my father and me. So one of my small portrait heads is just called *Butch*. With *Brown Sugar Vine*, I was making a fashion statement. Vine was the name for a suit. Certainly my birthday suit qualified. A British friend called me her brown sugar after the Rolling Stones song. Again, ta da!

8. Miss T and Others

After my first visit to Rome, Italy, I returned with a head full of inspirations besides the icons and gold leaf. The paintings in the Uffizi in Florence were mindblowers. Especially one by Giovanni Moroni. The figure in a black, skin-tight outfit made me see the illusion of form and simplicity in a different light. I realized from that painting that I could handle volume with a minimum of detail and still pull off the desired perception of weight and solidity in a style I had never worked with before. *Miss T* and *J.S.B. the III* are a direct by-product of that influence. There are several other works where I use a limited color palette and flat figure shapes to make my statements: *Sir Nelson, Solid*; *Miss Brown to You*; *Ms. Johnson*; and *George Jules Taylor* all had flat colors in them. The most recent in my limited palette series is *Roaring River Apostle*.

9. Lawdy Mama

Lawdy Mama was the portrait of my second cousin twice removed, Kathy Williams, not Angela Davis or Kathleen Cleaver. The title was inspired by lyrics from the songbook of Nina Simone about "sistas." My love of Greek and Roman icons had a great deal to do with the materials and composition of this work. In fact it was the first large-scale gold-leafed painting of my career. Beyond the inspiration it provided a wealth of knowledge and experience about the craft and art of gold leafing. The lunette top was one of four prepared after I cut two plywood circles in half. Three went to a basketball composition called *Father, Son and . . .* The fourth was *Lawdy Mama*.

10. The Three Graces Theme

Sir Charles, Alias Willie Harris; *October's Gone, Goodnight*; *Bahsir*; and *Northern Lights* sprang from that direct influence. I also felt one pose was not enough for those particular subjects. There was the shine of the green leather coat and the "bling" of the gold teeth that inspired the title for the painting of the Boston-based

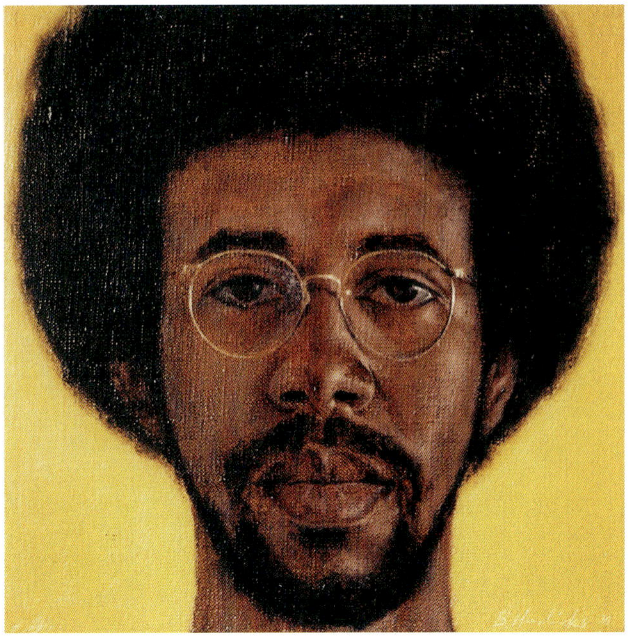

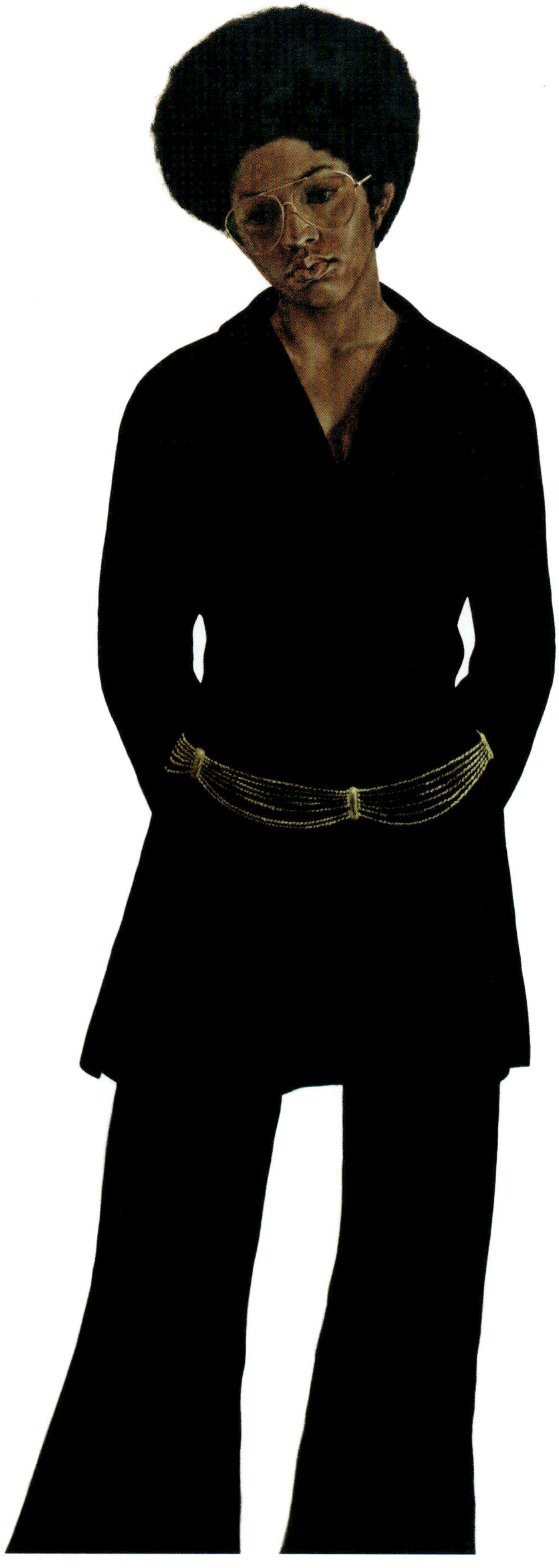

brother. He was also in a double portrait I called *Yocks*. *Yock* was the name given to a dude who knew how to "rag." Rick Powell would call them dandies. (Thanks, Rick, for recognizing several other of my "stylers" to include in one of his essays.) The street styles from various locales around America have spread globally, then and now, whether we like it or not. Someone once referred to the figure I did in the *Northern Lights* painting as a pimp. It was his big hat and large fur-collared coat that was behind the assessment. I said I once saw Ronald Reagan in the same large fur-collared coat. Did that make him a pimp? You'll have to answer that one. Sometimes clothes do make the man. Hail to the chief.

11. Brothers from the Hood

When I went to the Pennsylvania Academy of the Fine Arts for four years for art, William Corbett went to another Pennsylvania institution for five years for armed robbery. Each time I would encounter him on my visits to the hood, he would ask, "Hey, man, you still drawing?" He would then tell me, "When I was in the joint, I did some art." On one occasion, he said in the pen upstate, "Us North Philly niggahs had to stick together." Having had none of Corbett's lockdown experiences, I was, however, fully aware of the perils we from Tioga could be in if the smell of North Philadelphia was detected on you when you strayed away from those boundaries.

As an arts and crafts instructor who was assigned to various playgrounds around District 10, I was fully aware of the ass whippings many thugs were ready to give you if they thought North Philly was discovered.

Subjects like *Toast* and *Reggie* and *Buck* and *Li'l Bits* were all portraits I did in the office at Amos Playground. Before I started to travel to other locations in District 10, I taught checkers and chess and supervised several tournaments. I also had the job of trying to stop the local gang members and thugs from drinking wine and smoking various weed products in the toilets. I remember once I was dispatched by Mrs. Jarrett to chase them from the toilet. Well I moseyed up to the urinal to take a pee. While there, I said in a nonchalant fashion that Mrs. Jarrett said not to drink wine and smoke here. Well, Lucky said, "Look at this, Marshal Dillon just entered the saloon to stop us from drinking, dig it!" I zipped up and slowly made it to the door and beseeched them to give me a break. After they finished, they smashed the bottles into a million pieces that the custodian, Sam, had to clean up. So much for respecting the sheriff!

12. Serpent's Tooth or Taps for Sherman B

My first instrument purchase was a trumpet. Hot out of the music shop Sherman stole it from. Sherman Brown was a childhood chum who lived up the block on Westmoreland Street. He was a not-to-be-trusted associate who was always double-crossing and pulling fast ones on us. Sherman had the reputation of being able to steal the color out of your shirt or the taste out of your food.

Once on the way to the movies on a Saturday afternoon, we pried open a parking meter. Nickels spilled out in all directions. Sherman was like the Flash as he scooped up the majority of the coins and took off with the cash. We chased him for several blocks, but he was

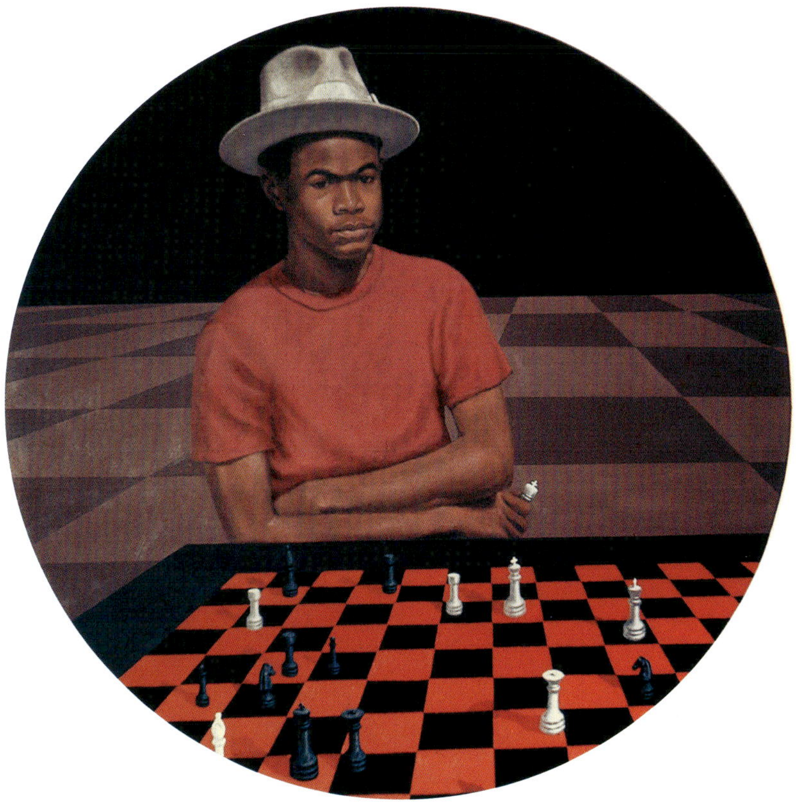

cat. 9 (opposite page)
Miss T, 1969
Oil and acrylic on linen canvas
78 x 56 inches

fig. 9
Buck, 1967
Oil on canvas
46 inch diameter

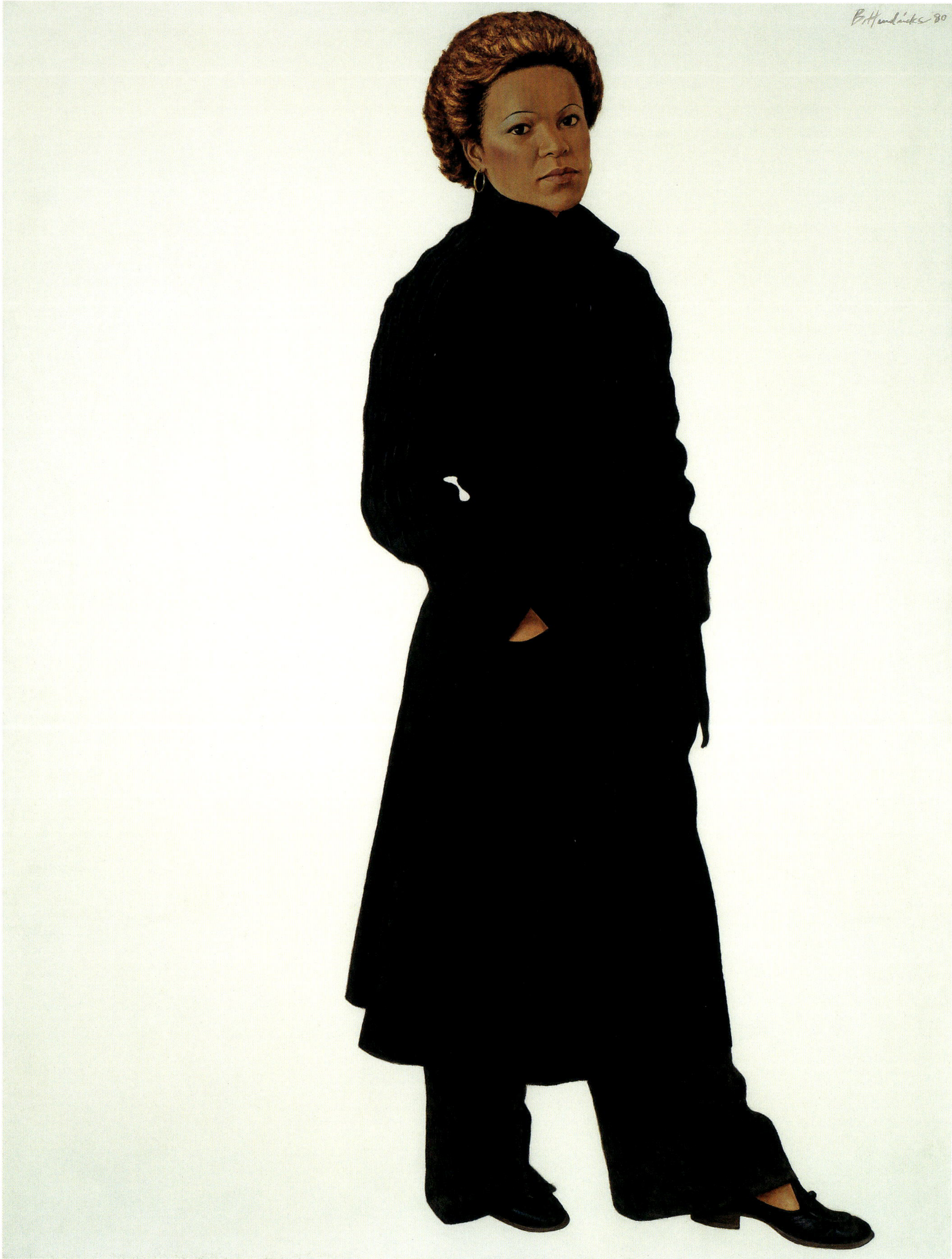
B. Hendricks '80

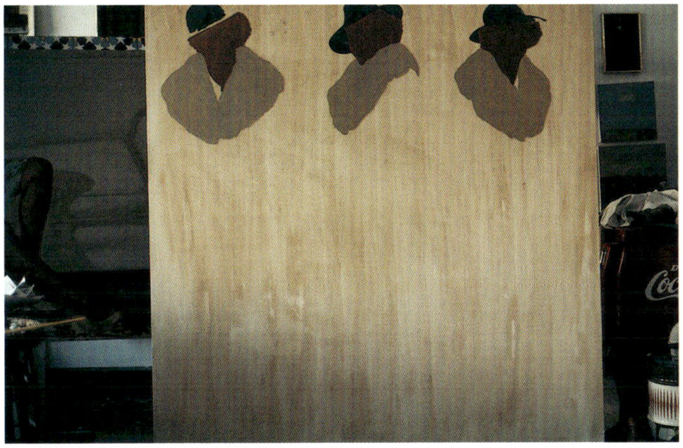
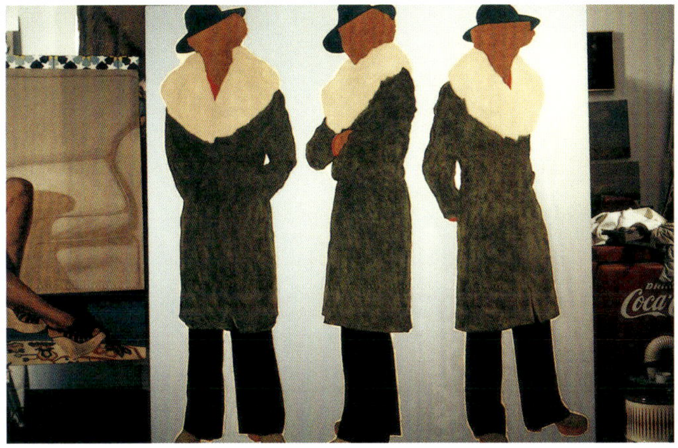
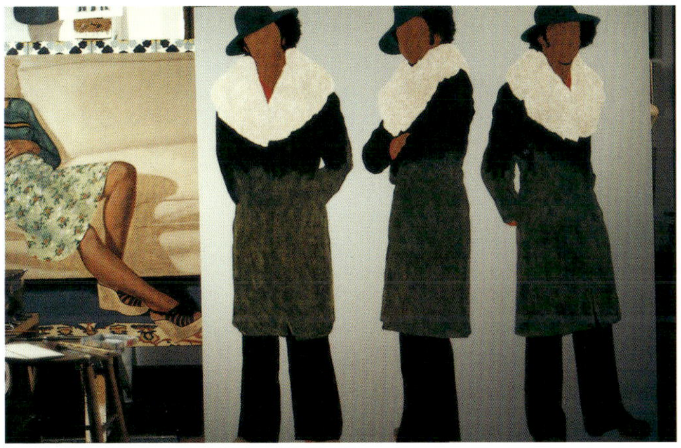
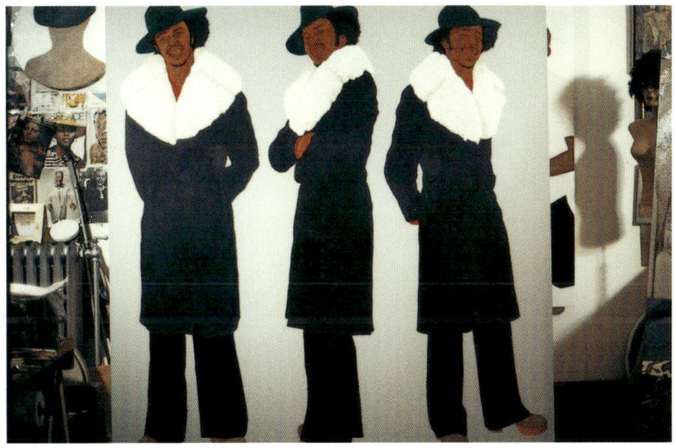
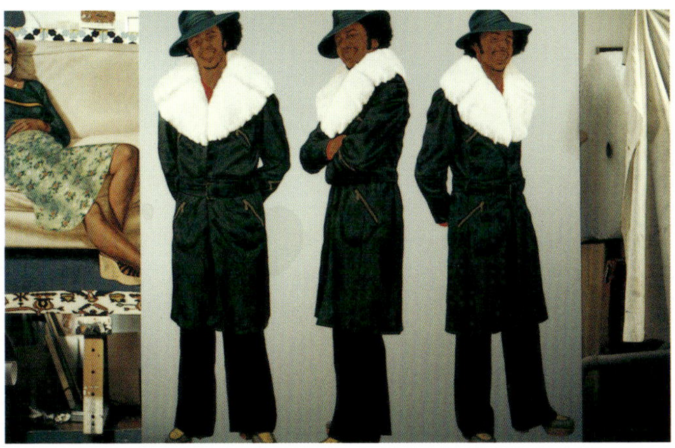
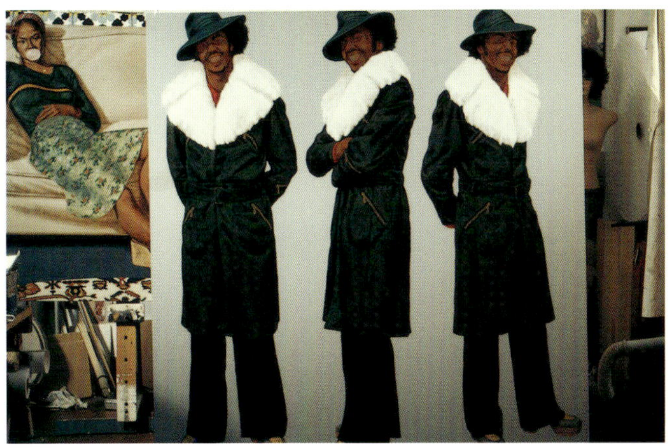
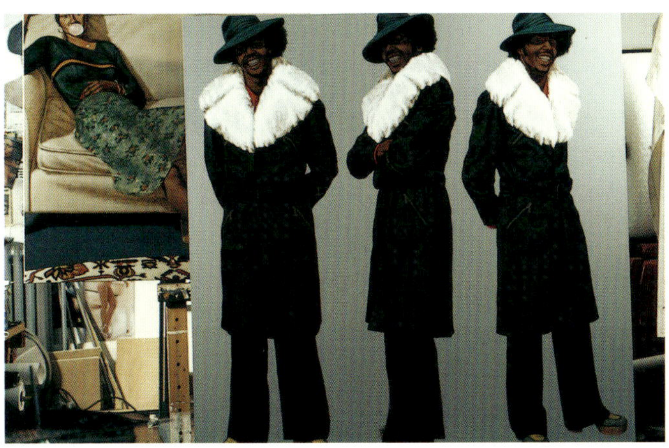
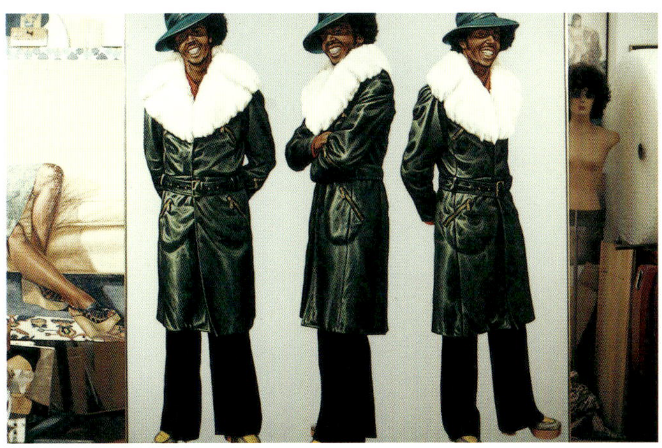

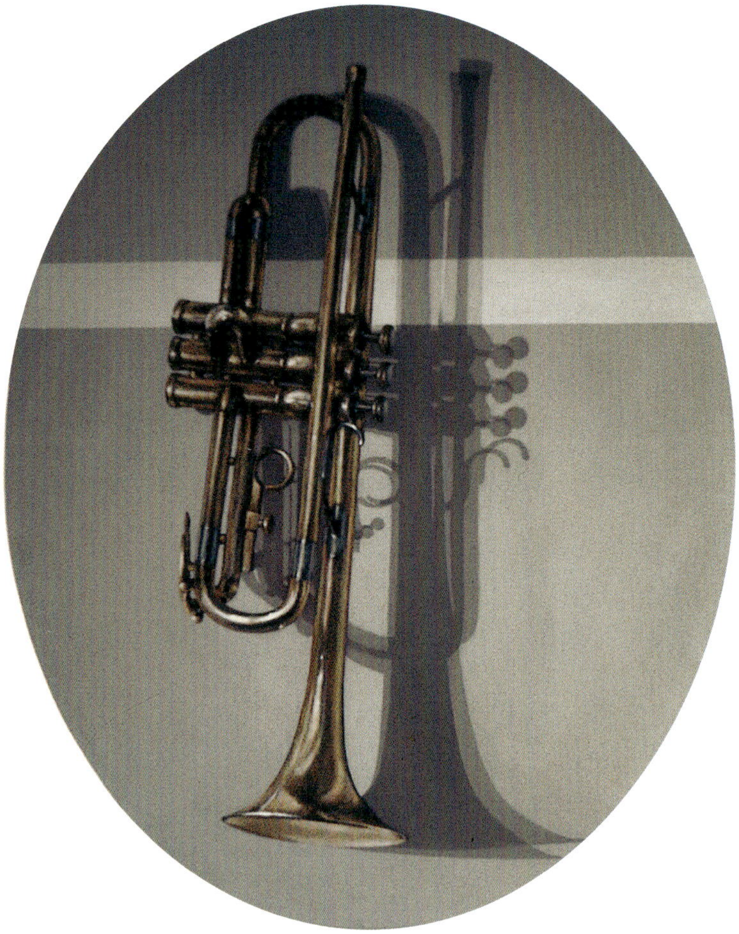

fast and had too much of a head start on us. We promised to "kick his ass when we caught him." Well, that didn't happen that day.

When we grew up and departed from the block, Sherman took his slimy ways with him. One day I got a knock on my studio door and it was Sherman with a shiny brass trumpet in a brown paper bag. He said, "Butch, do you want to buy a horn?" Being a major jazz lover, I always wanted to play some kind of instrument. I saw this as my chance. I didn't have too much guilt about the fact it was a "five-finger discounted" horn. He wanted fifty bucks, but took forty because it was all I had.

Since Sherman didn't provide the mouthpiece with the horn, I needed one. Not knowing anything about the variety of sizes that can be custom-fitted for one's mouth for different sounds, I bought the first thing that was put in front of me. A mistake. After taking it back to my studio and trying it out on the horn, that error became clear. Nothing happened but swooshing wind sounds when I blew through that beautiful piece of brass. This went on for weeks. My frustration level moved me to do a painting of that attractive shiny yellow still life. After the painting was completed, I sold the painting and then I sold the horn.

One Saturday, my brother Lamont and I were digging an afternoon jazz recording session by Julian "Cannonball" Adderley and his group. With him on that date were Charles Lloyd and Jimmy Heath on the tenor saxophones. During one of the periods between songs I overheard part of a conversation where Jimmy was telling the band he had a tune that Miles Davis stole from him. Given the origins of the horn that was now history, I titled the previously unnamed painting *Serpent's Tooth* after the tune that Jimmy said Miles stole.

A decade or more after the stolen horn incident, my brother refreshed my memory

cat. 39 (page 108)
Latin from Manhattan... the Bronx Actually, 1980
Oil and acrylic on linen canvas
66 1/8 x 50 1/4 inches

figs. 10–17 (page 109)
Hendricks's sequence of painting *Northern Lights*, 1976
Oil and acrylic on cotton canvas
72 x 72 inches

fig. 18 (above)
Serpent's Tooth, 1968–1969
Oil on canvas
23 x 27 inches

cat. 2 (opposite page)
Self-Portrait, 1966
Oil on canvas
42 x 28 inches

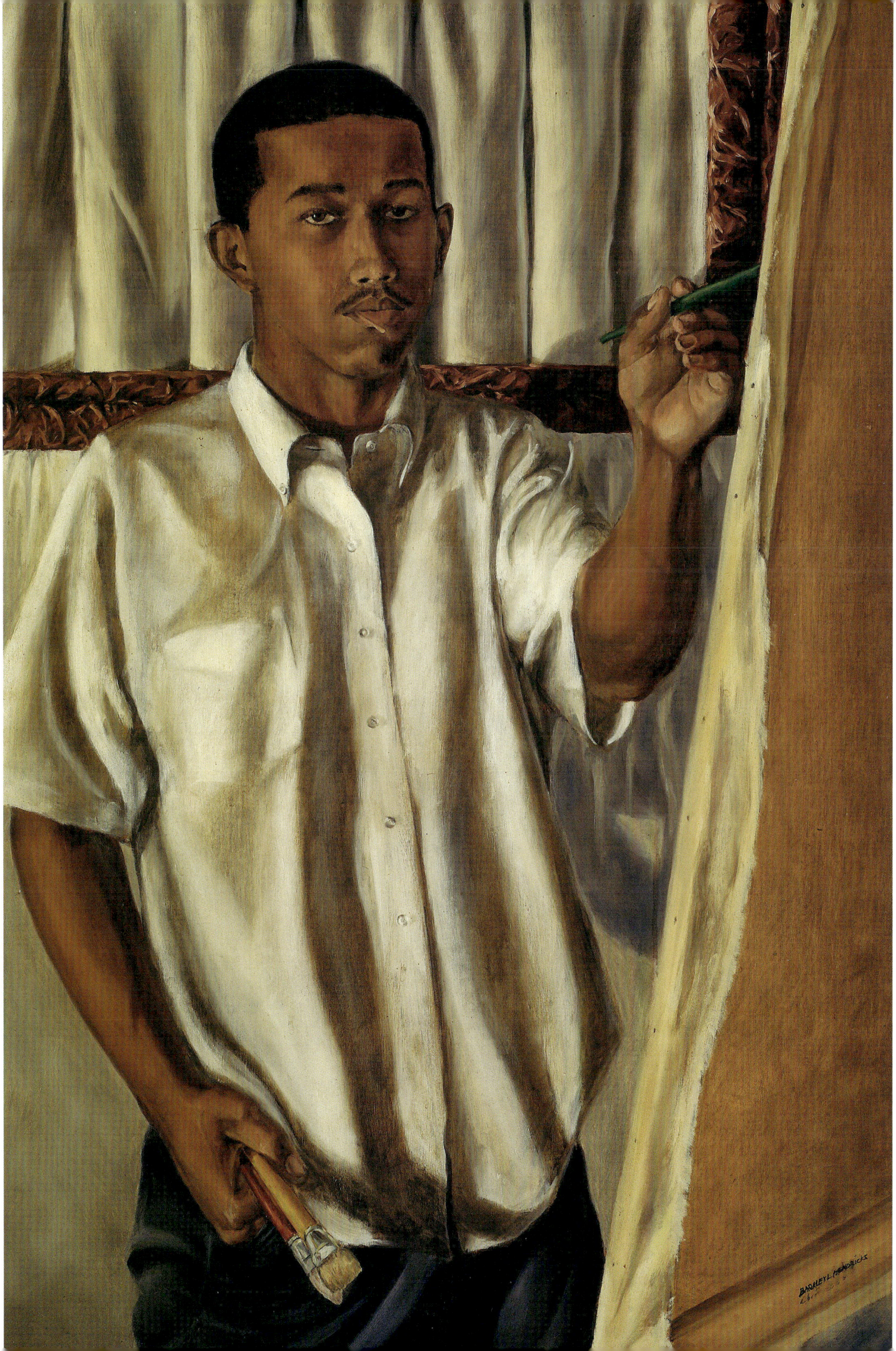
BARKLEY L. HENDRICKS

about our childhood pal Sherman—how he never changed and how it cost his life. Sherman and the thugs he hooked up with robbed a bank. Sherman beat feet with the cash and left them to do the time. When they finally caught up with him, their payback was to put a bullet in his head. He crawled to his front steps and died. As my brother reflected on the sad tale, he said, "Some habits and behaviors die hard."

13. George Jules Taylor Series

Jules proved to be an excellent subject and friend. While at Yale, I was a painting assistant for Bernard Chaet, and Jules was one of his students. Once in class I remember Jules saying, "Every time Chaet says something about my work, you would come and say something completely opposite." Jules was great for saying things that would make you laugh like hell. I once asked him about New Orleans music. Well, he cracked me up with his answer: "Just because a niggah's from New Orleans, you think they know about jazz. Well, I'm a niggah from New Orleans and I hate jazz!" He once said to me while posing during one of our sessions where we always had spirited conversations, "Every niggah I ever met from Philadelphia has been crazy, including you!"

Paintings of Jules are:
Jules
Family Jules
New Orleans Niggah
George Jules Taylor

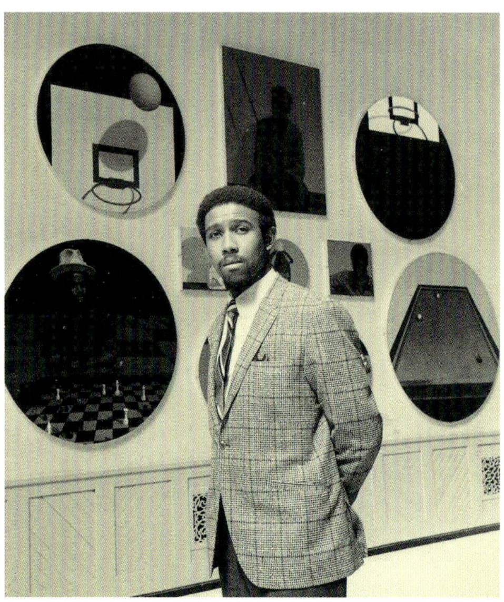

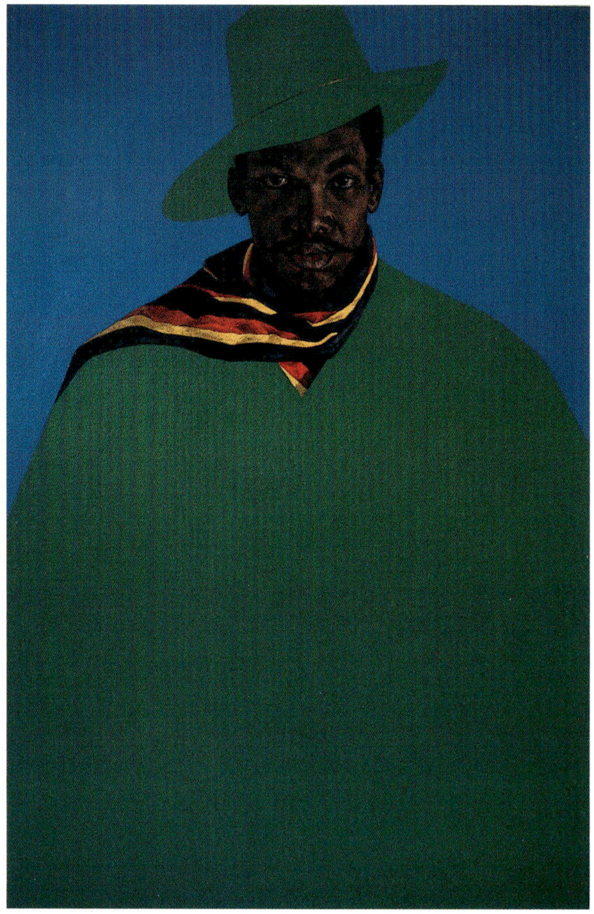

14. Traveling

In May 1966 I was awarded the William Emlen Cresson traveling scholarship from the Pennsylvania Academy of the Fine Arts in Philadelphia. It paid for the following year's tuition but more significantly, it financed three months' travel and stay in Europe. My travels took me to the major museums and art sights in Italy, France, Holland, Great Britain, Spain, Turkey, and Greece. There were several countries along the way that provided stopovers and adventures of the unforgettable kind.

The following year, 1967, I was the recipient of the Henry Scheidt Memorial Traveling Scholarship. Unlike the Cresson that was for European travel, the Scheidt was a passport with bucks for the planet. Mother Africa beckoned this time. So after landing back in Luxembourg, I headed south to Morocco, and that got my travel started across Algeria, Tunis, and Libya to Egypt. These two awards were unquestionably the instigators of a life of global look-seeing.

fig. 19
Hendricks and his paintings presented on "Scheidt Scholarship" wall at the Pennsylvania Academy of the Fine Arts, May 3, 1967

fig. 20
Sir Nelson, Solid, 1970
Oil on canvas
46 x 30 inches

15. My First Sale

My first gallery sale was a portrait of Morris Blackburn, a three-inch by five-inch print from a plastic engraved plate, which sold at the Woodmere Art Gallery for $5. Mr. Blackburn inspired my love of printmaking and painting in the great outdoors, especially at the Jersey shore. *En plein air* painting made me fall in love with tropical settings, especially Jamaica.

16. Historical Perspectives

Today is Wednesday, August 22, 2007, several days after Hurricane Dean stormed over Jamaica. A good friend lost her relatively newly built house when the roof was liberated from the cinderblock walls and foundation. When the New Year of 2007 opened, we were enjoying the warmth of the "land of wood and water." 2007's start was significant to the island given the commemoration of the 1807 ban on the slave trade in Britain and several other places in the Caribbean. Chinua Achebe, visiting from Nigeria, was one of the honored speakers for several events surrounding the 200th anniversary. Jamaicans were reminded of the role their country played in the sad history of those poignant centuries before slavery was abolished.

I have visited the mountain retreat of the Maroons on January 6 for many years. They celebrate the defeat of the British in their fight to exit the bonds of slavery. One year, there were representatives from Ghana at the celebrations. The connection between that region of Mother Africa was fully acknowledged and documented. When the speakers talked about the forts along the coast of Ghana where many humans were shuttled through, I recalled the churning of my stomach on that hot afternoon when I visited the female dungeon of Elmina Castle. The stench almost made me lose my breakfast. So now some of those Africans had their offspring to thank for not forgetting their pain and ordeal. Those offspring were now in the "new world." The new world with the same old mind, with a new technological twist.

When I sit down to paint, occasionally I am reminded of the history of Jamaica and its associations beyond my narrow perspectives of aesthetics. The roads and fields I find myself on and in have many stories to tell beyond my creative motivations and responses to what I see around me. Do I really have to say the history was an important footnote to some of the vistas and perspectives I have painted? I mention the history because at times, it cannot be avoided as I move about the country that is now made famous by ganja, reggae, and Bob Marley.

fig. 21
Hendricks painting beach scene in Jamaica, 1998

fig. 22 (pages 114–115)
Studio at 58 State Street, New London, CT with wall of unfinished self-portraits, c. 1980

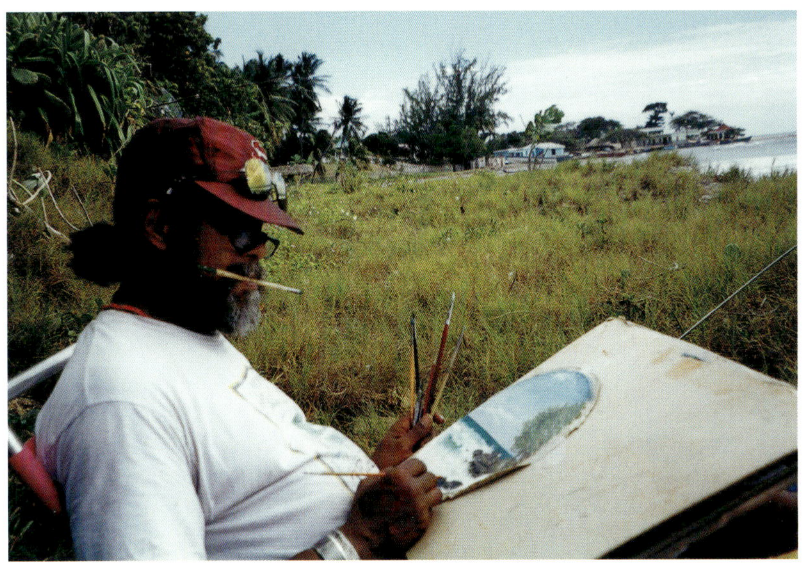

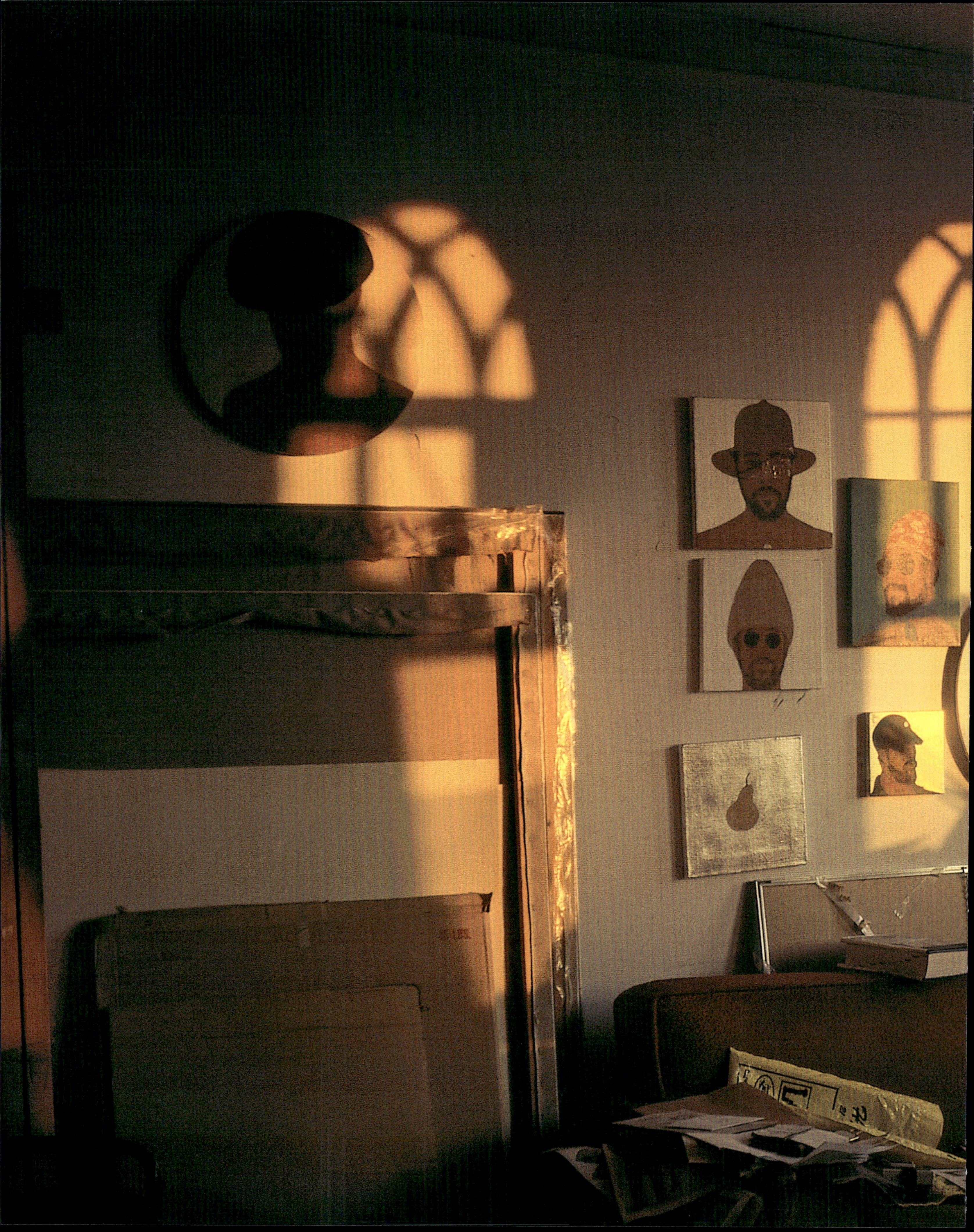

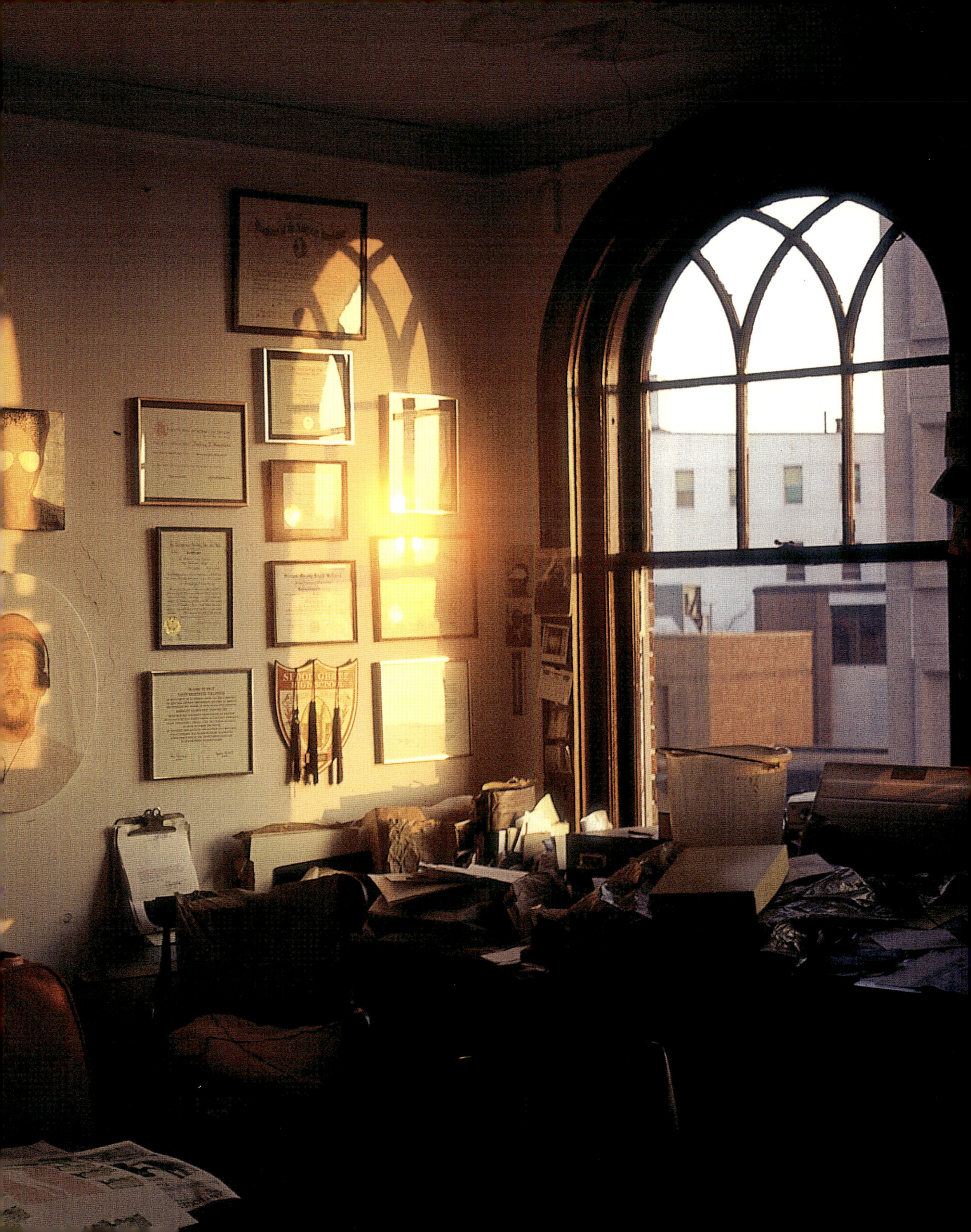

Selected Artist Chronology Barkley L. Hendricks Compiled 2008

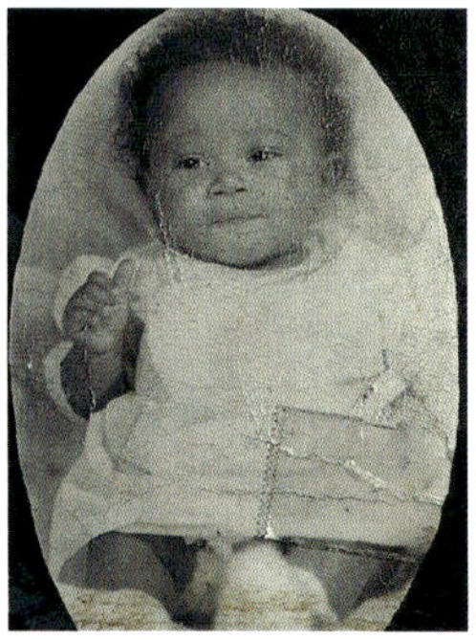

fig. 1
Barkley's baby picture, 1945

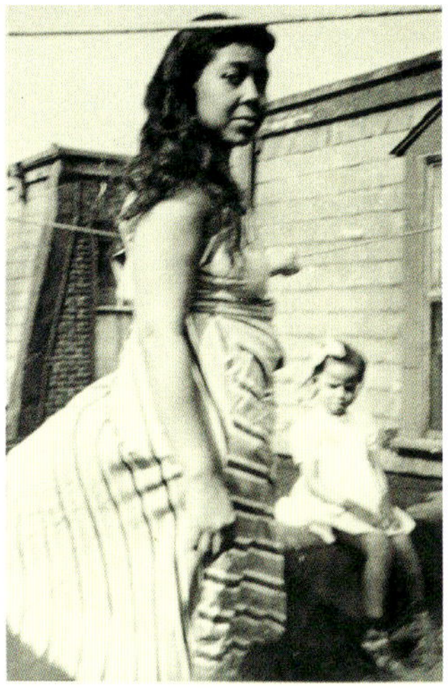

fig. 2
Ruby Powell Hendricks on rooftop in Philadelphia, early 1950's

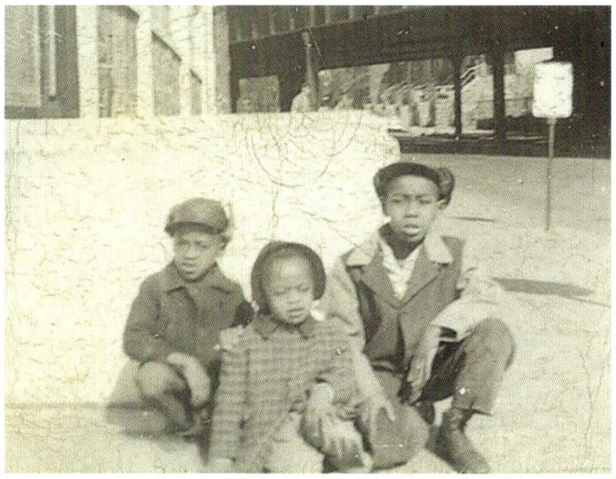

fig. 3
Lamont (brother), Denise (sister) and Barkley, ages 6, 3, and 8, at corner of 19th Street and West Westmoreland Street, Philadelphia, 1953

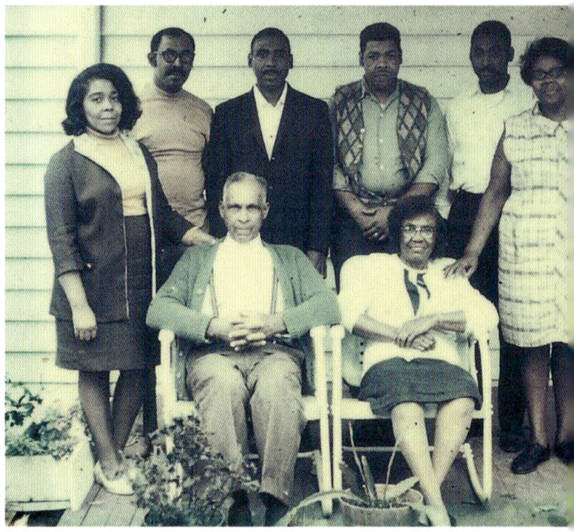

fig. 4
Ruby Powell Hendricks (mother) and her siblings and parents at their home in Meadville, VA, c. 1970

Barkley Leonnard Hendricks

Born April 16, 1945
Philadelphia, PA
Died April 18, 2017
Twin sister died at birth

Parents and Siblings

Father: Barkley Herbert Hendricks
Born September 27, 1923
Halifax, VA
Died January 2, 1975

Mother: Ruby Arlene Powell Hendricks
Born February 24, 1926
Halifax, VA

Brother: Dwight Lamont Hendricks
Born October 13, 1947
Philadelphia, PA
Died October 6, 1999

Sister: Arlene Denise Hendricks
Born October 13, 1950
Philadelphia, PA

Brother: Andre Kevin Hendricks
Born July 17, 1954
Philadelphia, PA

Brother: Methun Levin Hendricks
Born April 5, 1962
Philadelphia, PA

Education

1951–1957

Grover Cleveland Elementary School
Philadelphia, PA

1957–1960

Elizabeth Dune Gillespie Junior High School
Philadelphia, PA

1960–1963

Simon Gratz High School
Philadelphia, PA

1963–1967

Pennsylvania Academy of the Fine Arts
Philadelphia, PA

First African American to be awarded two consecutive travel grants

William Emlen Cresson European Traveling Scholarship, 1966

J. Henry Scheidt Traveling Scholarship, 1967

1970–1972

Yale University, New Haven, CT

In addition to painting, I studied photography with Tom Brown and Walker Evans.

My photo essay for Tom Evans's advanced class featured the New York Port Authority as subject matter. Walker Evans remarked that I was the first student ever to bring him a tondo photograph. Tondo is a description that Julian Levi from PAFA used to describe the circular paintings I brought to our crit sessions on Wednesday afternoons at the academy.

Awarded painting assistantship with Bernard Chaet in 1971

Selected Exhibitions Highlights

1966

Student solo exhibition at Pennsylvania Academy of the Fine Arts, Philadelphia, PA

Met my first dealer, Harry Kulkowitz, which led to annual group and solo exhibitions through 1975 at his Kenmore Gallery and the Woodmere Gallery, both in Philadelphia, as well as the Butler Institute and the National Academy of Design Museum, both in New York City, among other shows.

1967

32nd Annual Midyear Show at Butler Institute of American Art, Youngstown, OH

Led to subsequent *Annual Mid-year Shows*. *Reggie* exhibited in 1967, *Sweet Thang* in 1977, *Steve* in 1978, *Tuff Tony* in 1979, *Tequila* in 1980, *Have You Met Ms. Jones* in 1981, and *Vitamin K for Fun* in 1982. Awarded second-place merit medal for *Tuff Tony*.

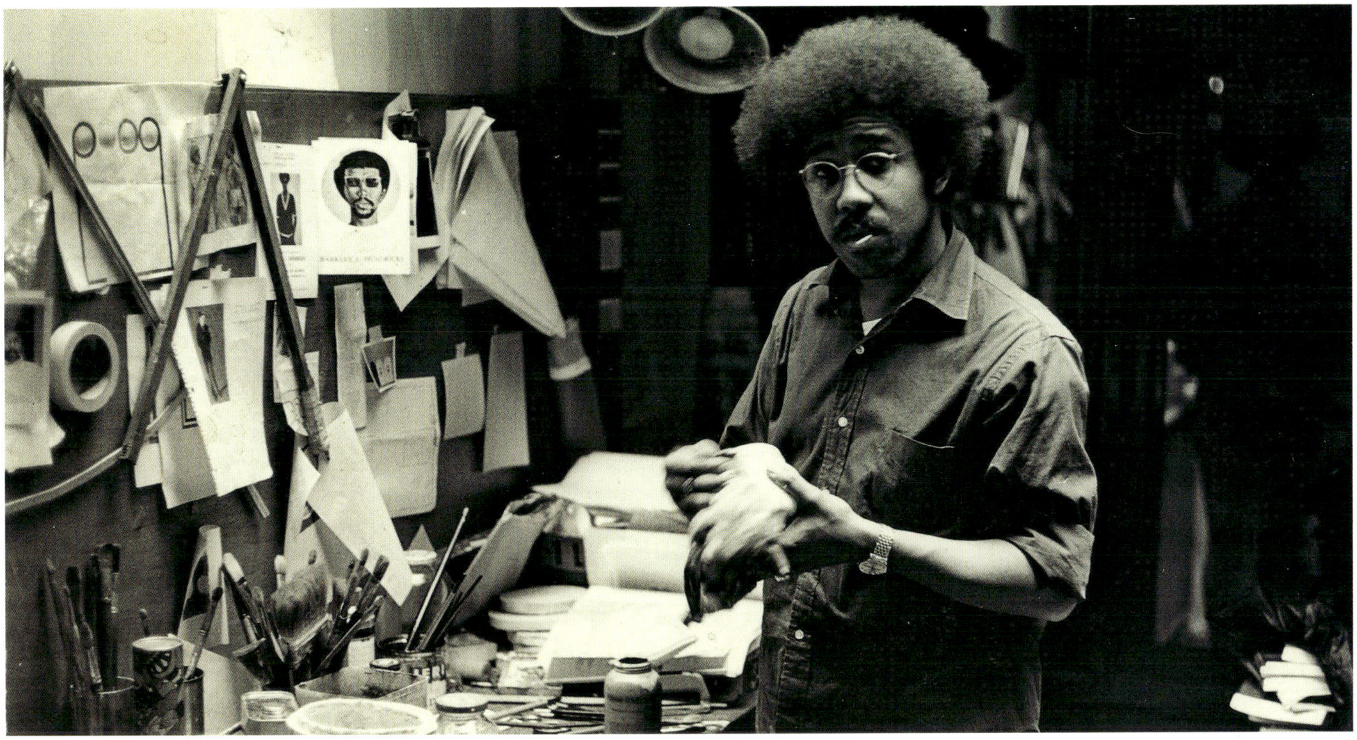

fig. 5
Hendricks in his studio at Yale University, New Haven, CT, 1971

1968

Barkley Hendricks and June Weingarten at Philadelphia Art Alliance, Philadelphia, PA

Twenty oil and acrylic paintings by Hendricks exhibited.

1969

Afro-American Artists, 1800–1969 at Philadelphia Civic Center, Philadelphia, PA

Miss T exhibited.

1970

First solo exhibition at Kenmore Galleries, Philadelphia, PA

1971

Contemporary Black Artists in America

First exhibition at Whitney Museum of American Art, New York, NY

Robert Doty, Curator

Brown Sugar Vine exhibited.

1971

Group exhibition at Carnegie Mellon University, Pittsburgh, PA

Brooks Dendy, Curator

Awarded prize in Black and White Photography for image of a boy at a pool table.

1973

Millennium at Museum of the Philadelphia Civic Center, co-sponsored by the Philadelphia Museum of Art

Jacqueline Y. Teamor, Exhibition Coordinator

Beautiful Like a Woman, a Real Woman; *Bid 'Em In/Slave (Angie)*, *Mayreh*, *Miss Johnson (Angie)*, and *Mr. Johnson (or Sammy from Miami)* exhibited.

1973

Second solo exhibition at Kenmore Galleries, Philadelphia, PA

1973

First solo exhibition at Connecticut College galleries, New London, CT

1974

The Second World Black and African Festival of Art and Culture, Inc., *North American Zone*, *Southeastern Regional Exhibition* at University Museum, Philadelphia, PA

Wallace X. Conway, Curator (New Jersey State Museum)

Arriving Soon, *Little Old Man*, *Napoleon*, *Vertical Hold*, and *Woody* exhibited.

1975

First solo exhibition in the South at Greenville County Museum of Art in Greenville, SC

I was told I would not be able to show any nudes. I later discovered they had white nudes in their collection. My black nudes were just too "black," so I've been told. This museum is now home to *Foxie Roxie*, a painting with condition issues that is unfortunately unable to travel to the Nasher Museum for *Birth of the Cool*.

1975

Solo exhibition at Gibbes Museum of Art, Charleston, SC

1975

First exhibition at CRT Craftery Gallery, Hartford, CT

1975

Jubilee: Afro-American Artists on Afro-America at the Museum of Fine Arts, Boston, MA. In cooperation with the Museum of the National Center of Afro-American Artists

Edmund Barry Gaither, Curator

Bahsir, *Family Jules: NNN (No Naked Niggahs)*, *Foxie Roxie (or Rox the Fox)*, *New London Niggah (Big Chuck)*, and *North Philly Niggah (William Corbett)* exhibited.

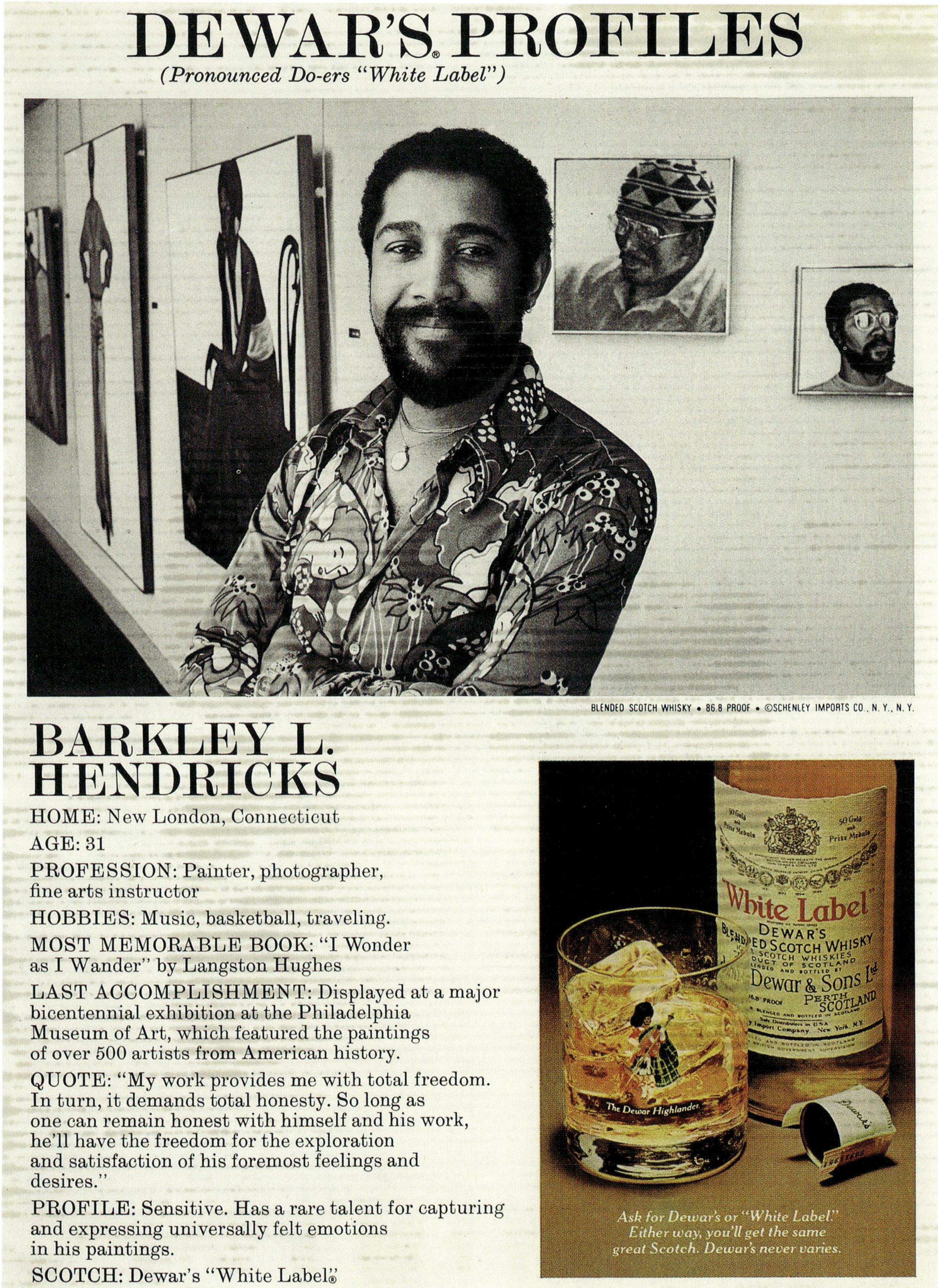

fig. 6
Dewar's Profile, c. 1976

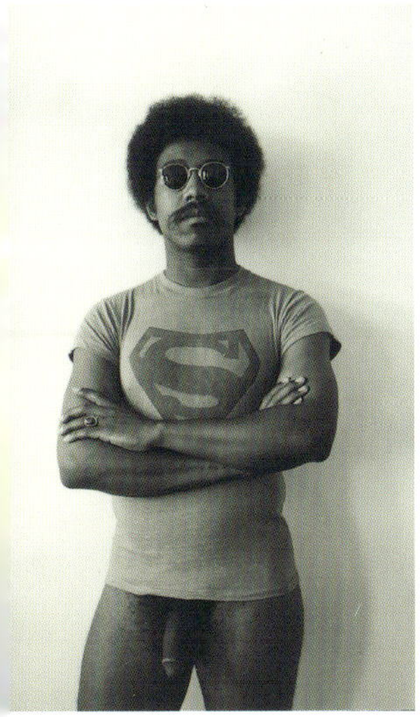

fig. 7
Hendricks as subject for *Icon for My Man Superman*, 1969

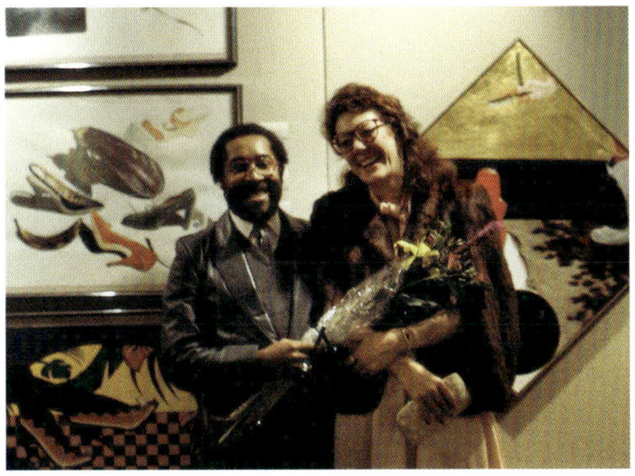

fig. 8
Barkley and wife, Susan, at opening reception of *Barkley L. Hendricks presents Barkley L. Hendricks 1967–1987*, Housatonic Museum of Art, Bridgeport, CT, 1988

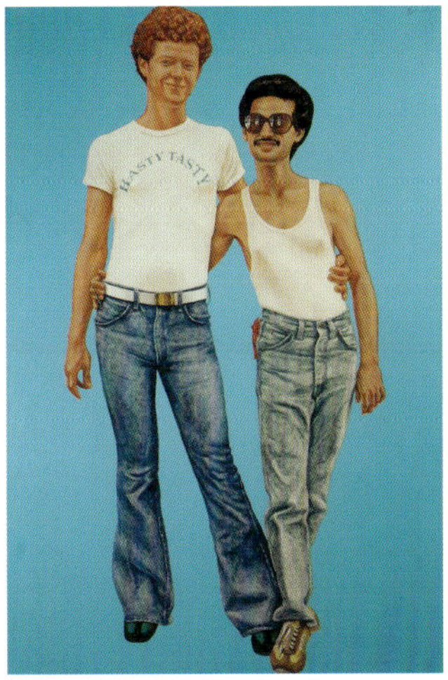

fig. 9
Hasty Tasty, 1977
Oil and acrylic on linen canvas
72 x 48 inches

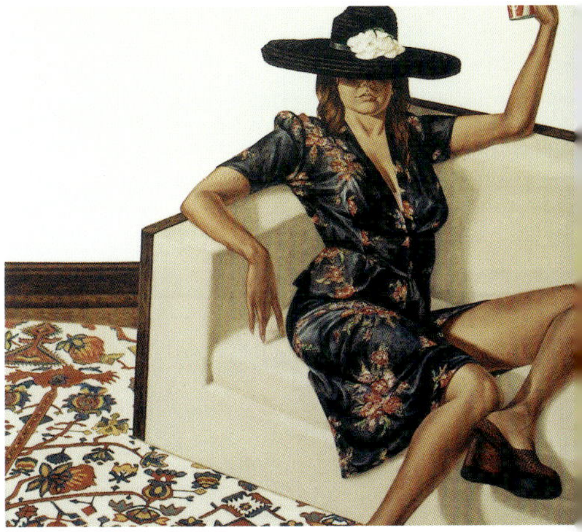

fig. 10
Jackie Sha-La-La (Jackie Cameron), 1975
Oil and acrylic on linen canvas
50 x 60 inches

1976

First exhibition at ACA Galleries, New York, NY

1976

Solo exhibition at Ulrich Museum of Art, Wichita State University, Wichita, KS

1976

Philadelphia: Three Centuries of American Art at the Philadelphia Museum of Art, Philadelphia, PA

Ralph and Alvin: Sikkayou exhibited.

1977

The Figure Today at the Slater Memorial Museum, Norwich, CT

Arriving Soon exhibited.

1978

Solo exhibition of photographs at Arch Street Gallery, Philadelphia, PA

Gallery director, John Phillips, a former student of mine at Connecticut College, later became an assistant to George Wein, founder and director of the Newport Jazz Festivals. This allowed me backstage access to photograph many jazz greats.

1978

Second solo exhibition at ACA Galleries, New York, NY

1978

Connecticut Painting, Drawing and Sculpture at Carlson Art Gallery at University of Bridgeport, Bridgeport, CT; the New Britain Museum of American Art, New Britain, CT; Cummings Art Center, Connecticut College, New London, CT; organized by Art Resources of Connecticut

North Philly Niggah (William Corbett) exhibited.

1978

Artist's Postcards Series II exhibition at Cooper-Hewitt National Design Museum, the Smithsonian National Museum of Design in Washington, DC

My contribution was the postcard-size painting self-portrait titled *Me*.

1978

The Southern New England Invitational Art Exhibition 1978 at Fairfield University, Fairfield, CT

Doc and Ruby's Oldest Boy, *Hasty Tasty*, *Noir*, *Sisters (Susan and Toni)*, *Tequila*, and *Tuff Tony* exhibited.

1979

Solo exhibition at Delaware Art Museum, Wilmington, DE

1979

First solo exhibition of watercolors at Lyman Allyn Art Museum, New London, CT

1980

First solo exhibition at Studio Museum in Harlem, New York, NY

Mary Schmidt Campbell, Curator

1980

First solo exhibition at CRT Craftery Gallery, Hartford, CT

Connie Thomas, Curator

1980

Spiral: Afro-American Art of the 70's at the Museum of the National Center of Afro-American Artists, Roxbury, MA

Edmund Barry Gaither, Curator

Misc. Tyrone and *Take All the Time You Need* exhibited.

1980

35 Under 35 at Lever House, New York, NY; organized by New York Urban League

Avel de Knight, Curator

Brenda's Sister, *Barbara Jean* exhibited.

1980

Retours Aux Sources Une Exposition en Afrique D'Artistes Afro-Americains at Galerie d'Art Mitkal, Abidjan, Ivory Coast, Africa

Arriving Soon exhibited.

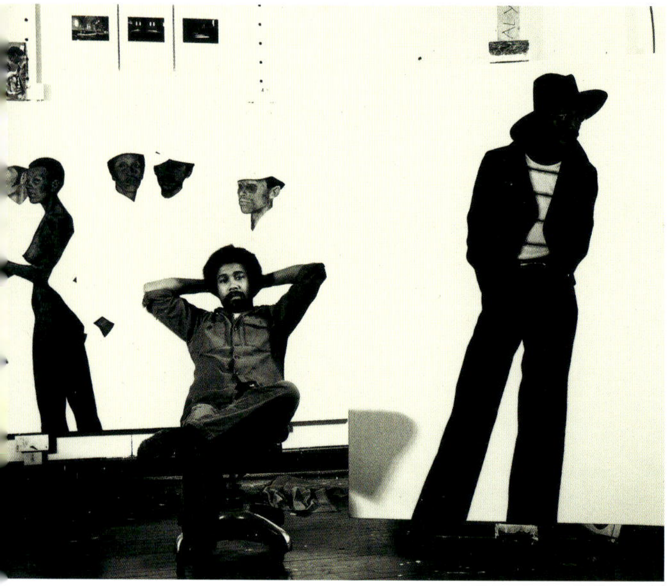

fig. 11
Hendricks in his studio at 58 State Street, New London, CT, mid-1970's

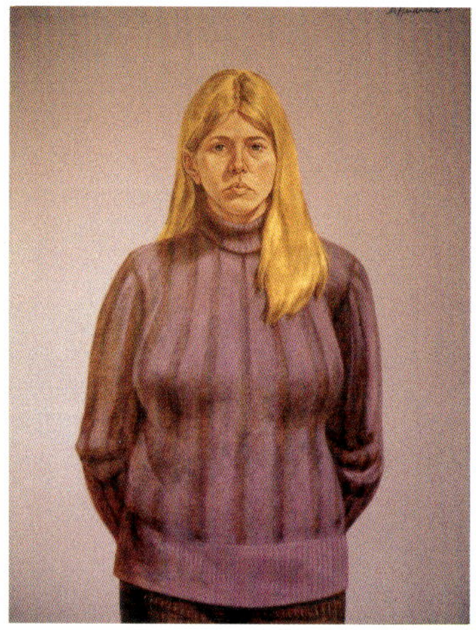

fig. 12
Claire, 1971
Oil and acrylic on cotton canvas
40 x 30 inches

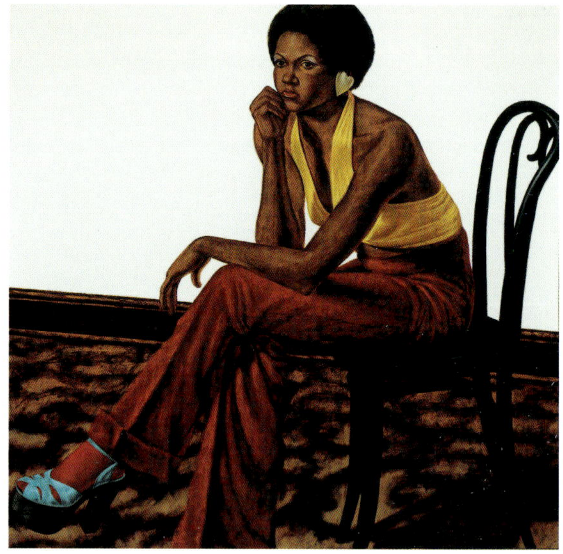

fig. 13
Foxie Roxie, 1975
Acrylic on canvas
48 1/2 x 48 1/2 inches

1981

First solo exhibition at Benjamin Mangel Gallery, Philadelphia, PA

1982

Third solo exhibition at ACA Galleries, New York, NY

1982, 1983, and 1984

Annual solo exhibitions at Spectrum Gallery on 57th Street, New York, NY

The now-defunct gallery was run by a friend from Philadelphia. This was a sports gallery where my basketball paintings were on view in the Big Apple for the first time. Other exhibition spaces and galleries had a very closed mind about showing any work that was not a black figure.

1983

Second solo exhibition at Connecticut College, New London, CT

1983

Celebrating Contemporary American Black Artists at Fine Arts Museums of Long Island, Hempstead, NY

Latin from Manhattan, *Misc. Tyrone*, and *Victory at 23* exhibited.

1983

Barkley, Barkley, a play about Barkley Hendricks and his art and life in Philadelphia.

Written, staged, and directed by Dr. J. Brooks Dendy. Presented at the Walnut Street Theatre.

Several of my paintings were on the stage. The actors in each scene emerged from behind the paintings for their spotlight moment. I never got to see the play. Harry Kulkowitz said he liked the play, and I trusted both Brooks and Harry.

1984

Third solo exhibition at Connecticut College, New London, CT

1984

Solo exhibition at Brattleboro Museum and Art Center, Brattleboro, VT

Due to concerns about potential offense to the local Christian constituency, my mixed media work with a gold cross and high heel shoes apparently was censored and removed.

1984–2002

A Dry Spell for Figures

As I prepared the timeline for this catalogue, I noticed something about my figurative painting output during the "Ronaissance" (the age of Ronald Reagan). As we have learned about this period of our nation's recent history, it in no way resembles the age of enlightenment we call the Renaissance. It was two steps forward and four steps backward in many aspects of us coming together as a nation and a thoughtful country on the planet.

En plein air painting was very important for my mental positioning, something that studio painting could no longer alone provide. Perhaps it was a rearrangement of my creative energies to buttress my sanity in the wake of my brother's murder in 1999. I can vividly see that it was a preparation under way for something important on my mental horizon. It would be an understatement to say I needed those hours *en plein air*, under the blue skies of Jamaica, that winter of 1999. My other art expressions came to a screeching halt. The circles and oval landscapes were significant barometers at a time when I needed messages from the core of my talent nerve center.

Significant personal health experiences during the winter of 2005 made it necessary for me to call upon that core once again. Those planetary portraits of Jamaica were (and remain) prescriptions equally vital for the healing of my mind and heart. Irie.

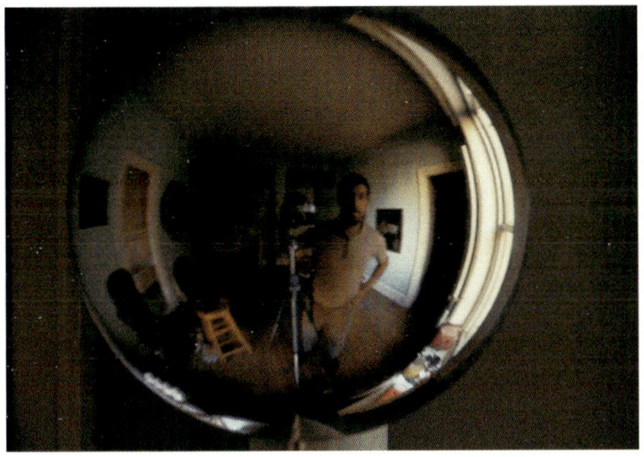

fig. 14
Self-portrait photograph taken in hubcap at Peale House studio, Philadelphia, c. 1967

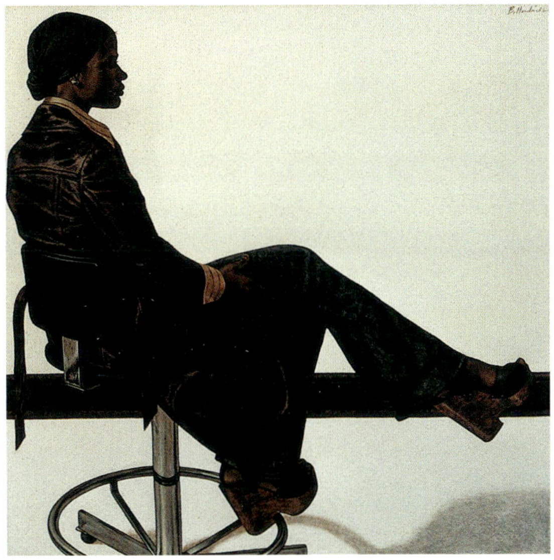

fig. 15
Brenda's Sister, Barbara Jean, 1977
Oil, acrylic, and magna on linen canvas
50 x 50 inches

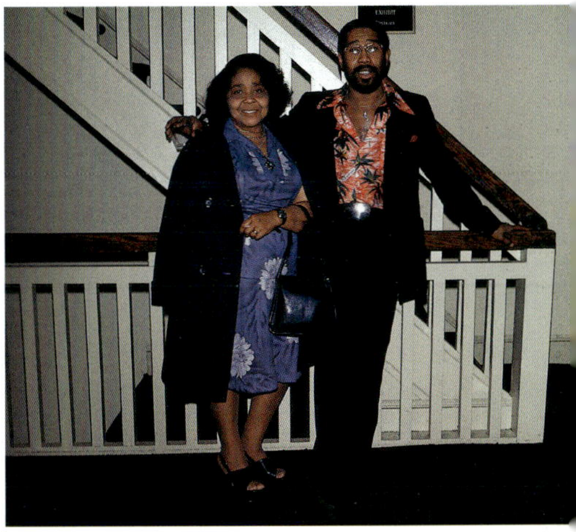

fig. 16
Barkley and Ruby (mother) at opening of solo exhibition at ACA Galleries, New York, 1978

1985

Solo exhibition at Peale House Gallery, Pennsylvania Academy of the Fine Arts, PA

Musical and models performance at opening choreographed by Dr. J. Brooks Dendy.

1985

15 Painters + 15 Sculptors at John Slade Ely House, New Haven, CT

Elizabeth L. Greeley and Raymond W. Smith, Curators

Ma Petite Kumquat, *Someone Has to Do It (Thee Game Series)*, and *Someone Has to Do It, II* exhibited.

1986

Connecticut Circumscribed at Erector Square Gallery, New Haven, CT

Someone Has to Do It, II exhibited.

1987

The Art of Black America in Japan group exhibition, Tokyo, Japan

Sweet Thang exhibited.

1988

Barkley L. Hendricks Presents Barkley L. Hendricks 1967–1987 solo exhibition at Housatonic Museum of Art, Bridgeport, CT

Benjamin Ortiz, Curator

1989

Connecticut/Collage at Art at 100 Pearl, Hartford, CT

Jonathan Talbot, Curator

Confirmation (Charles Christopher Parker Series) exhibited.

1990

Directions: African-American Artists Now at the Newport Art Museum, Newport, RI

Lovers Leap # 1 and *Lovers Leap # 2* exhibited.

1992

First in the Heart Is the Dream: African-American Artists in the 20th Century, The Philadelphia Connection at Philadelphia Art Alliance, Philadelphia, PA

Something Like a Bird: Double Barbara exhibited.

1993

Second solo exhibition of watercolors at Benjamin Mangel Gallery, Philadelphia, PA

1993

The Many Faces of Barkley Hendricks solo exhibition at Norwalk Community Technical College, Norwalk, CT

Sandy Lefkowitz, Curator

A mixed media installation of *Virgin Pin* works is deemed "inappropriate" by the college president and censored. I was asked to reinstall the window with other work. The censored piece was replaced with yellow crime scene tape and a special new drawing done for the censored window installation area.

1993

Group exhibition of photographs taken while on Citizen Ambassador Program in China at Laura Knott Gallery at Bradford College, Bradford, MA

1994–1997

The Studio Museum in Harlem: 25 Years of African-American Art organized by the Studio Museum in Harlem and traveled by the Gallery Association of New York State to twelve national venues

Valerie Mercer, Curator

An ink on paper homage to Charles Mingus titled *Self-Portrait in Three Colors* exhibited.

1994–1995

Black Male: Representations of Masculinity in Contemporary American Art at the Whitney Museum of American Art, New York, NY

Thelma Golden, Curator

George Jules Taylor, *North Philly Niggah*, and *Tuff Tony* exhibited.

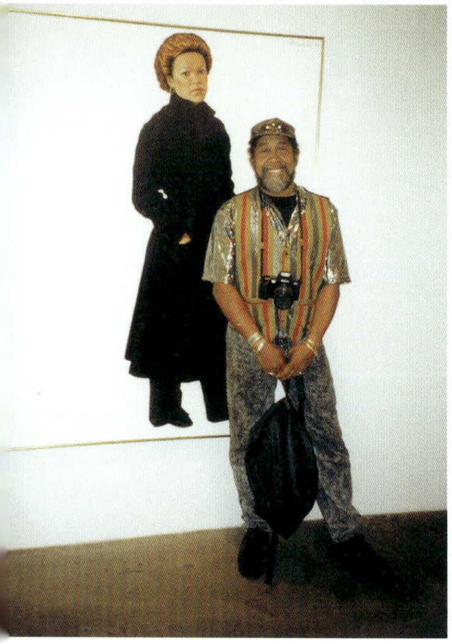

fig. 17
Hendricks at Brent Sikkema, New York, for opening of *The Magic City*, 2000

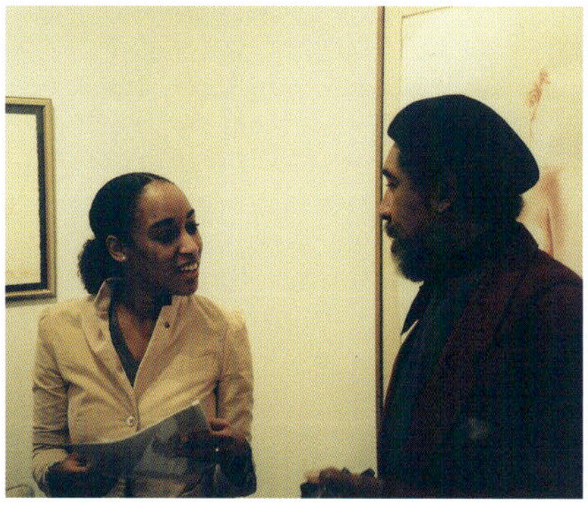

fig. 18
Teka Selman and Barkley at Mitchell Algus Gallery, New York, for opening of solo exhibition, 2005

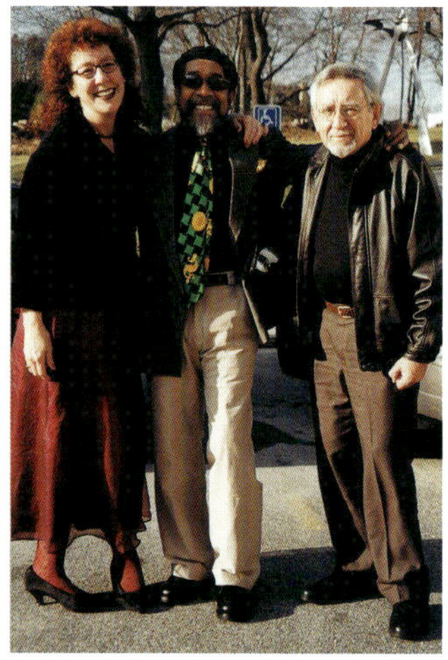

fig. 19
Susan Hendricks (wife) and Barkley with Harry Kulkowitz at opening of *The Barkley L. Hendricks Experience*, New London, CT, 2001

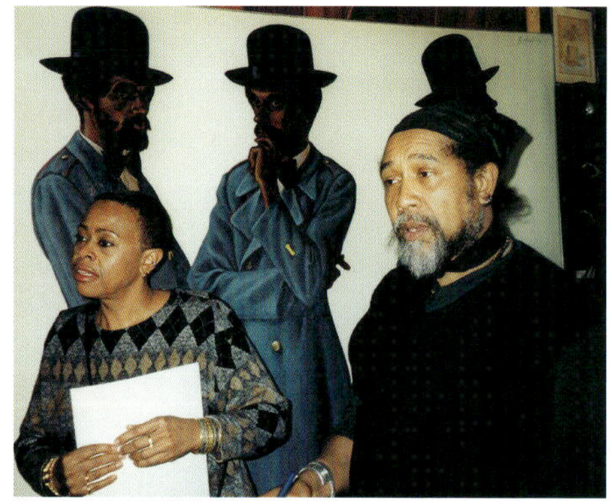

fig. 20
Denise (sister) and Barkley at Hendricks's home in New London, CT, 2001

Black Male traveled to the Armand Hammer Museum, Los Angeles, CA, in 1995.

1996

Four figure paintings used as backdrop for launch of Black Entertainment Television (BET) at ACA Galleries, New York, NY

Blood, *Hasty Tasty*, *Misc. Tyrone* and *North Philly Niggah (William Corbett)* exhibited.

1997

Solo exhibition of watercolor landscapes at Laura Knott Gallery at Bradford College, Bradford, MA

1999

To Conserve a Legacy: American Art from Historically Black Colleges and Universities opens at the Studio Museum in Harlem, New York, NY

Richard J. Powell, Chair of Art and Art History Department at Duke University and Jock Reynolds, Director, Yale University Art Gallery, Curators

Dixwell exhibited.

To Conserve a Legacy traveled to Addison Gallery of American Art, Phillips Academy, Andover, MA, 1999

The Corcoran Gallery of Art, Washington, DC, 2000

The Art Institute of Chicago, Chicago, IL, 2000

Clark Atlanta University Art Galleries with the High Museum of Art, Atlanta, GA, 2000

North Carolina Central University Art Museum with Duke University Museum of Art and the Center for Documentary Studies, Durham, NC, 2000

Fisk University with Tennessee State Museum, Nashville, TN, 2001

Hampton University Museum, Hampton, VA, with the Chrysler Museum, Norfolk, VA, 2001

2000

The Magic City at Brent Sikkema Gallery, New York, NY

First collaboration with Trevor Schoonmaker, Curator

Latin from Manhattan and *Noir* exhibited.

2001

The Barkley L. Hendricks Experience solo exhibition at Lyman Allyn Art Museum, New London, CT

2001

Art of the Commonwealth: Realism in Pennsylvania Painting at Southern Alleghenies Museum of Art, Loretto, PA

Blood exhibited.

Art of the Commonwealth traveled to Erie Art Museum, Erie, PA, 2001

James A. Michener Art Museum, Doylestown, PA, 2001–2002

2002

Hairitage at the Amistad Foundation at the Wadsworth Atheneum Museum of Art, Hartford, CT

Lawdy Mama exhibited.

2003

Black President: The Art and Legacy of Fela Anikulapo-Kuti opens at New Museum, New York, NY

Trevor Schoonmaker, Curator

Fela: Amen, Amen, Amen, Amen . . . was the first figure painting I completed between 1984 and 2002. (Although there were and are a number of works on easels and stacked against the walls in my studio, waiting for ongoing inspiration or "direction from my muse"). The impetus that compelled me to paint Fela was multi-faceted. I have thirty or forty vinyl records and CDs of Fela's music. I saw him perform four times and photographed him at each of those venues, including an extraordinary moment sitting down with him in his trailer backstage in Norwich, Connecticut. Fela told me I could blow my horn with his band. I never got the opportunity to take him up on that invitation. So when Trevor told me about his exhibition concept for *Black President*, I wanted to be a part

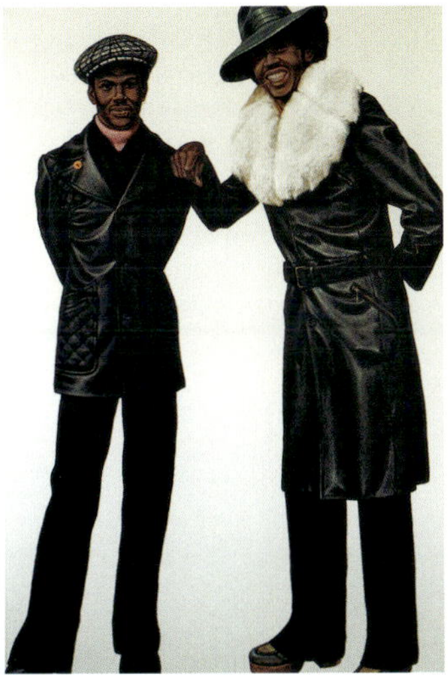

fig. 21
Yocks, 1975
Oil and acrylic on linen canvas
72 x 48 inches

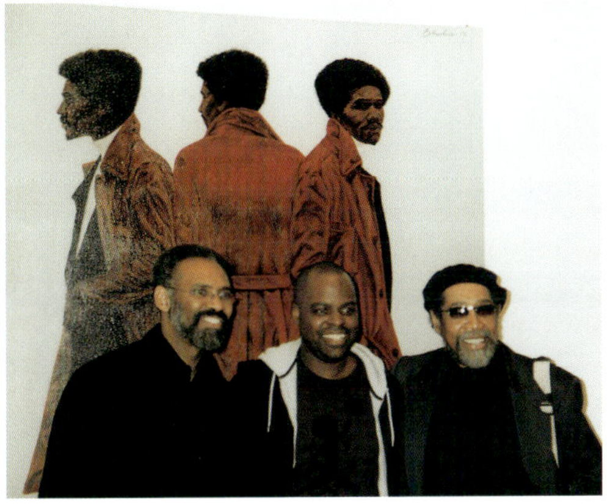

fig. 22
Curators Richard J. Powell and David A. Bailey with Barkley at Whitechapel Gallery, London, for opening of *Back to Black*, 2005

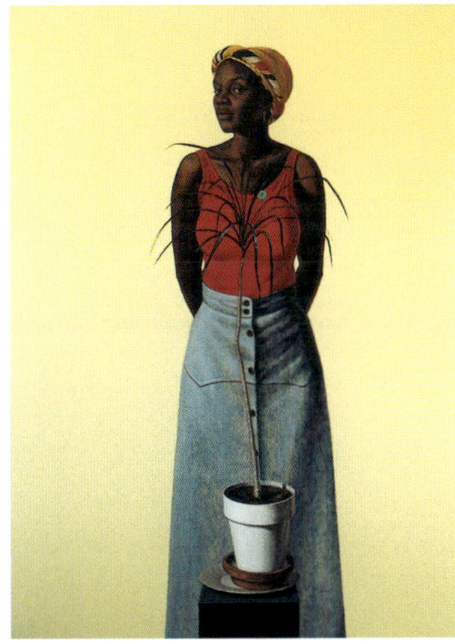

fig. 23
Pretty Peggy's Black Box, 1976
Oil and acrylic on linen canvas
66 x 48 inches

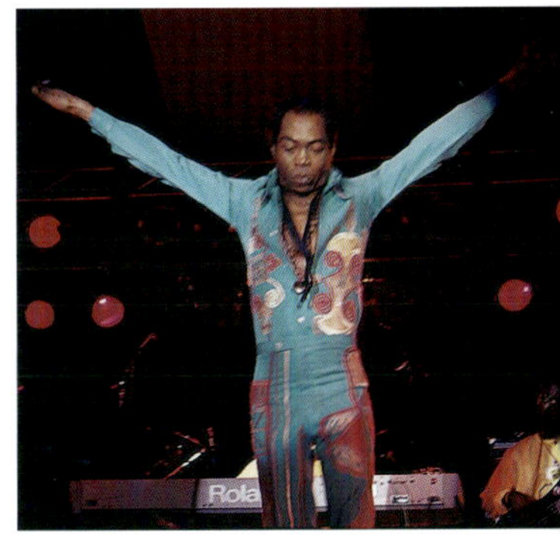

fig. 24
Hendricks's photograph of Fela Kuti at Rose Arts Festival, Norwich, CT, July 1990

of it as an exhibitor and the portrait of Fela was born.

Black President traveled to The Curve Gallery at the Barbican Centre, London, England, 2004

Yerba Buena Center for the Arts, San Francisco, CA, 2004

Contemporary Art Center, Cincinnati, OH, 2005

2003

After Matisse Picasso group exhibition at P.S.1 Contemporary Art Center, New York, NY

Jeffrey Uslip, Curator

Lunch with Picasso or Curry Goat for Two self-portrait exhibited.

2003

The Human Figure group exhibition at ACA Galleries, New York, NY

2005

Two concurrent solo exhibitions, New York, NY

Barkley Hendricks 1972–1983 at Projectile Gallery

Beautiful Like a Woman, a Real Woman at Mitchell Algus Gallery

2005

The Whole World Is Rotten: Free Radicals and the Gold Coast Slave Castles of Paa Joe at Jack Shainman Gallery, New York, NY

Claude Simard, Curator

Isolde Brielmaier and Trevor Schoonmaker, Curatorial Advisors

APB's exhibited.

Jack sold the painting *APB's* from this show to my MFA alma mater, Yale University. The painting *Noir*, the subject of which is one of the same figures in *APB's*, is in the traveling exhibition *Black Panther: Rank and File*, which is a reconfigured and updated version of the exhibition at Jack Shainman Gallery.

2005

African Queen at the Studio Museum in Harlem, New York, included *Lawdy Mama* from their collection. Since acquiring that work many years ago, Thelma Golden, director and chief curator, tells me it is one of the works in the collection most frequently inquired about. The same can be said for *Miss T* at the Philadelphia Museum and *Slick* at the Chrysler Museum of Art, Norfolk, VA.

2005

Back to Black: Art, Cinema and the Racial Imaginary at the Whitechapel Art Gallery, London, England

Richard J. Powell and David A. Bailey, Guest Curators.

Traveled to The New Art Gallery in Walsall, England

Blood, *Lawdy Mama*, and *Sir Charles, Alias Willie Harris* exhibited.

2006

Black Panther: Rank and File opened at the Yerba Buena Center for the Arts, San Francisco, CA, 2006

Claude Simard and René de Guzman, Co-Curators

Noir exhibited.

Traveled to Southeastern Center for Contemporary Art, Winston-Salem, NC, 2007

Maryland Institute College of Art, Baltimore, MD, 2007

2006

Day for Night: The Whitney Biennial at the Whitney Museum of American Art, New York, NY

This is my third group exhibition at the Whitney and the first time I have shown photographs. I was gratified that my provocative Ku Klux Klan images were selected for inclusion in this show.

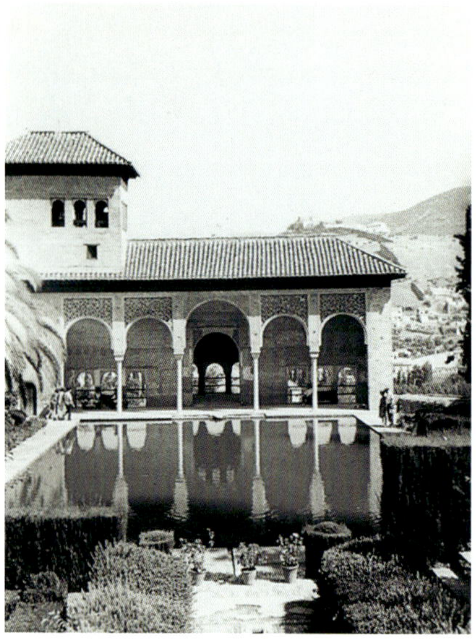

fig. 25
Hendricks's photograph of Alhambra palace, in Granada, Spain, 1966

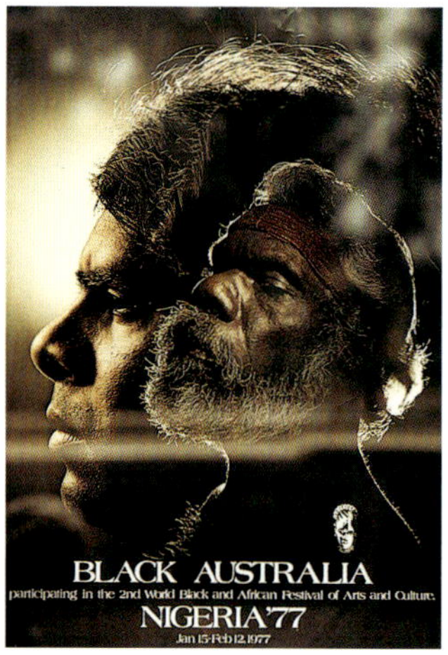

fig. 26
Hendricks's photograph of Black Australia FESTAC poster, Lagos, Nigeria, February 1977

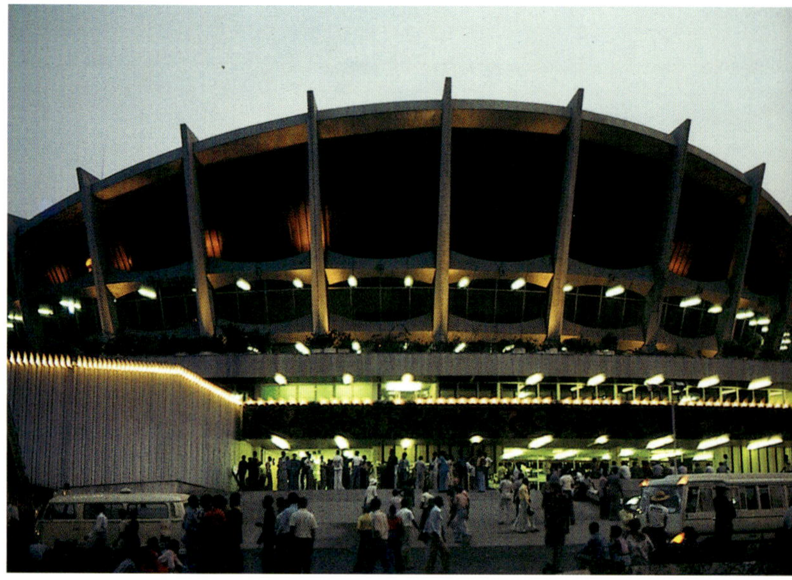

fig. 27
Hendricks's photograph of main FESTAC performance pavilion, Lagos, Nigeria, February 1977

2006

REPRESENT: Selections from the Permanent Collection of the Studio Museum in Harlem at New York State Museum, Albany, NY

Lawdy Mama exhibited.

2007

Connecticut Contemporary exhibition at the Wadsworth Atheneum Museum of Art, Hartford, CT

Joanna Marsh, Curator

This is the fourth time I have shown at the Atheneum and the first major venue where my Jamaican landscapes have been presented together with one of my figure paintings; the subject of *Roaring River Apostle* is a native Jamaican. In addition to seeing my own works on the walls, it's always inspiring to see paintings by two of my favorite artists: the Atheneum owns and has on almost permanent view a gorgeous Caravaggio and an excellent Ribera.

2007

New at the Nasher at the Nasher Museum of Art at Duke University, Durham, NC

The show presents *Bahsir*, recently acquired by the museum.

Travel

1966

Awarded the William Emlen Cresson European Traveling Scholarship from the Pennsylvania Academy of the Fine Arts, Philadelphia. Traveled to England, France, Holland, Italy, Greece, Spain, and Turkey.

1967

Awarded the J. Henry Scheidt Traveling Scholarship from the Pennsylvania Academy of the Fine Arts, Philadelphia. Traveled to Morocco, Tunisia, Algeria, Libya, and Egypt.

1977

Traveled to Lagos, Nigeria, for FESTAC '77 (Second World Black and African Festival of Arts and Culture). Two weeks in Lagos, with day trip to Ibadan, Nigeria.

1978

Returned to Nigeria and also traveled to Ghana, Benin, and Togo in a five-week trip.

1983

First trip to Jamaica for honeymoon with Susan in Montego Bay. Returned 1984 and 1985 to north side of the island. Started landscape watercolor series which is still ongoing twenty-five years later.

1986

Returned to Jamaica, first trip to mountains on south side of the island. Have returned to this area in December and/or January every year since. Early 1990s started tondo, oval, and lunette oil landscapes series, ongoing.

1987

Traveled to Tokyo for opening of *Black American Art in Japan* group exhibition.

1991

Travel to China with the Citizen Ambassador Program. Visited Beijing, Xian, Shanghai, and Hong Kong. Color photography fashion shoot at Modeling School in Xian.

1996

Returned to Ghana: five-month study away program with students through Connecticut College. Painted ten *Warrior Women* watercolors, a series based on the Ghanaian legend of Zaria the warrior queen. Painted sixteen oil landscapes in *View of the Gulf of Guinea*. Neither of these series has been exhibited.

2000–2003

Returned to Rome and Florence, Italy, annually.

2006

Returned to Amsterdam, Holland, specifically to view *Rembrandt-Caravaggio* exhibition at the Van Gogh Museum.

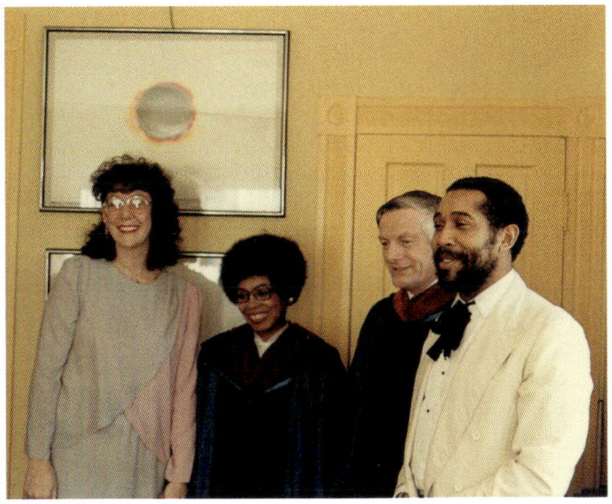

fig. 28
Barkley L. Hendricks marries Susan Weig at their home in New London, CT, on April 2, 1983
Married by Minister James Pratt and Thelma Waterman

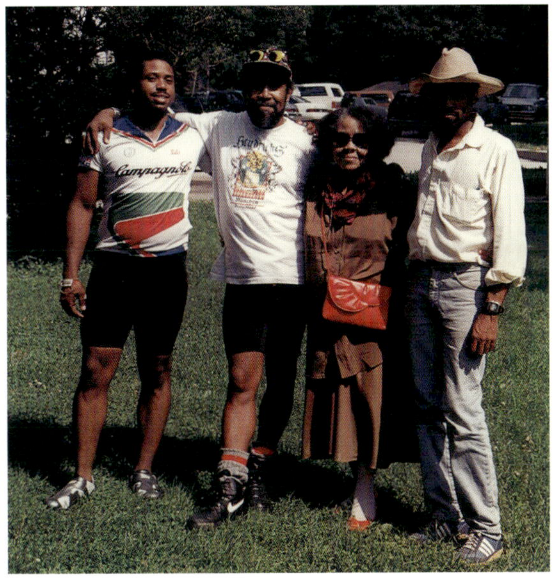

fig. 29
Methun (brother), Barkley, Ruby (mother), and Lamont (brother) at family reunion in Philadelphia, early 1990s

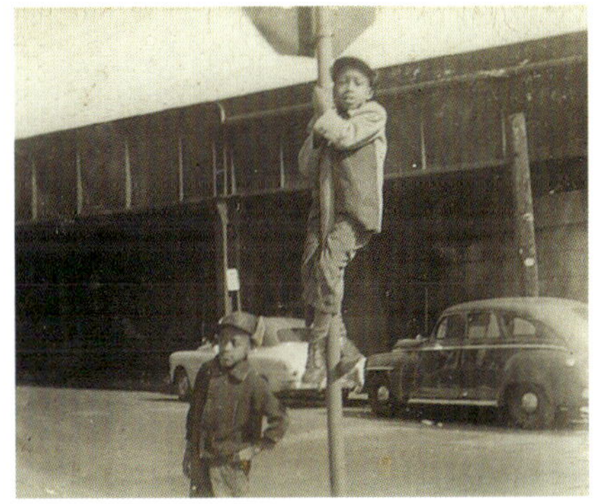

fig. 30
Barkley (climbing the stop sign) and Lamont at ages 8 and 6, in Philadelphia, 1953

Personal Details

1966–1970

Employed as a recreation leader with the Philadelphia Department of Recreation. One of my most memorable duties, besides marble tournaments, arts and crafts classes, stopping the theft of basketballs, and ending fights, was being an usher at a Nina Simone concert. That was a good gig.

1968–1974

Joined New Jersey National Guard and completed obligation after six years.

1971–1972

Instructor of painting at the Pennsylvania Academy of the Fine Arts in Philadelphia, PA.

1972

Moved from New Haven to New London, CT.

1972

Started as instructor of art at Connecticut College, New London, CT.

1975

The death of my father, Barkley H. Hendricks, in January got the year off to a helluva start. Doc was a very strong and skillful man. His hands were indeed his tools. He would be amazed at the number of tools I have accumulated since I stopped working for him. It even blows my mind given how much I hated the work.

1978

Awarded tenure as professor at Connecticut College.

1979

Met Susan Weig (future wife) in Aldo's Jazz Club, New London, CT.

1979

Bought and renovated home and studio space in New London, CT.

April 2, 1983

Married Susan Weig at our home in New London. We had two ministers, one male and one female, perform the nuptials and thirteen people in attendance.

1987

Promoted to full professor at Connecticut College.

October 6, 1999

The death of my brother Lamont just a week shy of his fifty-second birthday hit me hard. When we were kids, it was always Butch and Lamont, Butch and Lamont. Where I went, Lamont was sure to follow. Or, as my mother would say, "Take Lamont with you" (or else you don't go was the implied message). People took his size for granted because he was thin, but he was a scrappy little dude whenever we were in a fair fight. Lamont was one of my most vocal supporters. I know he pissed off several artists in Philly when he would regularly say, "My brother is the best artist to come out of Philadelphia." I miss his mouth on that subject and really wish he could be at the PAFA opening for this show.

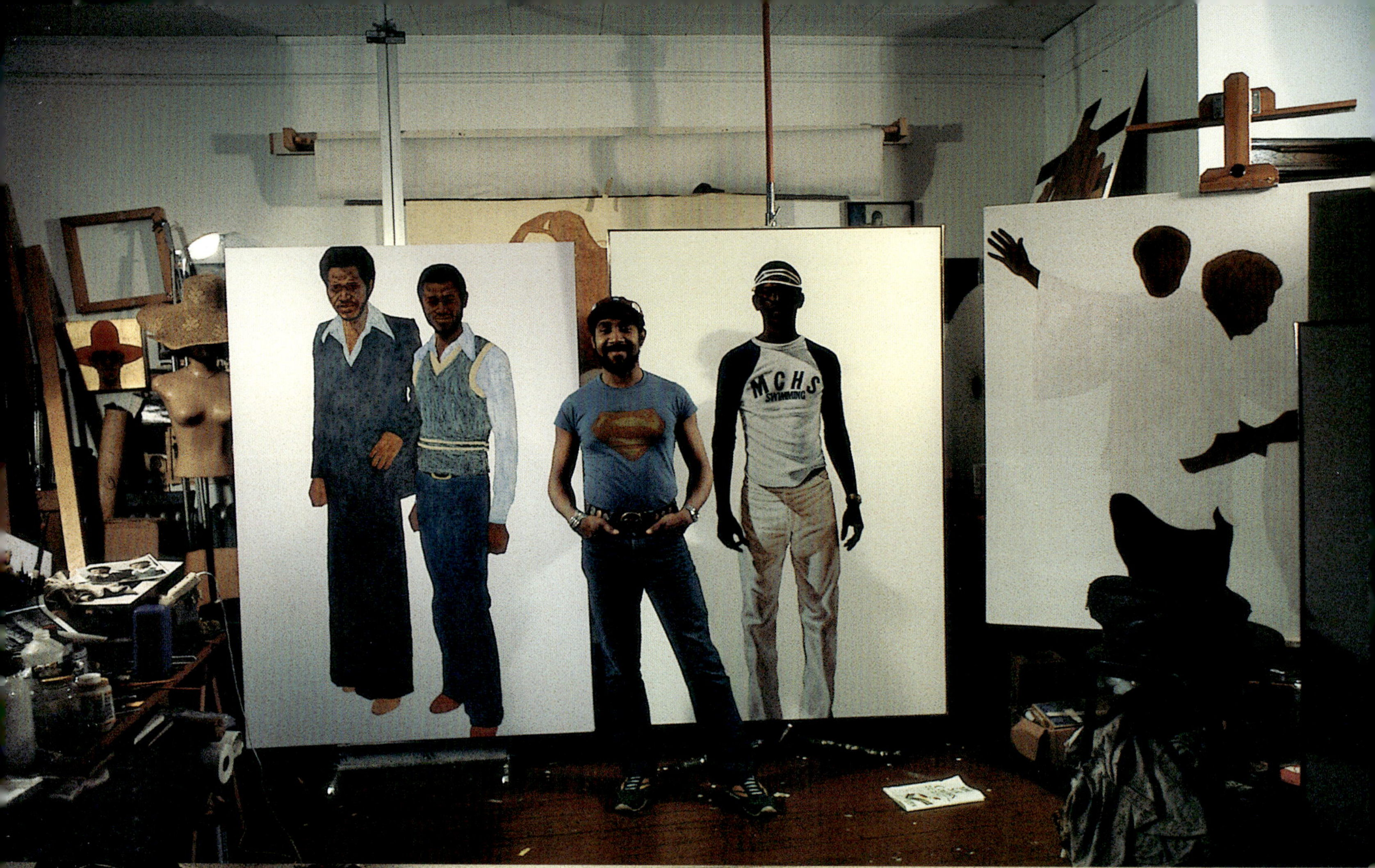
MCHS
SWIMMING

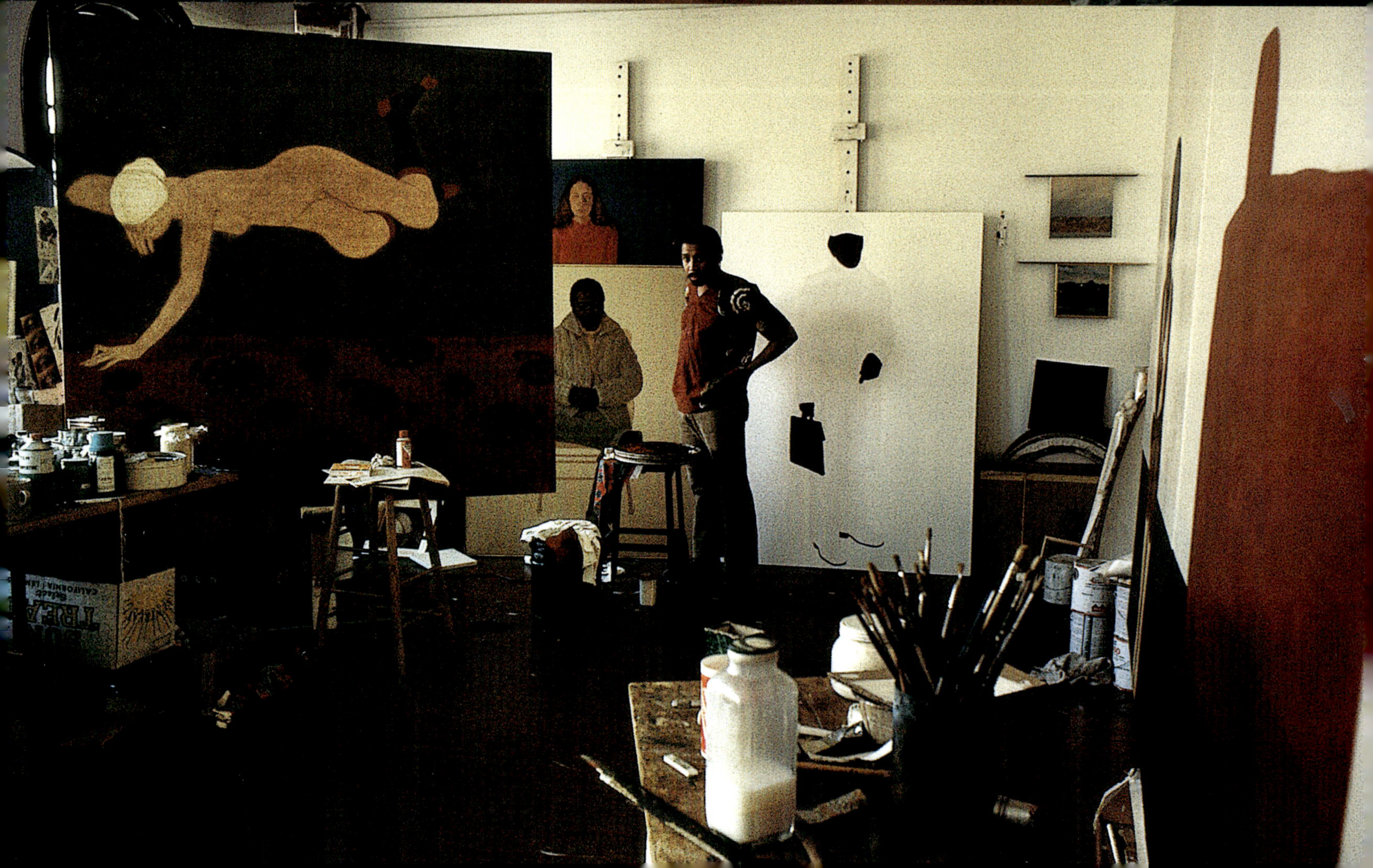

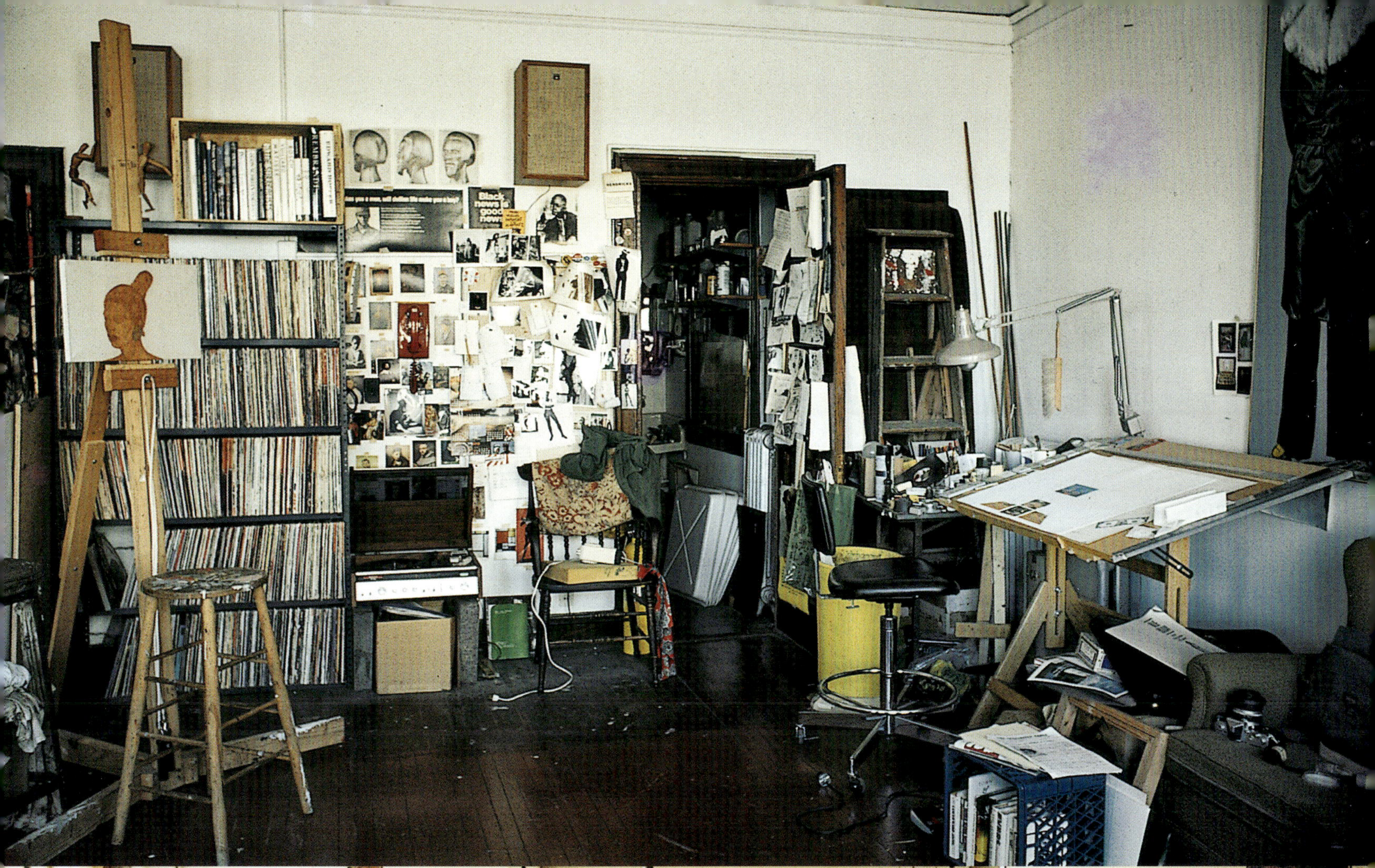

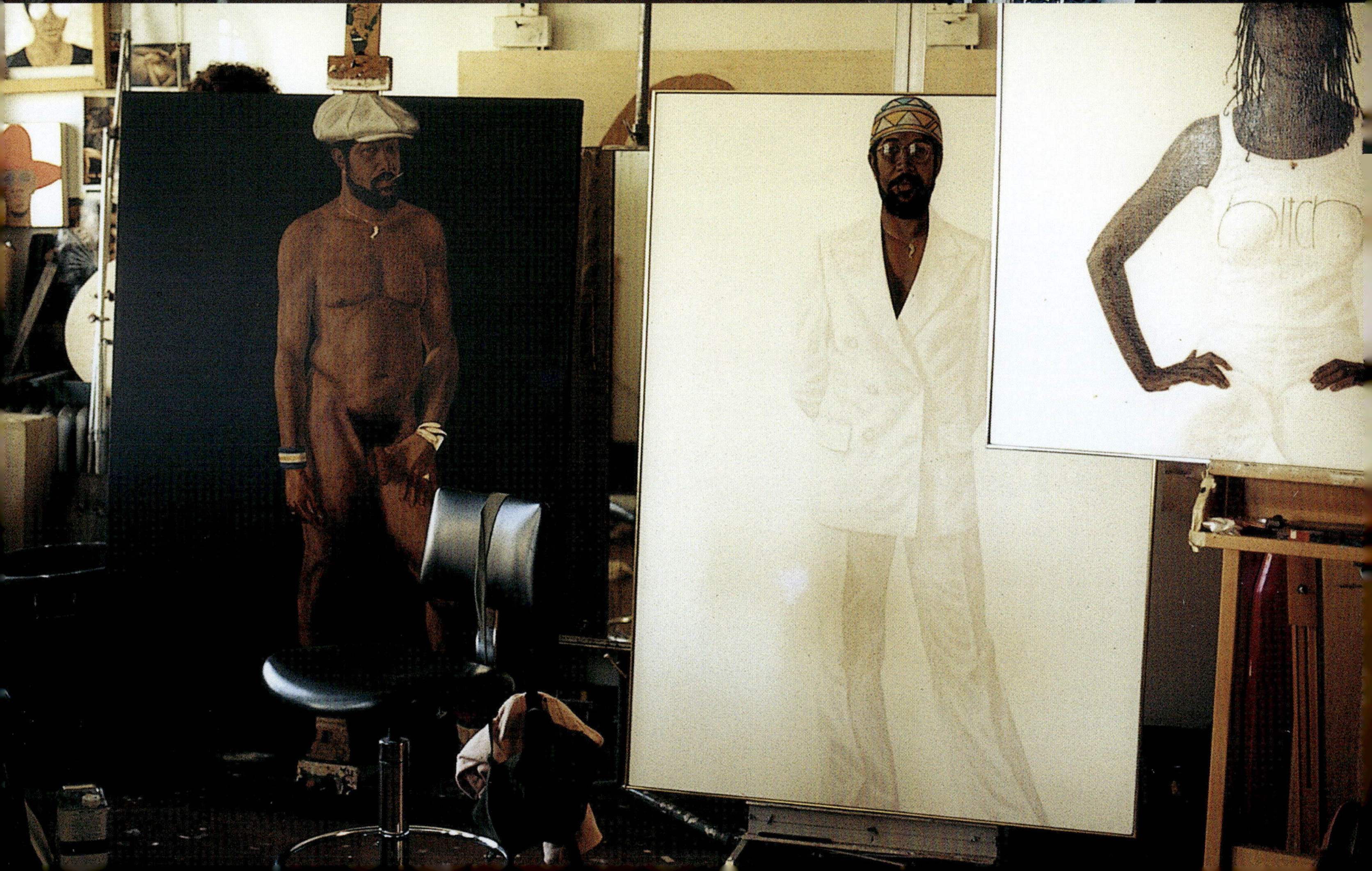

About the Contributors Compiled 2008

Thelma Golden is Director and Chief Curator of the Studio Museum in Harlem. Golden began her career at the Studio Museum in 1987 before joining the Whitney Museum of American Art in 1988. In a decade at the Whitney, she organized numerous groundbreaking exhibitions, including *Black Male: Representations of Masculinity in Contemporary American Art* (1994) and *Bob Thompson* (1998). She also served as Director of the Whitney Museum at Phillip Morris (now Altria). She returned to the Studio Museum in 2000 as Deputy Director for Exhibitions and Programs and was named Director and Chief Curator in 2005. At SMH, Golden has organized many notable exhibitions, including *Chris Ofili: Afro Muses 1995–2005* (2005), *Black Romantic* (2002), *Freestyle* (2001), *Frequency* (2005), *Glenn Ligon: Stranger* (2001), *Martin Puryear: The Cane Project* (2001), and *Isaac Julien: Vagabondia* (2000). Golden holds a B.A. in art history and African-American Studies from Smith College and honorary doctorates from Smith and the Moore College of Art and Design. She is an active guest lecturer, curator, and panelist, and was a *Glamour* Magazine "Woman of the Year" in 2005.

Richard J. Powell is the John Spencer Bassett Professor of Art and Art History at Duke University, where he has taught since 1989. He studied at Morehouse College and Howard University before earning his doctorate in art history at Yale University. Along with teaching courses in American art, the arts of the African diaspora, and contemporary visual studies, he has written on topics ranging from primitivism to postmodernism, including such titles as *Homecoming: The Art and Life of William H. Johnson* (1991), *Jacob Lawrence* (1992), and *Black Art: A Cultural History* (1997 and 2002). His latest book, *Cutting a Figure: Fashioning Black Portraiture* (2008), is about nineteenth-, twentieth-, and twenty-first-century portraits of peoples of African descent. Powell has also helped organize several exhibitions, most notably *The Blues Aesthetic: Black Culture and Modernism* (1989); *Rhapsodies in Black: Art of the Harlem Renaissance* (1997); *To Conserve a Legacy: American Art at Historically Black Colleges and Universities* (1999); *Beauford Delaney: The Color Yellow* (2002); *Circle Dance: The Art of John T. Scott* (2005); *Back to Black: Art, Cinema, and the Racial Imaginary* (2005); and *Conjuring Bearden* (2006). In 2007 Powell became Editor-in-Chief of *The Art Bulletin* for a three-year term.

fig 1 (page 126, top)
Hendricks in 58 State Street studio, New London, CT, in front of *APB's*, *Steve*, and unfinished *Full Moon*, 1978

fig 2 (page 126, bottom)
Hendricks in 58 State Street studio, New London, CT, in front of *Dr. Kool*, *Little Old Man*, *Mayreh (Mary Sheehan)*, and unfinished *Take All the Time You Need*, c. 1974

fig. 3 (page 127, top)
Studio at 58 State Street, New London, CT, 1980

fig 4. (page 127, bottom)
Studio at 58 State Street, New London, CT, 1977

Trevor Schoonmaker is Curator of Contemporary Art at the Nasher Museum of Art at Duke University. His first exhibition at the Nasher was *Street Level: Mark Bradford, William Cordova & Robin Rhode* (2007), which traveled to the Contemporary Arts Center, New Orleans (2007–2008) and the Institute of Contemporary Art, Boston (2008). Prior to joining the Nasher Museum he was organizer of numerous exhibitions including *The Magic City*, Brent Sikkema, New York (2000); *Black President: The Art and Legacy of Fela Anikulapo-Kuti*, New Museum of Contemporary Art, New York (2003), Yerba Buena Center for the Arts, San Francisco (2004), Barbican Centre, London (2004), and the Contemporary Arts Center, Cincinnati (2004/2005); *DTroit*, Gigantic ArtSpace, New York (2003–2004) and Urbis, Manchester, U.K. (2004); *Propeller*, Steve Turner Gallery, Los Angeles (2005); and co-curator of *The Beautiful Game: Contemporary Art and Fútbol* for BICA at Roebling Hall and the Brooklyn Academy of Music, New York (2006). He is the editor of *Fela: From West Africa to West Broadway* (2003). Schoonmaker holds a B.A. in art history from the University of North Carolina at Chapel Hill and an M.A. in art history from the University of Michigan.

Franklin Sirmans is Curator of Modern and Contemporary Art at the Menil Collection in Houston, where he has organized *Everyday People: 20th Century Photography from The Menil Collection*, *The David Whitney Bequest*, and *Otabenga Jones: Lessons from Below*. Since 2005 he has been a Curatorial Advisor at P.S. 1 Contemporary Art Center, New York. He is curator of *For the Love of the Game: Race and Sport in America* at the Amistad Center/ Wadsworth Athenaeum Museum of Art, Hartford (2007). He was co-curator of *Basquiat* (Brooklyn Museum, Los Angeles Museum of Contemporary Art and the Museum of Fine Arts, Houston, 2005–2006), *Make it Now: New Sculpture in New York* (Sculpture Center, NY, 2005), and *One Planet Under a Groove: Contemporary Art and Hip Hop* (Bronx Museum of the Arts, Walker Art Center, Spelman College Art Gallery, and Villa Stuck, Munich, 2001–2003). A former Editor of *Flash Art* and *Art AsiaPacific* magazines, Sirmans has written for several publications, including the *New York Times*, *Essence Magazine*, *Art in America*, *Grand Street*, and *Gulf Coast*. He has taught art history at Maryland Institute College of Art and Princeton University. He is the 2007 recipient of the David C. Driskell Prize awarded by the High Museum of Art, Atlanta. He is also a Contributing and Advisory Editor for *Callaloo*. He is currently at work on the exhibition *NeoHooDoo: Art for a Forgotten Faith*.

Exhibition Checklist

1. *My Black Nun*, 1964
Oil on masonite board
11 3/4 x 7 1/4 inches
Courtesy of the artist

2. *Self-Portrait*, 1966
Oil on cotton canvas
42 x 28 inches
Courtesy of the artist

3. *Vertical Hold*, 1967
Oil, acrylic, and metallic silver on cotton canvas
47 x 44 inches
Courtesy of the artist

4. *FTA*, 1968
Oil on linen canvas
32 x 30 inches
Collection of Charlotte and Gordon Moore, Cambridge, MA

5. *J.S.B III (James Sherman Brantley)*, 1968
Oil on linen canvas
48 x 34 3/8 inches
Pennsylvania Academy of the Fine Arts, Philadelphia; gift of Mr. and Mrs. Richardson Dilworth

6. *Dippy's Delight*, 1969
Oil and acrylic on cotton canvas
46 inch diameter
Courtesy of the artist

7. *Icon for My Man Superman (Superman never saved any black people—Bobby Seale)*, 1969
Oil, acrylic, and aluminum leaf on linen canvas
59 1/2 x 48 inches
Courtesy of the artist

8. *Lawdy Mama*, 1969
Oil and gold leaf on linen canvas
53 3/4 x 36 1/4 inches
The Studio Museum in Harlem, New York; gift of Stuart Liebman, in memory of Joseph B. Liebman

9. *Miss T*, 1969
Oil and acrylic on linen canvas
78 x 56 inches
Philadelphia Museum of Art; purchased with the Philadelphia Foundation Fund, 1970

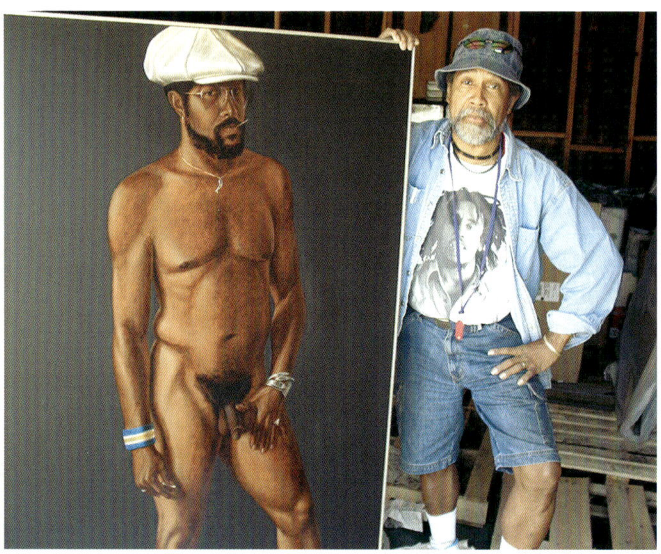

fig. 1
Hendricks at storage in New London, CT, May 13, 2007

10. *Brown Sugar Vine*, 1970
Oil and acrylic on linen canvas
50 x 48 inches
Collection of Dr. and Mrs. John T. Williams Sr., Philadelphia

11. *Granada*, 1970
Oil and acrylic on cotton canvas
48 x 46 inches
Collection of Dr. and Mrs. John T. Williams Sr., Philadelphia

12. *Dixwell*, 1971
Oil and acrylic on linen canvas
38 1/4 inches diameter
North Carolina Central University Art Museum, Durham, NC

13. *Down Home Taste*, 1971
Oil and acrylic on linen canvas
48 3/4 x 48 5/8 inches
Courtesy of the Office of the Dean of Students, Cornell University
Gift of Michael Straight to the Willard Straight Hall Art Collection

14. *George Jules Taylor*, 1972
Oil and acrylic on cotton canvas
91 1/2 x 60 1/4 inches
National Gallery of Art, Washington, DC; William C. Whitney Foundation

15. *Ms. Johnson (Estelle)*, 1972
Oil and acrylic on linen canvas
73 1/4 x 50 3/4 inches
Gibbes Museum of Art/ Carolina Art Association, Charleston, SC

16. *Sergio*, 1972
Oil and acrylic on linen canvas
60 x 44 inches
Collection of Dr. and Mrs. Robert and Joan Clark, Philadelphia

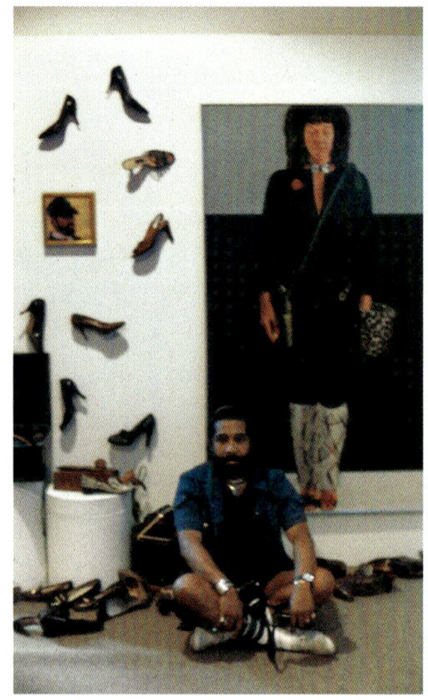

fig. 2
Hendricks in front of installation and *Ma Petite Kumquat* at solo exhibition at Brattleboro Museum and Art Center, Brattleboro, VT, 1984

17. *Sir Charles, Alias Willie Harris*, 1972
Oil and acrylic on linen canvas
84 1/8 x 72 inches
National Gallery of Art, Washington, DC; William C. Whitney Foundation

18. *Bid 'Em In/Slave (Angie)*, 1973
Oil and acrylic on linen canvas
72 x 50 inches
Searles/Spicer Collection, New York

19. *Dr. Kool*, 1973
Oil and acrylic on linen canvas
72 3/4 x 52 3/4 inches
Collection of Dr. and Mrs. Robert and Joan Clark, Philadelphia

20. *Mayreh (Mary Sheehan)*, 1973
Oil and acrylic on linen canvas
72 1/4 x 52 inches
Courtesy of the artist

21. *New Orleans Niggah*, 1973
Oil and acrylic on cotton canvas
72 x 52 inches
National Afro-American Museum and Cultural Center, Wilberforce, OH; Gift of Joseph Erdelac, Cleveland, OH

22. *What's Going On*, 1974
Oil, acrylic, and magna on cotton canvas
65 3/4 x 83 3/4 inches
Courtesy of ACA Galleries, New York

23. *Bahsir (Robert Gowens)*, 1975
Oil and acrylic on linen canvas
83 1/2 x 66 inches
Nasher Museum of Art at Duke University, Durham, NC

24. *Bedroom Eyes (Self-Portrait)*, 1975
Oil and acrylic (iridescent) on cotton canvas
10 x 10 inches
Courtesy of the artist

25. *Blood (Donald Formey)*, 1975
Oil and acrylic on cotton canvas
72 x 50 1/2 inches
Collection of Dr. Kenneth Montague / The Wedge Collection

26. *North Philly Niggah (William Corbett)*, 1975
Oil and acrylic on cotton canvas
72 1/2 x 48 1/2 inches
Collection of Blake Byrne, Los Angeles

27. *Take All the Time You Need (Adrienne Hawkins)*, 1975
Oil on linen canvas
72 1/4 x 72 1/4 inches
Courtesy of the artist

28. *Sweet Thang (Lynn Jenkins)*, 1975–1976
Oil on linen canvas
52 1/8 x 52 3/4 inches
Courtesy of the artist

29. *Misc. Tyrone (Tyrone Smith)*, 1976
Oil and magna on linen canvas
72 x 50 1/4 inches
Courtesy of the artist

30. *Steve*, 1976
Oil, acrylic, and magna on linen canvas
72 x 48 inches
The Forbes Collection, New York

31. *Brilliantly Endowed (Self-Portrait)*, 1977
Oil and acrylic on linen canvas
66 x 48 1/4 inches
Courtesy of the artist

32. *Doc and Ruby's Oldest Boy (Self-Portrait)*, 1977
Oil and acrylic on linen canvas
72 x 48 inches
Columbus Museum of Art, OH; Museum Purchase, Derby Fund, from the Philip J. and Suzanne Schiller Collection of American Social Commentary Art 1930–1970

33. *Sisters (Susan and Toni)*, 1977
Oil and acrylic on linen canvas
66 x 48 1/4 inches
Courtesy of the artist

34. *Slick (Self-Portrait)*, 1977
Oil, acrylic, and magna on linen canvas
67 x 48 1/2 inches
Chrysler Museum of Art, Norfolk, VA; gift of the American Academy and Institute of the Arts and Letters, New York, Childe Hassam Purchase Funds

35. *Vendetta*, 1977
Oil, acrylic, and magna on linen canvas
36 x 48 1/8 inches
Collection of Monica and Rick Segal, New York

36. *APB's (Afro-Parisian Brothers)*, 1978
Oil and acrylic on linen canvas
72 x 50 inches
Yale University Art Gallery, New Haven, CT; The Janet and Simeon Braguin Fund

37. *Tequila*, 1978
Oil and acrylic on linen canvas
60 3/4 x 50 1/4 inches
The Butler Institute of American Art, Youngstown, OH; Museum Purchase 1980

38. *Tuff Tony*, 1978
Oil and acrylic on linen canvas
72 x 48 inches
The Forbes Collection, New York

39. *Latin from Manhattan . . . the Bronx Actually*, 1980
Oil and acrylic on linen canvas
66 1/8 x 50 1/4 inches
Collection of Mr. and Mrs. Alexander Miller, Grand Rapids, MI

40. *Icon for Fifi*, 1982
Oil and combination leaf on linen canvas
60 1/4 x 50 1/4 inches
Courtesy of the artist

41. *Ma Petite Kumquat*, 1983
Oil, acrylic, white gold, and silver leaf on linen canvas
72 1/4 x 40 1/8 inches
Courtesy of the artist

42. *View from Behind the School*, 2000
Oil on linen canvas
22 inch diameter
Courtesy of the artist

43. *View from Red Banks School*, 2000
Oil on cotton canvas
12 x 21 inches
Courtesy of the artist

44. *Mustard YS Falls*, 2002
Oil on linen canvas
12 x 21 inches
Courtesy of the artist

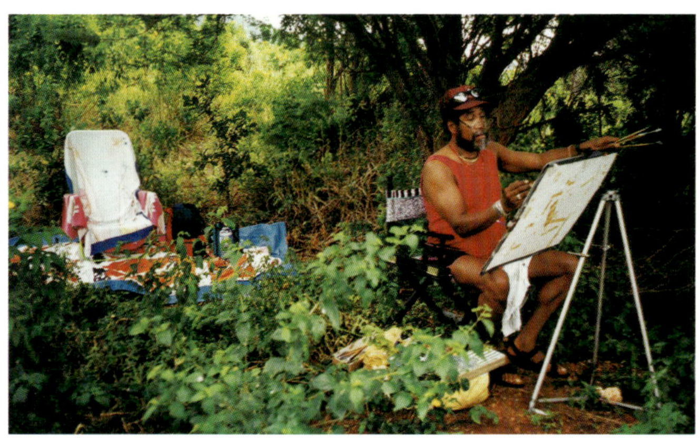

fig. 3
Hendricks painting in Jamaica, c. late 1990s

45. *Fela: Amen, Amen, Amen, Amen . . .* , 2002
Oil and variegated leaf on linen canvas, wooden frame, altarpiece armature, 27 pairs of high heels
66 3/4 x 46 3/4 inches (60 x 40 inches unframed), with 60-inch altarpiece
Courtesy of the artist

46. *Lunch with Picasso: Curry Goat for Two*, 2003
Oil, acrylic, and gold variegated leaf on cotton canvas
15 3/4 x 19 3/4 inches
Courtesy of the artist

47. *Roaring River Apostle (Serious Smoker Series)*, 2004
Oil on linen canvas, wooden frame
72 1/4 x 40 inches
Courtesy of the artist

48. *Boxing Day in the Quarry #3*, 2004
Oil on linen canvas
16 1/2 x 28 inches
Courtesy of the artist

49. *Alligator's Head*, 2005
Oil on linen canvas
12 x 21 inches
Courtesy of the artist

50. *Black River from the Elgin Road View*, 2005
Oil on linen canvas
16 1/2 x 28 inches
Courtesy of the artist

51. *Lyrical View from the Villa*, 2005
Oil on linen canvas
12 x 21 inches
Courtesy of the artist

52. *New Year's Day in the Quarry (Marl Hole)*, 2006
Oil on linen canvas
18 3/4 x 26 1/2 inches
Courtesy of the artist

53. *The Anglican Perspective on January 3rd*, 2006
Oil on linen canvas
14 x 24 inches
Courtesy of the artist

54. *Cold Day on the Mountain*, 2006
Oil on linen canvas
17 1/2 x 27 3/4 inches
Courtesy of the artist

55. *Boxing Day in the Quarry (Marl Hole)*, 2006
Oil on linen canvas
18 3/4 x 26 1/2 inches
Courtesy of the artist

56. *St. Mary's Blues (Sky)*, 2006
Oil on linen canvas
14 x 24 inches
Courtesy of the artist

57. *New Year's Marl Hole*, 2007
Oil on linen canvas
18 3/4 x 26 1/2 inches
Courtesy of the artist

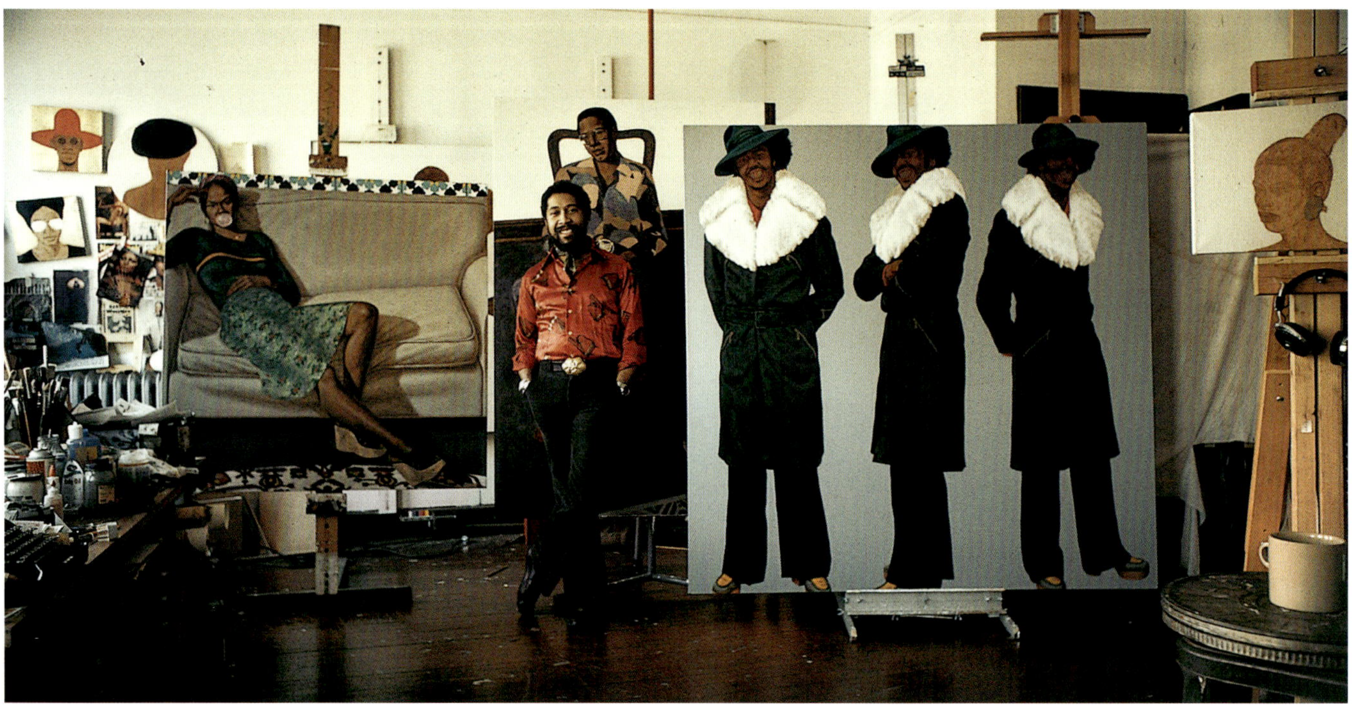

fig. 4
Hendricks in 58 State Street studio, New London, CT, in front of *Sweet Thang*, *Northern Lights*, and unfinished *Greg*, 1976

Selected Bibliography

Articles and Talks by Barkley L. Hendricks

Art Talk Program #12. Videocassette. New London, CT: Griffis Art Center, 1993.

Barkley Hendricks: A Lecture. Videocassette. Art Institute of Boston, 1998.

Barkley L. Hendricks Presents Barkley L. Hendricks, 1967–1987. Bridgeport, CT: Housatonic Museum of Art, 1988.

Barkley L. Hendricks: Recent Paintings. Greenville, SC: Greenville County Museum of Art, 1975.

Barkley Leonnard Hendricks. New York: ACA Gallery, 1976.

Hendricks, Barkley, and Maureen M. McCabe. *Connecticut Painting, Drawing and Sculpture 78*. New Haven: Art Resources of Connecticut, 1978.

"Rome Rendezvous: Rendezvous with Myself." In *The Barkley L. Hendricks Experience*. New London: Lyman Allyn Museum of Art, Connecticut College, 2001.

Catalogues, Books, and Catalogue Essays

32nd Annual Midyear Show. Youngstown, OH: Butler Institute of American Art, 1979.

Afro-American Artists, 1800–1969. Philadelphia: School District of Philadelphia, 1969.

The Art of Black America in Japan. Exhibition catalogue. Tokyo, Japan, 1987.

Campbell, Mary Schmidt, ed. *Barkley L. Hendricks: Oils, Watercolors, Collages and Photographs, January 20–March 30, 1980*. New York: Studio Museum in Harlem, 1980.

Collins, Lisa Gail, and Margo Natalie Crawford, eds. *New Thoughts on the Black Arts Movement*. New Brunswick, NJ: Rutgers University Press, 2006.

Connecticut Circumscribed. New Haven, CT: Erector Square Gallery, 1986.

Contemporary Black Art: A Selected Sampling. Miami: Florida International University, 1977.

Conway, Wallace X. *The Second World Black African Festival of Art and Culture, Inc., North American Zone, Southeastern Regional Exhibition*. Philadelphia: University of Pennsylvania, 1974.

Directions: African-American Artists Now. Newport, RI: Newport Art Museum, 1990.

Doty, Robert. *Contemporary Black Artists in America*. New York: Whitney Museum of American Art, 1971.

Flomenhaft, Eleanor. *Celebrating Contemporary American Black Artists*. Hempstead, NY: Fine Arts Museum of Long Island, 1983.

Fonvielle-Bontemps, Jacqueline. *Choosing: An Exhibit of Changing Perspectives in Modern Art and Art Criticism by Black Americans, 1925–1985*. Hampton, VA: Jacqueline Fonvielle-Bontemps, 1985.

Four Young Realists: Anne Besser, Rebecca Davenport, Barkley Hendricks, Mark Rendleman. New York: ACA Gallery, 1977.

Gaither, E. Barry, ed. *Jubilee: Afro-American Artists on Afro-America*. Boston: Museum of Fine Arts, 1977.

Gaither, E. B. "Spiral: Introduction." *Spiral: Afro-American Art of the 1970's*. Roxbury, MA: Museum of the National Center of Afro-American Artists, 1980.

Gaither, E. B. "Introduction." *Directions: African-American Artists Now*. Newport, RI: Newport Art Museum, 1990.

Golden, Thelma. "My Brother." In Thelma Golden, ed., *Black Male: Representations of Masculinity in Contemporary American Art*. New York: Whitney Museum of American Art, 1994.

Greeley, Elizabeth L., and Raymond W. Smith. *15 Painters + 15 Sculptors*. New Haven, CT: John Slade Ely House, 1985.

Gubert, Betty Kaplan. "Hendricks, Barkley (L.)." In Thomas Riggs, ed., *St. James Guide to Black Artists*. New York: St. James Press, 1997.

Haggin, Virginia Mann. "Introduction." *Connecticut Painting, Drawing and Sculpture*. New Haven, CT: Art Resources of Connecticut, 1978.

Mangan, Doreen. "Barkley Hendricks." In Susan E. Meyer, ed., *Twenty Figure Painters and How They Work from the Pages of American Artist*. New York: Watson-Guptill, 1979.

Mercer, Kobena. "Introduction." In Kobena Mercer, ed., *Pop Art and Vernacular Cultures*. Cambridge, MA: MIT Press and Institute of International Visual Arts, 2007.

Millennium at Museum of the Philadelphia Civic Center. Philadelphia: Philadelphia Civic Center, 1973.

New York Urban League and Avel De Knight. *35 Under 35: An Exhibition of Paintings, Sculpture, Graphics and Photography by 35 Minority Artists Under Age 35*. New York: Urban League, 1980.

Philadelphia: Three Centuries of American Art: Bicentennial Exhibition, April 11–October 10, 1976. Philadelphia: Philadelphia Museum of Art, 1976.

Powell, Richard J. *Black Art and Culture in the 20th Century*. New York and London: Thames and Hudson, 1997.

Powell, Richard J. *Cutting a Figure: Fashioning Black Portraiture*. Chicago: University of Chicago Press, 2008 (forthcoming).

Powell, Richard J. "To Be Real." In *The Barkley L. Hendricks Experience*. New London: Lyman Allyn Museum of Art, Connecticut College, 2001.

Powell, Richard J. "Racial Imaginaries, from Charles White's *Preacher* to Jean-Paul Goude's & Grace Jones' *Nigger Arabesque*." In Richard J. Powell, David A. Bailey, and Petrine Archer-Straw, eds., *Back to Black: Art, Cinema & the Racial Imaginary*. London: Whitechapel Gallery, 2005.

Powell, Richard J. "Sartor Africanus." In Susan Fillin-Yeh, ed., *Dandies: Fashion & Finesse in Art & Culture*. New York: New York University Press, 2001.

Powell, Richard, and Jock Reynolds. *To Conserve a Legacy: American Art from Historically Black Colleges and Universities*. Andover, MA, New York, and Cambridge, MA: Addison Gallery of American Art, Studio Museum in Harlem, distributed by MIT Press, 1999.

Retour aux sources: Une exposition en Afrique d'artistes Afro-Americains 1980. Côte d'Ivoire: Galerie d'Art Mitkal, 1980.

Schoonmaker, Trevor, ed. *Black President: The Art and Legacy of Fela Anikulapo-Kuti*. New York: New Museum of Contemporary Art, 2003.

Schoonmaker, Trevor, ed. *Fela: From West Africa to West Broadway*. New York: Palgrave Macmillan, 2003.

Selleck, Jack. *Exploring Visual Design*. Worcester, MA: Davis, 1978.

The Southern New England Invitational Art Exhibition 1978. Fairfield, CT: Fairfield University, 1978.

The Studio Museum in Harlem: 25 Years of African-American Art. New York: Studio Museum in Harlem, 1994.

Talbot, Jonathan. *Connecticut/Collage*. Hartford, CT: Art at 100 Pearl, 1989.

Thomas, Connie, ed. *The CRT's Craftery Gallery Presents Barkley L. Hendricks*. Hartford, CT: CRT's Craftery Gallery, 1980.

Thomas, Floyd R. "A Personal Reflection on the Barkley L. Hendricks Experience— As I See It." In *The Barkley L. Hendricks Experience*. New London: Lyman Allyn Museum of Art, Connecticut College, 2001.

Articles and Reviews

Adams, Sarah. "Black President: The Art and Legacy of Fela Anikulapo-Kuti." *African Arts* 37 (Spring 2004): 83–86.

Bertan, Britton. "8. Barkley Hendricks." *Art or Idiocy?* (May 20, 2005), artoridiocy.blogspot.com.

"Black President." *New Yorker* 79 (August 11, 2003): 14–15.

"Business of Fine Arts." *Black Enterprise Magazine* (December 1975).

Caplan, Nina. "Art Review: Back to Black: Art, Cinema and the Racial Imaginary." *Metro* [London] (June 8, 2005), www.erniebarnes.com/pressreleases/backtoblack-review.html.

Cotter, Holland. "Imaginings of Africa, Chained or Unchained, Dispersed or Together." *New York Times* (February 25, 2005).

Cotter, Holland. "King of Music (and of All He Surveyed)." *New York Times* (July 18, 2003).

Damsker, Matt. "Portrait of the Artist." *Hartford Courant* (June 8, 1986).

Dendy, J. Brooks. "Lancaster, Wade, Hendricks." *Scoop USA Newspaper* (July 30, 1993).

DeShazo, Edith. "Hendricks' Cool Realism on View." *Sunday News Journal* (Wilmington, DE) (February 11, 1979).

Donohoe, Victoria. "Barkley Hendricks: Ben Mangel Show." *Philadelphia Enquirer* (October 30, 1989).

Eagan, Matt. "A Different State of Mind: Connecticut Artists Stretch Beyond Conventional Perceptions." *Hartford Courant* (April 15, 2007).

"Flashbacks: Barkley L. Hendricks." *Connecticut College Magazine* (Spring 1999).

Gopnik, Adam. "Black Studies." *New Yorker* (December 5, 1994): 135–140.

"Group Show: A Look at Different Artists, Their Works, Styles and Techniques." *Black Enterprise* (December 1975): 54.

Hendricks, Barkley. "Newport: The Jazz Festival." Photographs in *Southeastern Magazine* (January 1981): 55.

Hirsch, Linda Blaker. "Barkley Hendricks' Variations on a Theme." *Hartford Advocate* (August 1980).

Johnson, Ken. "The Magic City." *New York Times* (August 4, 2000).

Kimmelman, Michael. "Constructing Images of the Black Male." *New York Times* (November 11, 1994).

Knight, Dustan. "The Lamont Gallery, Phillips Exeter Academy/Exeter: American Visions." *Art New England* 28 (April/May 2007): 24.

Kramer, Hilton. "Art: Portraiture by Hendricks." *New York Times* (March 11, 1980).

Kramer, Hilton. "Art: To the Last Detail." *New York Times* (June 17, 1977).

Loughery, John. "Faded Glory." *Hudson Review* 48 (Spring 1995): 115–120, 117.

MacLean, Ruairidh. "Exultation/Blaxplotation." *Socialist Review* [London] (July 2005), www.socialistreview.org.uk/article.php?articlenumber=2472.

Mangan, Doreen. "Barkley Hendricks and His Figurative Drama." *American Artist* (July 1976): 34–38, 68–70.

Martin, Courtney J. "Black President." *Flash Art International* 36 (October 2003): 56–57.

Ogunnaike, Lola. "Celebrating the Life and Impact of the Nigerian Music Legend Fela." *New York Times* (July 17, 2003).

Olujobi, Gbemi. "Far from Home, a Nigerian Journalist Finds Fela's Legacy Alive and Well in Art." *San Francisco Chronicle* (May 4, 2004).

Pantalone, John. "Directions: African American Artist Now." *Newport This Week* (September 20, 1990).

Pollack, Barbara. "The Afrobeat Generation: Finding Inspiration in an African Pop Icon." *Village Voice* (July 18, 2003), www.villagevoice.com/art/0330,pollack,45664,13.html.

Potter, Melissa. "Conversations with Don Carroll and Christian Haye." *NYFA Current Special Edition* (October 5, 2005), www.nyfa.org/level3.asp?=id=409&fid=6&sid=17.

Raynor, Vivien. "Barkley Hendricks, a Tale of Two Artists." *New York Times* (March 26, 1982).

Raynor, Vivien. "Artists Champion Other Artists." *New York Times* (January 30, 1983).

Raynor, Vivien. "In Bridgeport, More Than a Touch of the '60s Revisited." *New York Times* (May 7, 1995).

Seymour, Gene. "The City's Black Art Tradition." *Philadelphia Daily* (March 26, 1986).

Smith, Roberta. "Art in Review; Barkley Hendricks." *New York Times* (October 28, 2005).

Starger, Steve. "Lyman Allyn Art Museum/New London: Barkley L. Hendricks Experience." *Art New England* 22 (August/September 2001): 32.

Stein, Jerry. "CAC Exhibit Salutes African Musician." *Cincinnati Post* (January 6, 2005).

Strohkorb, Julie. "Work of the Month: *Slick, Self Portrait*, 1977." *Chrysler Museum of Art* (May 2001), www.chrysler.org/wom/wom0501.asp.

Thomas, Floyd. "Collecting the Art of Black Protest and Black Nationalist Movements." *International Review of African American Art* 15 (1998): 8–13.

Tomlinson, Glenn C., and Rolando Corpus. "A Selection of Works by African American Artists in the Philadelphia Museum of Art." *Philadelphia Museum of Art Bulletin* 90 (Winter 1995): 1, 4–47.

Tomlinson, Glenn C. "Barkley Hendricks." *Philadelphia Museum of Art Bulletin* 90 (Winter 1995): 20–21.

Tyler, Betty. "Barkley Hendricks—Contrast and Controversy." *Darien* (CT) *News—Review* (February 11, 1993).

Wasserman, Burton. *Exploring the Visual Arts*. Worcester, MA: Davis Publications, 1976.

Wasserman, Burton. "Making the Gallery Scene." *School Arts Magazine: The Art Education Magazine for Teachers* 73, no. 7 (March 1974): 38–41.

"We're All Nigerian!" *Chimurenga* 8 [South Africa] (December 2005).

Wilson, Judith. "Beauty Rites: Towards an Anatomy of Culture in African American Women's Art." *International Review of African American Art* 11 (1994): 11–17, 47–55.

Zimmer, William. "Private Visions Dare the Public Eye to See." *New York Times* (February 28, 1993).

Zimmer, William. "On the Trail of Art and Its Inspiration." *New York Times* (May 6, 2001).

Ziolkowski, Thad. "The Magic City." *ArtForum* 39 (October 2000): 146.

fig 5 (page 136)
Tequila, (detail) 1978
Oil and acrylic on linen canvas
60 3/4 x 50 1/4 inches

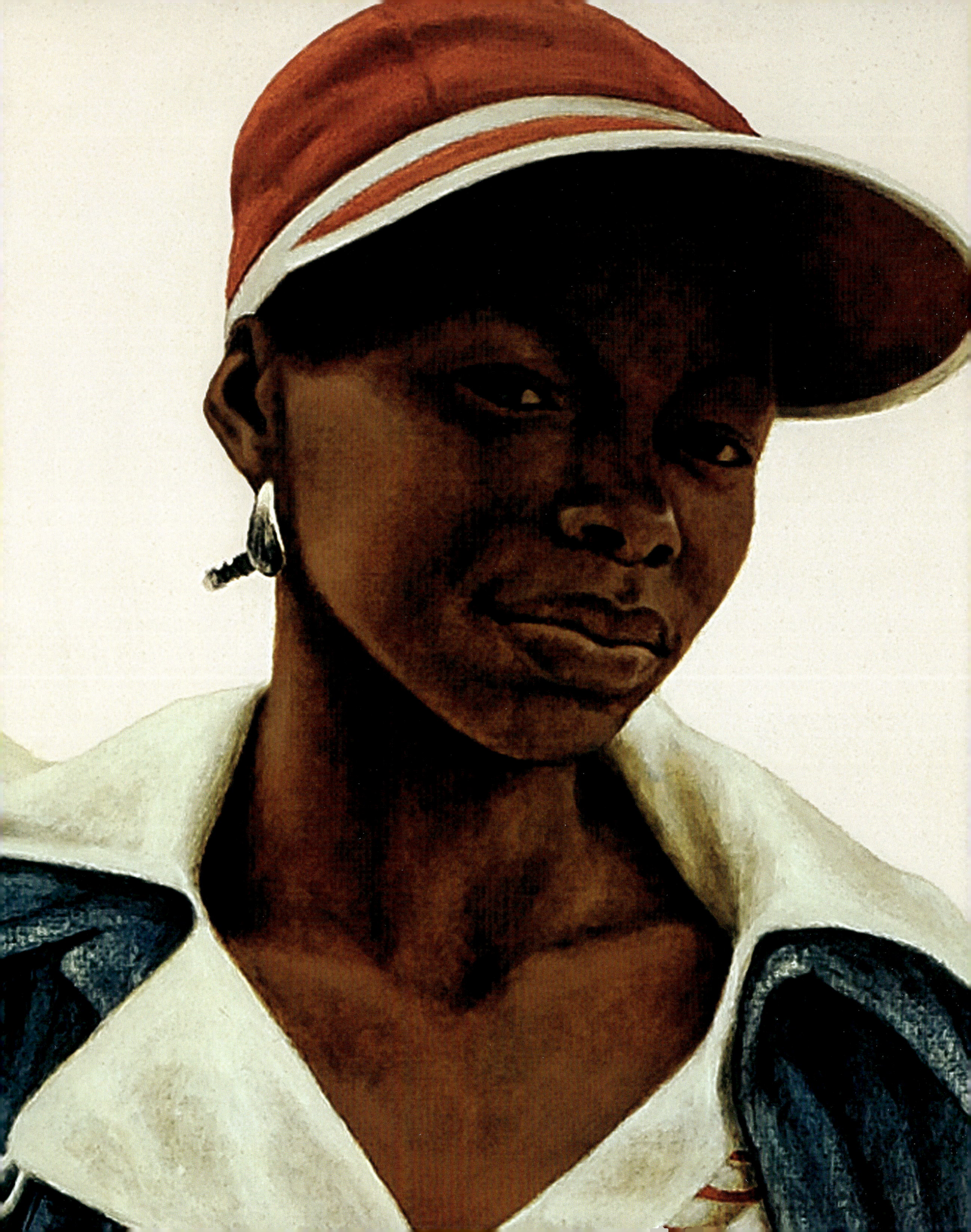

Reproduction Credits

All works by the artist © The Estate of Barkley L. Hendricks

Pages 1–11

Fig. 1. Hendricks with *Butch*, 1968

Location unknown; Courtesy of the artist

Fig. 2. Hendricks with self-portrait in pith helmet, mid 1970s

Courtesy of the artist

Cat. 25. *Blood (Donald Formey)*, 1975

Collection of Dr. Kenneth Montague / The Wedge Collection; Photo: Peter Geoffrion

Cat. 26. *North Philly Niggah (William Corbett)*, 1975

Collection of Blake Byrne, Los Angeles; Photo: Peter Geoffrion

Artist's Acknowledgments

Fig. 1. Barkley L. Hendricks *Self-Portrait with Black Hat*, 1980

Courtesy of the artist

Schoonmaker

Cat. 29. *Misc. Tyrone (Tyrone Smith)*, (detail) 1976

Courtesy of the artist; Photo: Peter Geoffrion

Cat. 1. *My Black Nun*, 1964

Courtesy of the artist; Photo: Peter Geoffrion

Cat. 45. *Fela: Amen, Amen, Amen, Amen...*(detail) 2002

Courtesy of the artist; Photo: Peter Geoffrion

Fig. 1. *Me (Self-Portrait)*, 1978

Location unknown. Courtesy of the artist

Cat. 11. *Granada*, 1970

Collection of Dr. and Mrs. John T. Williams Sr., Philadelphia; Photo: Joseph Painter

Cat. 31. *Brilliantly Endowed (Self-Portrait)*, 1977

Courtesy of the artist; Photo: Peter Geoffrion

Cat. 37. *Tequila*, 1978

The Butler Institute of American Art, Youngstown, OH; Museum Purchase 1980; Photo: Peter Geoffrion

Cat. 7. *Icon for My Man Superman (Superman never saved any black people-Bobby Seale)*, 1969

Courtesy of the artist; Photo: Peter Geoffrion

Fig. 2. *Family Jules: NNN (No Naked Niggahs)*, 1974

Courtesy of the artist

Fig. 3. Rembrandt Harmensz van Rijn

Self-portrait as a Young Man, c. 1629

Mauritshuis, The Hague, The Netherlands

© Scala/Art Resource, NY

Fig. 4. Caravaggio (Michelangelo Merisi da)

Youth Bitten by a Lizard

Longhi Collection, Florence, Italy

Alinari/ Art Resource, NY

Fig. 5. *A Man in a Red Turban (Self-portrait of Jan van Eyck)*, 1433

National Gallery, London

Erich Lessing/ Art Resource, NY

Fig. 6. Hendricks painting *Sir Charles, Alias Willie Harris*, Yale, 1972

Courtesy of the artist

Cat. 24. *Bedroom Eyes (Self-Portrait)*, 1975

Courtesy of the artist; Photo: Peter Geoffrion

Cat. 29. *Misc. Tyrone (Tyrone Smith)*, 1976

Courtesy of the artist; Photo: Peter Geoffrion

Cat. 46. *Lunch with Picasso: Curry Goat for Two*, 2003

Courtesy of the artist; Photo: Peter Geoffrion

Cat. 41. *Ma Petite Kumquat*, 1983

Courtesy of the artist; Photo: Peter Geoffrion

Cat. 40: *Icon for Fifi*, 1982

Courtesy of the artist; Photo: Peter Geoffrion

Cat. 12. *Dixwell*, 1971

North Carolina Central University Art Museum, Durham, NC; Photo: Peter Geoffrion

Cat. 48. *Boxing Day in the Quarry # 3*, 2004

Courtesy of the artist; Photo: Peter Geoffrion

Cat. 49. *Alligator's Head*, 2005

Courtesy of the artist; Photo: Peter Geoffrion

Cat. 53. *The Anglican Perspective on January 3rd*, 2006

Courtesy of the artist; Photo: Peter Geoffrion

Cat. 50. *Black River from the Elgin Road View*, 2005

Courtesy of the artist; Photo: Peter Geoffrion

Cat. 57. *New Year's Marl Hole*, 2007

Courtesy of the artist; Photo: Peter Geoffrion

Cat. 56. *St. Mary's Blues (Sky)*, 2006

Courtesy of the artist; Photo: Peter Geoffrion

Fig. 7. *Lagos Ladies (Gbemi, Bisi, Niki, Christy)*, 1978

Location unknown; Courtesy of the artist

Fig. 8. *Fela: Amen, Amen, Amen, Amen....*, (installation view) 2002

Courtesy of the artist; Photo: Peter Geoffrion

Powell

Cat. 35. *Vendetta*, (detail) 1977

Collection of Monica and Rick Segal, New York; Photo: Peter Geoffrion

Fig. 1. Vendetta (subject) with painting *Vendetta*, 1977; Photo: Richard J. Powell

Cat. 14. *George Jules Taylor*, 1972

William C. Whitney Foundation. Courtesy of the Board of Trustees, National Gallery of Art, Washington, 1972

Fig. 2. Chuck Close

Nancy, 1968

Milwaukee Art Museum, Gift of Herbert H. Kohl Charities, Inc.; Photo: Larry Sanders

Fig. 3. Kathy Williams (subject of *Lawdy Mama*) in Barkley's studio, 1970

Courtesy of the artist

Cat. 8. *Lawdy Mama,* 1969

The Studio Museum in Harlem, New York; Gift of Stuart Liebman, in memory of Joseph B. Liebman

Fig. 4. Philip Pearlstein, *Model with Legs Up*, 1975

Collection of the Akron Art Museum, Purchased, by exchange, with funds raised by the Masked Ball 1955-1963

Fig. 5. *Fast Eddie–JN (Jive Niggah|Eddie Clanton)*, 1975

Courtesy of the artist

Fig. 6. Jeff Donaldson

Ala Sango, 1968

Southside Community Art Center

Fig. 7. *Black on Black in Black*, 1967

Location unkown. Courtesy of the artist

Fig. 8. Kerry James Marshall

SOB, SOB, 2003

Courtesy of Jack Shainman Gallery

Cat. 18. *Bid 'Em In|Slave (Angie),* 1973

Searles / Spicer Collection, New York; Photo: Peter Geoffrion

Cat. 28. *Sweet Thang (Lynn Jenkins)*, 1975- 1976

Courtesy of the artist; Photo: Peter Geoffrion

Fig. 9. Till Freiwald

Untitled, 2003

Courtesy of Jack Shainman Gallery

Fig. 10. *New Michael*, 1971

Location unknown. Courtesy of the artist

Fig. 11. *Rooftop View*, 1999

Courtesy of the artist

Cat. 47. *Roaring River Apostle (Serious Smoker Series),* 2004

Courtesy of the artist; Photo: Peter Geoffrion

Cat. 23. *Bahsir (Robert Gowens),* 1975

Nasher Museum of Art at Duke University, Durham, NC; Photo: Peter Geoffrion

Cat. 13. *Down Home Taste,* 1971

Courtesy of the Office of the Dean of Students, Cornell University, Ithaca, NY

Gift of Michael Straight to the Willard Straight Hall Art Collection

Fig. 12. *Jules*, 1971

Location unknown. Courtesy of the artist

Fig. 13. *Michael BPP (Black Panther Party)*, 1971

Location unknown. Courtesy of the artist

Golden

Cat. 34. *Slick (Self-Portrait),* (detail) 1977

Chrysler Museum of Art, Norfolk, VA; Gift of the American Academy and Institute of the Arts and Letters, New York, Childe Hassam Purchase Funds

Fig. 1. *Sophisticated Lady (Barbara Perry)*, 1976

Collection of Renee Zwickel. Courtesy of the artist

Cat. 30. *Steve*, 1976

The Forbes Collection, New York

Cat. 36. *APB's (Afro-Parisian Brothers),* 1978

Yale University Art Gallery, The Janet and Simeon Braguin Fund

Fig. 2. *Arriving Soon*, 1973

Collection of Bruce Llewellyn. Courtesy of the artist

Fig. 3. Photograph of Lynn Jenkins, 1976

Courtesy of the artist

Fig. 4. *The Way You Look Tonight|Diagonal Graciousness (Self-Portrait)*, 1981

Location unknown. Courtesy of the artist

Cat. 34. *Slick (Self-Portrait),* 1977

Chrysler Museum of Art, Norfolk, VA; Gift of the American Academy and Institute of the Arts and Letters, New York, Childe Hassam Purchase Funds

Cat. 16. *Sergio*, 1972

Collection of Dr. and Mrs. Robert and Joan Clark, Philadelphia; Photo: Peter Geoffrion

Fig. 5. *Noir*, 1978

Courtesy of the artist; Photo: Peter Geoffrion

Cat. 20. *Mayreh (Mary Sheehan)*, 1973

Courtesy of the artist; Photo: Peter Geoffrion

Fig. 6. *Salina|Star*, 1975

Courtesy of the artist; Photo: A. Vincent Scarano

Fig. 7. *October's Gone... Goodnight*, 1973

Courtesy of the artist; Photo: A. Vincent Scarano

Cat. 33. *Sisters (Susan and Toni)*, 1977

Courtesy of the artist; Photo: Peter Geoffrion

Cat. 42. *View from the Behind the School*, 2000

Courtesy of the artist; Photo: Peter Geoffrion

Cat. 51. *Lyrical View from the Villa*, 2005

Courtesy of the artist; Photo: Peter Geoffrion

Cat. 55. *Boxing Day in the Quarry (Marl Hole),* 2006

Courtesy of the artist; Photo: Peter Geoffrion

Cat. 44. *Mustard YS Falls*, 2002

Courtesy of the artist; Photo: Peter Geoffrion

Cat. 43. *View from Red Banks School,* 2000

Courtesy of the artist; Photo: Peter Geoffrion

Cat. 52. *New Year's Day in the Quarry (Marl Hole),* 2006

Courtesy of the artist; Photo: Peter Geoffrion

Cat. 54. *Cold Day on the Mountain*, 2006

Courtesy of the artist; Photo: Peter Geoffrion

Fig. 8. *Ralph and Alvin–Sikkayou*, 1974

Location unknown. Courtesy of the artist

Fig. 9. *Something Like a Bird: Double Barbara*, 1982

Courtesy of the artist

Fig. 10. *Father, Son, and...*, 1969

Location unknown. Courtesy of the artist

Cat. 17. *Sir Charles, Alias Willie Harris*, 1972

William C. Whitney Foundation, Image courtesy of the Board of Trustees, National Gallery of Art, Washington, 1972

Sirmans

Cat. 31. *Brilliantly Endowed (Self-Portrait),* (detail) 1977

Courtesy of the artist; Photo: Peter Geoffrion

Fig. 1. *New London Niggah/ Big Chuck (Charles Harvey)*, 1975

Courtesy of the artist; Photo: A. Vincent Scarano

Fig. 2. Rashid Johnson

Self-portrait in homage to Barkley Hendricks, 2005

Courtesy of artist and Monique Meloche Gallery, Chicago

Fig. 3. Kehinde Wiley

Conspicuous Fraud (Portrait Study), 2001

Private Collection. Courtesy of Kehinde Wiley Studio

Fig. 4. Jeff Sonhouse

Meeting at the Crossroads, 2003

Courtesy of the artist and Tilton Gallery

Cat. 5. *J.S.B. III* (*James Sherman Brantley*), 1968

Courtesy of the Pennsylvania Academy of the Fine Arts, Philadelphia.

Gift of Mr. and Mrs. Richardson Dilworth

Cat. 19. *Dr. Kool,* 1973

Collection of Dr. and Mrs. Robert and Joan Clark, Philadelphia; Photo: Peter Geoffrion

Cat. 35. *Vendetta,* 1977

Collection of Monica and Rick Segal, New York; Photo: Peter Geoffrion

Cat. 38. *Tuff Tony*, 1978

The Forbes Collection, New York

Fig. 5. Kehinde Wiley

St. John the Baptist II, 2006

Collection of Blake Byrne. Courtesy of Kehinde Wiley Studio

Hendricks

Cat. 32. *Doc and Ruby's Oldest Boy (Self-Portrait)*, (detail) 1977

Columbus Museum of Art, OH; Museum Purchase, Derby Fund, from the Philip J. and Suzanne Schiller Collection of American Social Commentary Art 1930–1970; Photo: Michael Tropea

Fig. 1. Photo of Hendricks painting in Jamaica, c. late 1990s

Courtesy of the artist

Fig. 2. Barkley L. Hendricks, "Miles Davis" at Canandaigua Jazz Festival, 1988

Courtesy of the artist

Cat. 32. *Doc and Ruby's Oldest Boy (Self-Portrait)*, 1977

Columbus Museum of Art, OH; Museum Purchase, Derby Fund, from the Philip J. and Suzanne Schiller Collection of American Social Commentary Art 1930–1970; Photo: Michael Tropea

Cat. 4. *FTA,* 1968

Collection of Charlotte and Gordon Moore, Cambridge, MA; Photo: Peter Geoffrion

Fig. 3. Hendricks's postcard from Amsterdam, 1966

Courtesy of the artist

Fig. 4. Barkley Herbert Hendricks and James Hendricks, c.1971

Courtesy of the artist

Fig. 5. Hendricks in National Guard, c. 1968

Courtesy of the artist

Cat. 21. *New Orleans Niggah,* 1973

Courtesy of the National Afro-American Museum and Cultural Center, Wilberforce, Ohio. Gift of Joseph Erdelac, Cleveland, Ohio

Cat. 27. *Take All the Time You Need (Adrienne Hawkins),* 1975

Courtesy of the artist; Photo: Peter Geoffrion

Fig. 6. *Miss Brown to You*, 1970

Location unknown; Courtesy of the artist

Cat. 6. *Dippy's Delight,* 1969

Courtesy of the artist; Photo: Peter Geoffrion

Cat. 3. *Vertical Hold,* 1967

Courtesy of the artist; Photo: Peter Geoffrion

Cat. 22. *What's Going On*, 1974

Courtesy of ACA Galleries, New York

Cat. 10. *Brown Sugar Vine*, 1970

Collection of Dr. and Mrs. John T. Williams Sr., Philadelphia; Photo: Joseph Painter

Cat. 15. *Ms. Johnson (Estelle),* 1972

Gibbes Museum of Art / Carolina Art Association, Charleston, SC

Fig. 7. *Innocence (Self-Portrait)*, 1977

Location unknown. Courtesy of the artist

Fig. 8. *BLH (Self Portrait)*, 1968

Location unknown. Courtesy of the artist

Cat. 9. *Miss T*, 1969

Philadelphia Museum of Art: Purchased with the Philadelphia Foundation Fund, 1970; Photo: Graydon Wood

Fig. 9. *Buck*, 1967

Location unknown. Courtesy of the artist

Cat. 39. *Latin from Manhattan... the Bronx Actually,* 1980

Collection of Mr. and Mrs. Alexander Miller, Grand Rapids, MI; Photo: Peter Geoffrion

Figs. 10–17 Hendricks's sequence of painting *Northern Lights,* 1976

Collection of Susan Katzev. Courtesy of the artist

Fig. 18. *Serpent's Tooth*, 1968–1969

Location unknown. Courtesy of the artist

Cat. 2. *Self Portrait,* 1966

Courtesy of the artist. Photo: Peter Geoffrion

Fig. 19. Hendricks and "Sheidt Scholarship" wall, 1967

Courtesy of the artist

Fig. 20. *Sir Nelson, Solid*, 1970

Location unknown. Courtesy of the artist

Fig. 21. Hendricks painting beach scene in Jamaica, 1998

Courtesy of the artist

Fig. 22. Studio at 58 State Street, New London, CT, c. 1980

Courtesy of the artist

Selected Artist Chronology

Fig. 1. Barkley's baby picture, 1945

Courtesy of the artist

Fig. 2. Ruby Powell, early 1950's

Courtesy of the artist

Fig. 3. Lamont, Denise, and Barkley, 1953

Courtesy of the artist

Fig. 4. Hendricks family in Meadville, Virginia, c. 1970

Courtesy of the artist

Fig. 5. Barkley in Yale studio, 1971

Courtesy of the artist

Fig. 6. Dewar's Profile, c. 1976

Courtesy of the artist

Fig. 7. Hendricks as subject for *Icon for My Man Superman,* 1969

Courtesy of the artist

Fig. 8. Barkley and Susan, Housatonic Museum of Art, 1988

Courtesy of the artist

Fig. 9 *Hasty Tasty*, 1977

Courtesy of the artist; Photo: A. Vincent Scarano

Fig. 10. *Jackie Sha-La-La (Jackie Cameron)*, 1975

Location unknown. Courtesy of the artist

Fig. 11. Barkley in his studio, mid-1970's

Courtesy of the artist

Fig. 12. *Claire*, 1971

Courtesy of the artist

Fig. 13. *Foxie Roxie*, 1975

Collection of the Greenville County Museum of Art, SC

Fig. 14. Self-portrait in hubcap, c. 1967

Courtesy of the artist

Fig. 15. *Brenda's Sister, Barbara Jean*, 1977

Courtesy of the artist

Fig. 16. Barkley and Ruby at ACA Galleries, 1978

Courtesy of the artist

Fig. 17. Hendricks at Brent Sikkema, 2000

Courtesy of the artist

Fig. 18. Teka Selman and Barkley at Mitchell Algus Gallery, 2005

Courtesy of the artist

Fig. 19. Susan and Barkley with Harry Kulkowitz, 2001

Courtesy of the artist

Fig. 20. Denise and Barkley, 2001

Courtesy of the artist

Fig. 21. *Yocks*, 1975

Location unknown. Courtesy of the artist

Fig. 22. Richard J. Powell and David A. Bailey with Barkley, 2005

Courtesy of the artist

Fig. 23. *Pretty Peggy's Black Box*, 1976

Location unknown. Courtesy of the artist

Fig. 24. Fela Kuti, 1990

Courtesy of the artist

Fig. 25. Alhambra palace, 1966

Courtesy of the artist

Fig. 26. Black Australia FESTAC poster, 1977

Courtesy of the artist

Fig. 27. FESTAC performance pavilion, 1977

Courtesy of the artist

Fig. 28. Barkley L. Hendricks marries Susan Weig, 1983

Courtesy of the artist

Fig. 29. Methun, Barkley, Ruby and Lamont, early 1990s

Courtesy of the artist

Fig. 30. Barkley and Lamont, 1953

Courtesy of the artist

About the Contributors

Fig. 1. Hendricks in 58 State Street studio, New London, CT, 1978

Courtesy of the artist

Fig. 2. Hendricks in 58 State Street studio, New London, CT, c. 1974

Courtesy of the artist

Fig. 3. Studio at 58 State Street, New London, CT, 1980

Courtesy of the artist

Fig. 4. Studio at 58 State Street, New London, CT, 1977

Courtesy of the artist

Exhibition Checklist

Fig. 1. Hendricks at storage in New London, CT, 2007

Photo: Trevor Schoonmaker

Fig. 2. Hendricks in front of installation and *Ma Petite Kumquat*, 1984

Courtesy of the artist

Fig. 3. Hendricks painting in Jamaica, c. late 1990s

Courtesy of the artist

Fig. 4. Hendricks in 58 State Street studio, New London, CT, 1976

Courtesy of the artist

Reproduction Credits

Fig. 5. *Tequila,* 1978

The Butler Institute of American Art, Youngstown, OH; Museum Purchase 1980

Photo: Peter Geoffrion

Back Cover

Barkley L. Hendricks *Self-Portrait with Red Sweater,* 1980

Courtesy of the artist

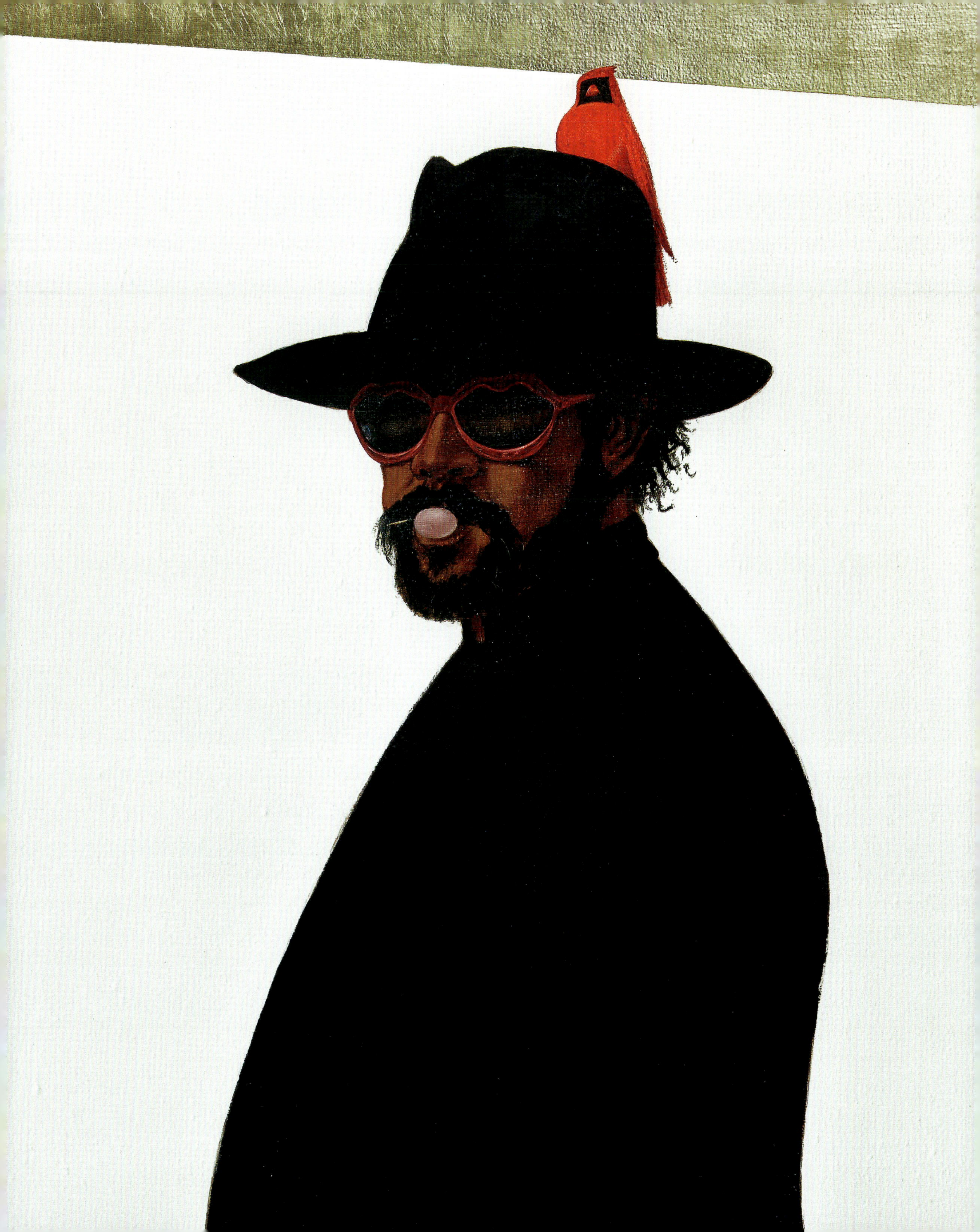

Barkley L. Hendricks April 16, 1945–April 18, 2017

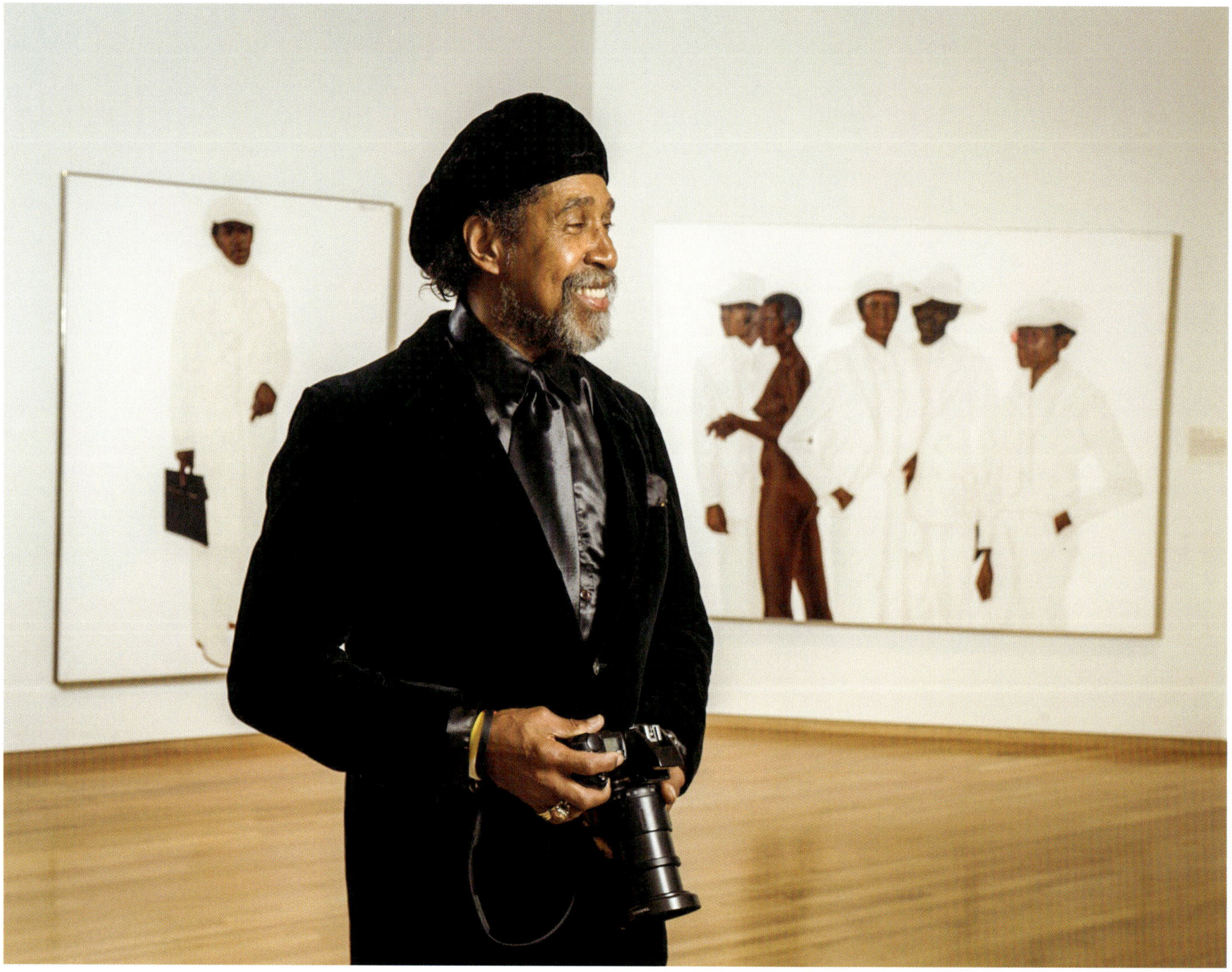

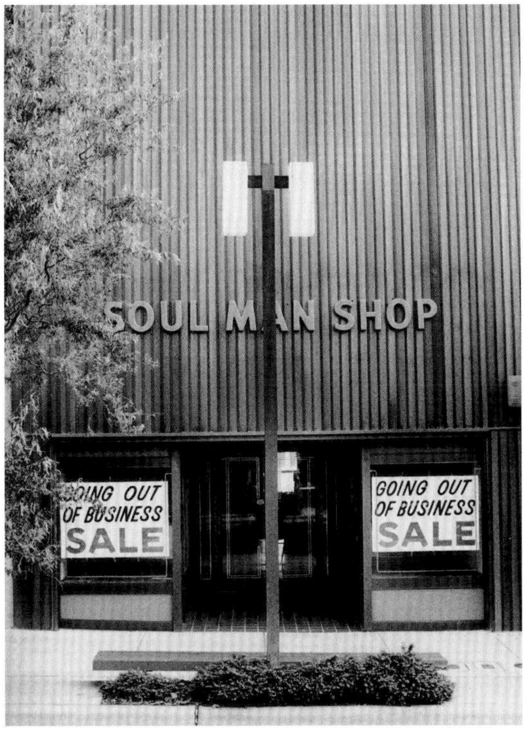

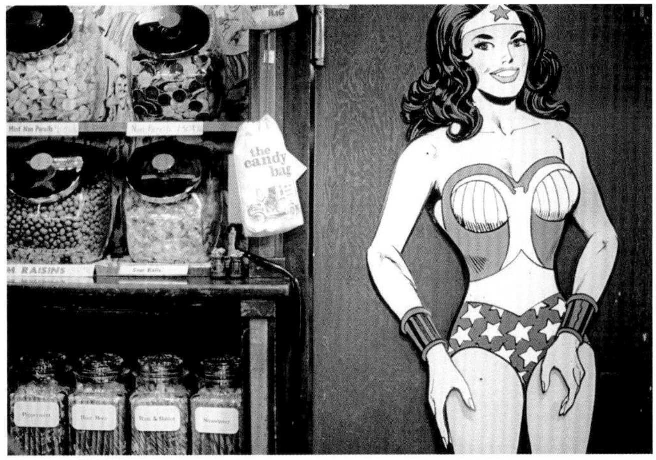

The Nasher Museum is proud to have worked with Barkley L. Hendricks to organize *Barkley L. Hendricks: Birth of the Cool* in 2008. The nationally touring exhibition rapidly produced new visibility for his work, which helped give rise to broadening interest, critical acclaim, scholarship, and institutional support that brought Hendricks more fully into the public eye. This new exposure also generated an increased awareness of other aspects of the artist's work, in particular his longstanding photography practice. Since *Birth of the Cool*, Hendricks's works have been included in numerous national and international exhibitions and acquired by many prominent public and private collections, including the Ackland Art Museum, University of North Carolina at Chapel Hill; Art Bridges, Bentonville; Luciano Benetton Collection; Harvard Art Museums/ Fogg Museum; Menil Collection; Museum of Fine Arts, Houston; Museum of Modern Art, New York; Rennie Collection; Rubell Family Collection; Tate Modern; Virginia Museum of Fine Arts; and the Whitney Museum of American Art. Thanks to the generosity of Susan and Barkley Hendricks, donors, and Duke University, the Nasher Museum today has a broad and rapidly growing collection of works by Hendricks, including figurative portraits, landscapes, mixed media works on paper, drawings, and photographs.

Hendricks has been represented by Jack Shainman Gallery, New York, since 2009. We extend our tremendous gratitude to the Estate of Barkley L. Hendricks for making the third printing of this exhibition catalogue possible.

above, left to right *Soul Man*, 1978 (printed 2010). Digital chromogenic print on Kodak Endura Matte paper, edition of 3, 30 x 20 inches. Collection of the Nasher Museum of Art at Duke University, Durham, North Carolina. Gift of the artist and Jack Shainman Gallery, New York; 2010.16.3. *Wonder Woman*, 1978 (printed 2010). Digital chromogenic print on Kodak Endura Matte paper, edition of 3, 20 x 30 inches. Collection of the Nasher Museum of Art at Duke University, Durham, North Carolina. Museum purchase, 2010.16.2. **opposite** Portrait of the artist at the Nasher Museum of Art, 2008. Photo by Duke Photography. **page 141** *The Way You Look Tonight/Diagonal Graciousness* (detail), 1981. Oil, acrylic, and white gold leaf on linen; 48 x 36 inches. All art by Barkley L. Hendricks: © Estate of Barkley L. Hendricks. Unless otherwise noted, images courtesy of the artist's estate and Jack Shainman Gallery, New York.

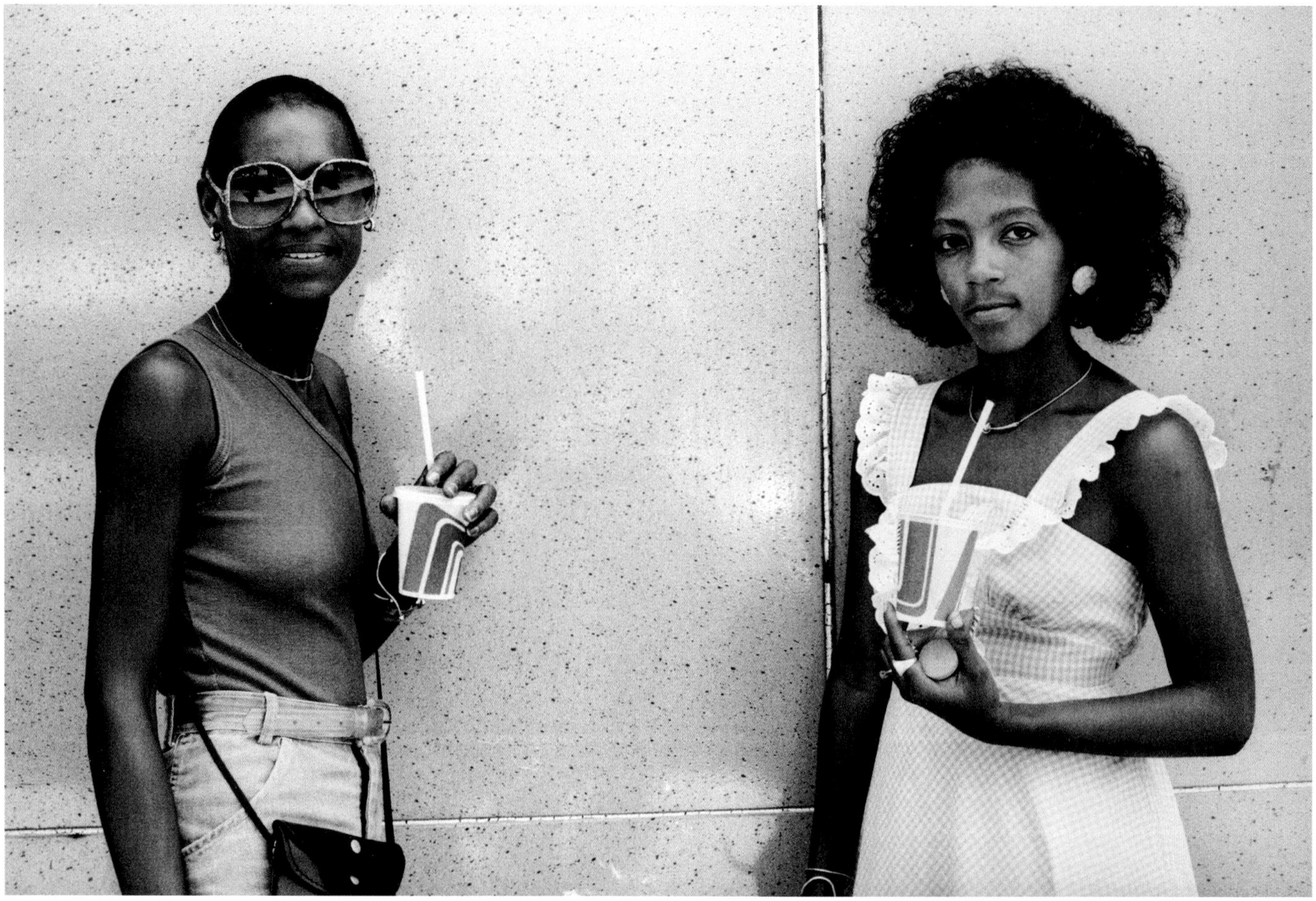

North Carolina Sisters, 1978 (printed 2010)
Digital chromogenic print on Kodak Endura Matte paper
Edition of 3, 20 x 30 inches
Collection of the Nasher Museum of Art at Duke University,
Durham, North Carolina
Museum purchase, 2010.16.1